The Guide to
Home Remodeling

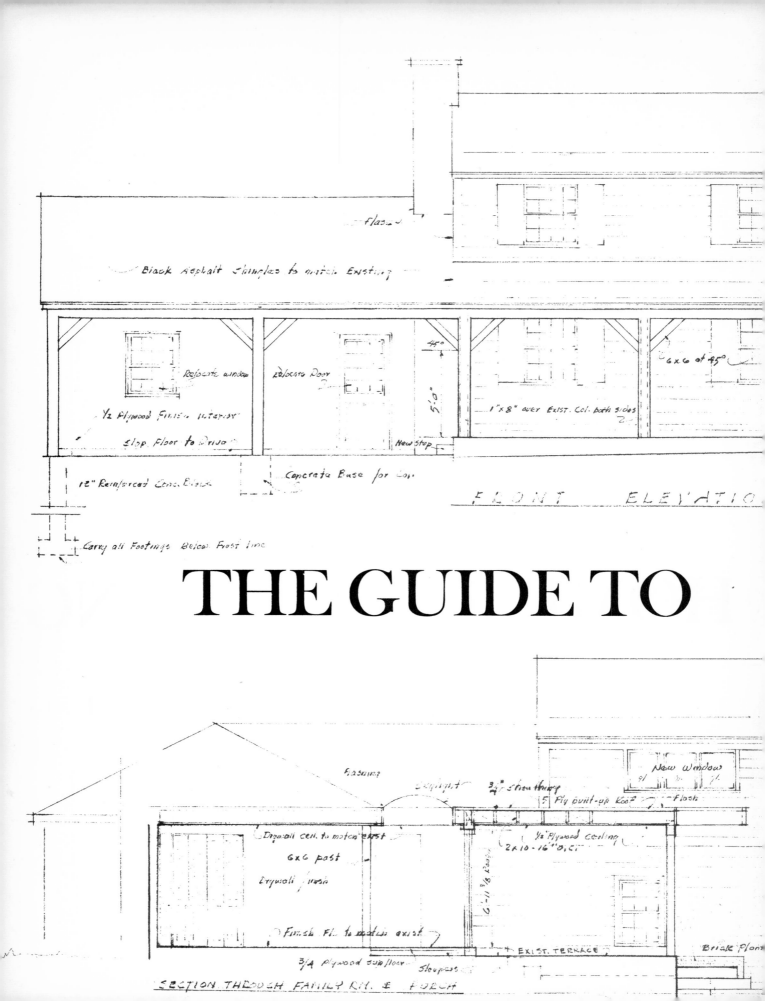

Flash

Black Asphalt Shingles to match Existing

Relocate window

Relocate Door

45°

5'-0"

6x6 at 45°

1/2 Plywood finish interior

Slop. Floor to Drive

1" x 8" over Exist. Col. both sides

New Step

12" Reinforced Conc. Block

Concrete Base for Col.

FRONT ELEVATIO

Carry all Footings Below Frost line

THE GUIDE TO

Flashing

Skylight

3/4" Sheathing

New Window

5 Ply built-up Roof

Flash

Drywall ceil. to match exist

6x6 post

Drywall finish

1/2 Plywood Ceiling

2x10-16" o.c.

6'-11 3/8" Rough

Finish Fl. to match exist

3/4 Plywood sub floor

Sleepers

EXIST. TERRACE

Brick Front

SECTION THROUGH FAMILY RM. & PORCH

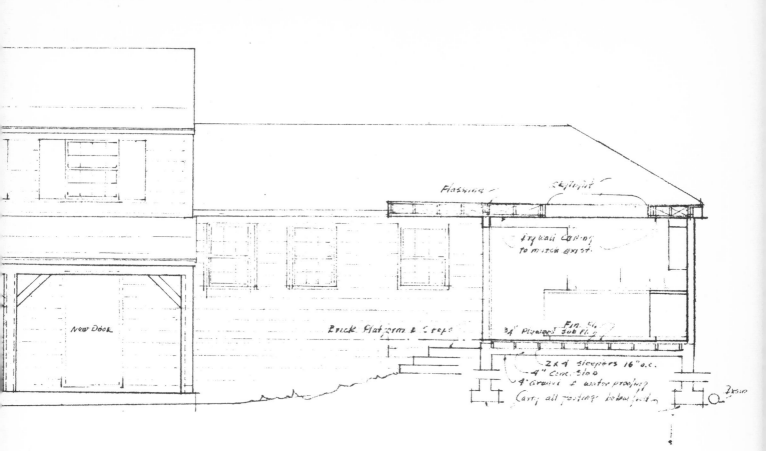

HOME REMODELING

A.J.Harmon A.I.A.

Holt, Rinehart and Winston
New York   Chicago   San Francisco

INTRODUCTION

This is a personal book written by an opinionated man. It is not a "do-it-yourself" guide or a handy man's instruction manual. It is material organized from the experience of a practicing architect with the purpose of helping you who are interested in remodeling to see where you are going and to decide if that is the direction you really want to go. Since about 90 per cent of the new houses being built today could benefit from some remodeling before a family moves in, this book should be as useful to those of you who are planning to buy or build a new house as to you who are planning to remodel an old one.

The skills and painstaking care of the old craftsmen have all but disappeared in today's automated society. And, although very little craftsmanship is available in the United States today, few reputable contractors do poor work in the sense of workmanship itself. This emphasizes the importance of the design. If your remodeling is well designed, you can expect it to be carried through to a successful result, but you cannot expect a transformation if you approach the task haphazardly.

To increase value and improve the usefulness of your home, each stage in your remodeling should be a real contribution to the house and not merely a change. For example, a new six-thousand-dollar kitchen will not increase the net value of a house by that amount if the rest of the house remains in poor condition. Every woman knows that it would be ridiculous to wear an expensive hat with a tired old housedress. We have all smiled at the African bushman wearing a homburg hat and very little else. Such incongruity looks no less foolish in a house. Although it may take a little longer to spot, it is just as illogical as a homburg in the veldt.

One of the first questions you will ask is "How much will the remodeling cost?" This is certainly to be expected. But do not assume that just because a remodeling is well done it is necessarily expensive. Many of us are so used to mediocre design that we associate good design with prohibitive expense.

This is not true . . . just ask your wife. She knows that although she may look as though she just stepped off the cover of the latest fashion magazine, she need not have spent all day at the beauty parlor or bought her dress from a designer's showroom. She also knows that unless she is a raving beauty or has unlimited funds to spend that she cannot throw just anything on and look well. She has learned to budget and plan exactly what she wears and how she wears it.

Now many women understand fashion but fail to realize that much the same kind of reasoning applies to their homes. When it comes to remodeling they let almost anyone with a hammer and saw and suit of overalls patch and piece their houses with little or no planning except to get the job done and done cheaply.

Of course you are going to need an architect, or at least some sort of professional help with your house, regardless of how much good taste you have. Taste is, after all, no adequate substitute for knowledge. If your wife plans to spend a thousand dollars on a new coat, hat, dress, gloves, bag, and shoes, you are hardly equipped to save money by sitting down with a needle one evening and sewing the costume yourself. You would spend two hundred dollars or so to pay a qualified designer to do it for you. Yet most people are reluctant to invest even this small amount in professional help with their homes, although they may be planning to spend thousands for the final result.

A remodeling project is a natural for stirring up comment, criticism, opinion, and free advice from friends and relatives. Try to ignore it and let the amateurs carry out any suggestions and experiments on their own homes, not yours.

Your home is yours to enjoy and it must do more than simply keep the rain off. It should not be static but an ever changing experience that contributes to your life and makes it more fun, more stimulating for you and your family. Although we cannot build our own world around us from the ground up, we can start with what we have and try to make it into what we want it to be. One place to start is with our homes. They are a very big part of our lives and what makes up our neighborhoods, our towns and cities, our country, and our world.

A. J. Harmon, A.I.A.

CONTENTS

The Guide to
Home Remodeling

SECTION ONE

The Philosophy of Remodeling

WHY REMODEL?

One of the most engaging love stories of our time, Shaw's *Pygmalion,* concerns the remodeling of Eliza Doolittle. And perhaps there is a bit of Professor Higgins in all of us, a desire to transform an unattractive, awkward something into a Cinderella. Making a house into an attractive and stimulating place to live is a rewarding experience, worth more than the time, trouble, and money it takes.

Why remodel a house? There are really only two reasons: because we must or because we want to. If we must, it is because the family has grown and we need more space . . . additional bedrooms, another bath, a family room, a garage. A desire to remodel which is not dictated by need usually stems from a changed pattern of living, a larger income, and, although we can afford to buy or build a better home now, we like our neighborhood, the street where we live.

Another consideration is not merely why we remodel but why we should remodel. A thoughtful look at any city and almost any town or suburb will make clear why we should and must do something about the houses and neighborhoods in which we live. The situation has grown so serious that the federal government has set up agencies and is trying to interest more people in improving the blighted areas of their towns and cities. By "blighted" areas I mean not only slums, but those sections occupied by people who have no interest or pride in their homes or communities. Neither color, race, nor religion sets them apart, and whatever their origin, their nationality is American. I do not mean migratory workers or other hapless people who truly cannot help themselves, but those who seem content to live in shacks, unpainted and ramshackle, with an expensive new car—and one or two others they have let rot—parked in the littered front yard. These people have set themselves apart by living in and putting up with conditions the rest of society finds intolerable.

On the other hand, it is important to try to understand the attitudes and problems of people whose living patterns are different from one's own. It is not a matter of money. Look at the small Greek town that is beautiful in its scrubbed and painted simplicity; the people earn far less than do those in an average American town, but they have a native pride, a sense of values that is becoming increasingly rare.

Some people are secure enough socially and financially to go on driving an old car, to read books instead of buying another television set. Others latch onto "things" as status symbols; a new car is more important than indoor plumbing, just as to a

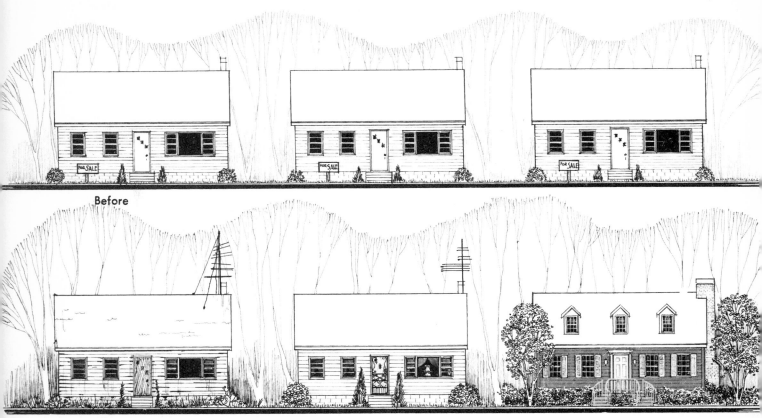

Before

After

child a bright tin toy is better than a good pair of shoes. By driving an expensive, fast automobile they can attain the same status, in their own view, as a big businessman or television hero, but they pay a high price, higher than they realize.

Our homes shape our lives and continually reflect our personalities. Drive through an established neighborhood development in which all the houses were identical when the families first moved in. Although only five or six years old, the houses have begun to divulge the character of the occupants. One house has deteriorated rapidly, with paint chipping, grass disappearing, and broken toys lying about. No effort has been made to maintain, let alone improve, the house, which has only been occupied and used. It will gradually wither and slip further into decay to become a poor neighbor, a bad house, and a risky investment.

The next house may be neat, the foundation planting exactly as advertised originally, a pointed evergreen on each side of the front door and one at each corner of the house, just where the contractor stuck them. The grass is cut, and the picture window displays the familiar lamp, the entrance the basic ugly storm door. The house is lived in, but joylessly maintained in a rigid manner that prevents it from becoming a home; its identity is lost in uniformity.

The third house started out like the others, but it is now more valuable both as a home and an investment. The lawn is not only well-kept but blooming; plantings screen the windows, and landscaping has softened the exterior. Dormers may have added light and scale to the attic; a fireplace may have been added to the living room. The property will intrigue you, make you curious to see the inside, even though you live in the same development or one just like it.

If you showed the three owners a piece of ground, the first would see a lot of dirt, the second a lot of crabgrass and work, and the third a garden.

We are no longer a nation of landlords and renters. In the United States more Americans can and expect to own their homes than in any other nation in history, but they have acquired along with their homes the obligation to improve them and the towns in which we live. Because it is so easy to buy a new house there are too many people ready to sell their old houses in the middle of town and join a movement to the suburbs or a new development. This usually solves few of the families' domestic problems and can create others that are far more aggravating and serious for both the family and the community. The new garden they longed for and slaved over may dry up, and the grass may turn brown because water is rationed, a problem common to many communities as sources of fresh water become more scarce and water tables continue to lower. All the problems they thought were left behind in the old house may be repeated, with the added dissatisfaction that they are farther away from work, church, and familiar shopping centers. In moving away they have left behind an area in which there are schools, hospitals, fire and police protection, public utilities, and public transportation, an area in which taxes are stable and roads are built. In a new neighborhood these may all be unknown quantities.

Moreover, as people move into the suburbs, properties in the cities and towns tend to become vacant or fall into careless hands, blighting the urban centers. This, in turn, tends to reduce the number of small businesses and private enterprises so that fewer people are left to pay taxes that keep going up and up in order to maintain the established government and public utilities.

Remodeling may be as much of an emotional decision as an economic one. People are like trees, and it is not easy to transplant them, to put down new roots. Children miss their old school and playmates. The "new boy" at school must always prove himself before he is accepted.

If we stay in familiar surroundings we know where the best butcher is, which grocer has the freshest vegetables, and which laundry irons our shirts with just the right amount of starch. Our neighbors like us, too, and when the remodeling is started there will be helping hands and pots of fresh coffee in every kitchen. There will be tours of inspection and admiring comments, new pride and satisfaction in our homes and in ourselves.

It is encouraging to see what can happen when neighbors get together and agree to improve their urban homes by remodeling. In Georgetown in the District of Columbia, New York's Greenwich Village, and San Francisco's Russian Hill—to cite just a few of the better-known projects—results have been revolutionary. Esthetics aside, property values in those areas more than doubled within five years, as did the income from rental property. These improvements were accomplished not by a government agency, but principally by individual homeowners working by themselves and with their neighbors to improve their homes.

Urban or suburban, the advantages of remodeling exist and we must, as homeowners in a free-enterprise system of government, develop them, or we will not have proved ourselves worthy or capable of ownership.

Before

After

WHAT TO REMODEL

After you have decided that something needs to be done to your home, the next question is, *what?* There are some preliminary questions which you should ask yourself.

How long do you plan to live in your home after you remodel it? How old are your children? Are your children old enough to benefit from what it will cost you, in time and money, to provide a better home and rooms of their own, or will it just complicate a child's senior year in high school? Do you expect to have another child; are your children about to leave home for college or to work on their own? Looking further, do you expect an older member of the family to come to live with you some day?

If you plan to move in a year or so and have already made your house as comfortable and attractive as possible, it is better to stick to maintenance and repair. It is most inadvisable, providing the house has no structural or mechanical defects, to make changes that you anticipate a new owner may want; people buying an older home want to make their own changes and do not expect to find everything exactly suited to their particular circumstances.

Most children under six years of age do not mind sharing a bedroom with a younger brother or sister. But after they start to school, each child wants a room of his own, no matter how small. And bedrooms can be quite small if you provide adequate storage, plenty of shelves, and good light, with a place to work and read. Often a partition down the middle of a larger room can be the answer, at least for a time.

If you expect to add to your family, have a room ready when the new baby gets home from the hospital. Babies require as much space and a lot more paraphernalia than a ten-year-old, and can be a problem to a child of school age; so do not try to double up.

When children are in grade school, rooms of their own are of much more value to them than, say, a playroom in the basement or a family room with a barbecue. After they get to high school, however, the appearance of their home and a pleasant place to have their friends congregate take precedence. They begin to feel accountable for their home and are conscious of their friends' opinion.

This sensitivity is often more marked in boys than in girls. A girl thinks more about her clothes and complexion than about whether the house needs a coat of paint. If she gets an invitation to the prom from the football captain, she is happy, and getting the dress she wants is more important than a hole in the roof. But a high school boy, though less conscious of personal appearance, is often acutely sensitive to having a house as good as his friends' homes. The size does not matter, but the appearance and atmosphere do.

If you anticipate that one or both of your parents or your wife's parents will move in with you in the not too distant future, remodel for this situation ahead of time and in relation to an over-all plan. A large guest room, preferably on the ground floor with a separate entrance through the garden, can be combined with bath and dressing-room space that also accommodates a small utility kitchen. Your week-end guests will enjoy getting their own breakfast coffee, and if it does happen that parents come to live with you, quarters will be ready for them, and they will feel wanted.

The same area can be used as a rentable apartment, which has obvious advantages in fact and in resale value, too. Most zoning ordinances permit one rentable apartment in a home if the owner occupies the residence. This is an advantage for older people who have retired or for a strictly budgeted family who can use the additional income. The time to plan these additional benefits is when you are designing your remodeling and deciding both your present and future needs.

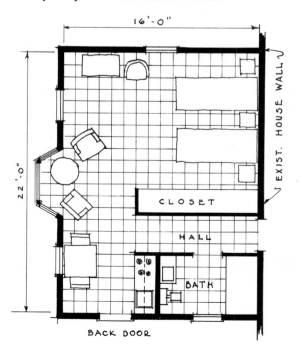

The basic question of what to modernize and change may be determined easily if you have lived in your house for some time and are familiar with its faults.

One of the best times to decide on what to remodel is just after you have returned from a vacation. Then, with the opportunity to take a fresh look at your home, you will probably see some things for the first time.

Make a list of all the things you have been wanting to do and of all items, large and small, that annoy you about the house. Plan to have essential things completed first; get the house in sound structural and mechanical shape along with any remodeling you do. An architect or contractor can tell you how serious the existing faults are and about how much it will cost to correct them. Sometimes the trivial things that annoy us most cost little to eliminate while the contractor is working on the house.

Does the house look too high and old-fashioned compared with the other houses on the street? This can be corrected in a variety of ways: for instance, the use of a low terrace wall with steps at the street, instead of at the front door can diminish the feeling of height. The apparent height of a house can also be lowered with appropriate plantings and the right choice of colors on the exterior. If overgrown foundation plantings are clambering over the roof, rip them out. Your house can look entirely different with well-designed landscaping and repainting.

Before

After

Is a picture window on the street making your living room too public? This may be remedied by a hedge or a properly placed fence. There are also many things you can do to the window itself, including screening it for more privacy and interior wall space.

If your house seems too close to the street and has a front porch, you may remove it and use low walls and terraces to lead up to the front door. It is almost always a waste of money to try to keep an ungainly wood porch in good repair. In the old horse-and-buggy days, it may have been pleasant enough to rock gently in a chair on the front porch, watching the carriages go by and greeting friends who strolled past in the shade of the tree-lined street. But today, with all the automobile fumes and noises, most front porches are pretty much of a liability. Even the elderly, who used to enjoy sipping their iced tea there in the summertime, seem to prefer the air-conditioned living room and watching their television friends.

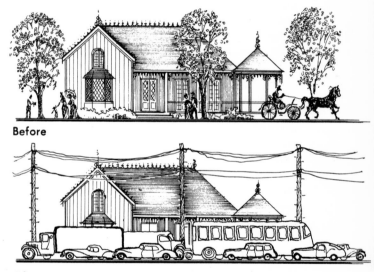

Before

After

An imperative aspect of remodeling is to maintain a good balance between the work to be done and the rest of the house. The overimprovement of any one room or section beyond the capabilities of the remaining areas tends to destroy the total design. Thus it is important to incorporate all ordinary maintenance and repairs (a matter of course in any home) in the over-all scheme. Each bit of paint, every nail, board, and light fixture should be placed so that it becomes a part of the ultimate remodeling.

WHEN TO REMODEL

When you remodel depends somewhat on your plans for the house and on its present condition. If it has been a bit neglected in the past few years, if repair and maintenance have run a little ahead of you, there is a substantial amount to be done, this is a good time also to add that needed bedroom or extra bath, to enclose a porch, or to take it off altogether and add a terrace in the back. If the walls have to be ripped up for installation of a new heating system, this may offer an economical opportunity to replace old wiring. Once the contractor is working on your house, it generally costs little more to do a complete job.

You must decide whether to have everything done at once or stretch the work out over a period of years. This depends on your financial situation, but the more you can do at one time, the less expensive each item will be in itself. The best thing to do is to have an architect draw up a master plan and work from that. Then do what you can when you can, with the knowledge that you are progressing toward a definite goal that will, when completed, be an entire remodeling project.

Spring and summer are the traditional times to remodel. When the smell of spring is in the air, everyone gets the urge to do something to the house. However eager you are to rush into the remodeling, do not hire the first contractor or carpenter you can find to do the work for you. Investigate several contractors or carpenters to be sure that you are getting only competent workmen. Plan your remodeling as far in advance as you can, in the autumn and early winter. Then get bids at the beginning of the year, so that the contractor you choose can include your work in his schedule and do it at the seasonally best time.

Have the essentials completed first. The furnace and heating work, of course, is best done in the summer months when heating contractors are not busy on emergency repair calls. You may want to consider installing air conditioning along with the new heating system. For best results in lower heating and cooling costs and for your own comfort the house should be fully insulated at this time.

Always plan to have exterior work finished by winter, so that when the weather gets rough, the contractor can carry on inside. Contractors usually charge less for indoor work in winter.

House #28 Before Remodeling

Intermediate Remodeling Steps

Frame walls can be erected at any time of the year in any region, although they should not stand exposed to rain and weather too long without being covered. Brief showers or snow do not affect lumber or exterior-grade plywood to any extent if the structure is covered within a short time from exposure.

If you live in the northern climates, masonry work for your house should be done in warm months. Footings, foundations, slabs, and so forth can be placed in cold, even freezing weather; but keeping masonry heated until it sets properly is more expensive, and you have to pay for this. If the concrete or mortar freezes, you might just as well try to stick the house together with graham cracker crumbs. Also, the excavation for footings or foundations is more difficult if the ground has frozen, and this, too, is reflected in higher costs.

Plaster work in northern zones should be done in the warm months, preferably in the spring. Then the windows can be left open to allow the plaster

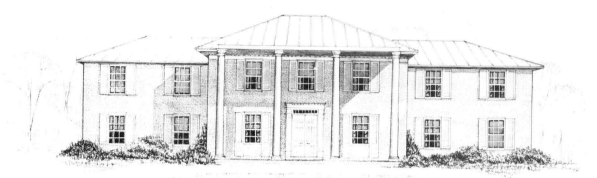

House #28 After Remodeling

to dry slowly. A closed house with a lot of wet plaster warps your floors and other woodwork, and if plaster dries too fast in the heat of summer, it cracks. In practical fact, it is best to avoid using plaster except where local building codes require it. You are better off replacing a whole ceiling with drywall instead of trying to patch up badly damaged plaster with more plaster. Drywall is quicker, better, and less expensive. Use half-inch or five-eighths-inch drywall; avoid the three-eighths-inch so frequently used in cheap developments.

Painting on the interior can be done at any time, but if you are allergic to the smell of fresh or drying paint, then paint in the warm months when you can leave the house wide open.

Exterior painting and staining are obviously better done when the paint and brushes cannot freeze. Early spring and late fall are the best times, between ten o'clock in the morning and four in the afternoon. Seasonally you are ahead of the

hatching of flies and bugs when you paint in early spring, and the first frost has got them by late fall. The ten-to-four restriction is recommended because moisture affects the color and, in some paints, the adhesive qualities.

Plan to do plumbing work in the kitchen and bathrooms at a time when your family can take off on a short vacation. Agree completely on what you have decided upon with your architect and contractor; then go away and let them do it.

Nothing slows down a contractor more than working around a house full of inquisitive children, unless it is a somewhat less than friendly pet or a lady of the house who changes her mind every minute about the color of the paint or tile and tries to keep things spotlessly clean all the time. If you must be in the house while major work is going forward, do not expect the contractor or his men to tidy up meticulously every evening before they leave. When they leave it need be only "broom clean" according to the contract.

WHERE TO REMODEL

Where you begin your remodeling depends entirely on your house, your family, and your pocketbook. If the plumbing, heating, and wiring are all in good condition and you have enough money to do an entire remodeling job, do it all at once. But if your budget limits you to a small project each year, do the important things first.

Most people who spend money redoing their house want the improvement reflected on the exterior. That is why certain "sacred cows" of our domestic architecture, the front porch and the picture window, may be the first to go, simply because many people now consider them useless and ugly.

The best place to start your remodeling would be in an architect's office. He will design a master plan that you can work from, with an eye to doing what you can when you can but always with entire remodeling the final goal. See him with your long-time list of things that are wrong with your house. Reappraise the exterior, and go through every room in the house. Note carefully what needs to be corrected, what you want changed, and what you would like to have done in relation to doors, windows, floors, walls, lighting, and other details.

Take into consideration the location of neighboring houses, their architecture, the views you want to see and the ones you want to ignore. Consider the orientation of the site, and whether its main axis is north and south or east and west.

You should read a copy of the local building code and be familiar with the zoning ordinances. These codes and ordinances govern your neighborhood and determine what you are permitted to do to your house.

Your grounds and house can be divided into three areas: public, private, and utility. Movement from area to area, known as "circulation," should be pleasing and comfortable. If the front entrance is in the living room, if you must go through one room to get to another, if you look into a bathroom from the living room, if there are stairs to the second floor or to the basement in the living room, these will be among the first things you will want to correct. Once the circulation problems are worked out, not only within the house but within the rooms themselves, half the job is done.

The way one is able to move about within individual rooms is also a circulation problem to be considered. We all know the saga of the housewife who is constantly moving the furniture. She knows there is something wrong the way it is, something that could be solved if she could just find the right combination. So she is always searching for a solution that does not exist. The furniture is as much a part of the house as seats are of an automobile, and must be anticipated and designed for in every room of the house. Of course the furniture could be wrong for the room—you cannot get the front seat of a Cadillac into the rumble seat of an old Ford—but just as often the fault is found in a poorly designed room, whose sole distinction is that it is an excellent indicator of where to start remodeling.

In old-fashioned houses and in a number of tract houses, there are so many doors and openings in the living room, front door, closet door, dining-room door, hallway to bedrooms, fireplace, and picture window, that there is no space for furniture. In a way, rooms are the same as closets; they are easier to keep clean and neat if everything has a place. Even if things are moved, they can be straightened quickly. If you trip over tables and bump into chairs, if a room is hard to clean and keep straightened, it is the fault of the room and should be corrected from the very beginning.

The work pattern and circulation of the kitchen can make preparing meals easier and cleaning up less tiring. The amount of space in a kitchen is not as important as how the space is used. A common fault, as in living rooms, is that so many doors are stacked around the walls that the kitchen ends up as a hallway; often so little space is provided for countertops that even minimum food preparation is a chore. Sometimes there is a back door, dining-room door, door to the hall, door to the garage, closet door, a door to the basement stairs, and a door to a terrace or porch. If possible there should never be more than three doors in a kitchen, the door to the dining room, a door to the front hall, and a door to the rear entrance.

So many bathrooms are the standard minimum five feet by seven feet that about the only thing you can do is to live with them. But if it is even smaller and you bump walls and fixtures when you clean, enlarge it, at the same time making it comfortable for two people to use at once.

In the last twenty years, bedrooms have become smaller. They lack the features necessary to make a comfortable, safe room to sleep in. Inept builders and designers have provided rooms 11¼ by 9½ feet with a window punched in the middle of each outside wall and called them bedrooms. These quasi-Pullman compartments are misnamed because there is barely room for a bed, let alone a chest of drawers and a comfortable chair with a reading light. If you want to put twin beds in the room, one or both invariably end up in front of a radiator or register and under a window. Bedrooms should have cross ventilation, but windows over beds are hard to open and close and cause drafts, and if it rains during the night, children and beds get soaked before the windows can be closed. Most corner windows in a bedroom are another misconception. They are, for the most part, ugly and difficult to curtain and provide no cross ventilation.

If the front porch is falling to pieces, take it off. A porch can be expensive to maintain and usually serves no other purpose than to keep rain and snow away from the front door.

In almost every house there is one area that is not being used as well as it could be because of the awkward placement of a staircase, the entrance, a hallway, or a window. This is especially true of houses built in the twenties or another more leisurely era. Before you add to your house, whether it is large or small, use well all the space in it from attic to basement.

Remodeling the House You Live In

WHAT'S WRONG WITH YOUR HOUSE?

It is just as important to know what is right with your house as to know what is wrong with it. Precious time and money can be saved by knowing what to leave alone and what to change. Sometimes it is less expensive to replace the windows instead of trying to patch and repair the old sash and window sills. New siding might, over a short period of years, be cheaper than scraping, sanding, repairing, and painting the existing house walls. The same may be true of the plumbing, heating, and electric work in the house, but these factors can be determined by getting alternate bids from a contractor. More difficult to decide in dollars and cents is the advantage of whether or not to turn and rebuild an old staircase that complicates the circulation within the house; whether to throw out an old kitchen and build another in a better location or in a new addition; whether to try and use an existing low attic for more bedrooms or add more in a new wing. After having lived in a house we are more apt to know what is wrong with it than what is right with it. The wrongs are ever present and constant reminders. The right things may not be apparent because we are used to them and expect them.

As noted earlier, regardless of how small or how large your property, each house and each site have three basic areas: public, utility, and private. The smaller the house and lot, the more important it is that these three areas be designed and defined accurately. If your home does not have these three definite areas inside and out, establish them. The more difficult this is to do, the greater the need to be done, because it is here that you will begin to see the real trouble with your property, aside from obvious mechanical, structural, and decorating faults.

On the outside, the public area is the driveway and the front yard; casual or formal, they present your impersonal side to the public. In the utility area you keep the garbage cans, store the lawnmower and garden equipment, dry the wash, keep the meters, and have a spot to pile and burn trash. A well-planned utility area is accessible from the driveway, the garage, and the back door, yet out of sight of the public area of the front and away from the private area of the garden. Hopefully, the private area is out of sight of the street and public areas, accessible through the house or by a garden gate, an area that is cool, sunny, inviting, and quiet.

On the interior, the public area includes the entrance hall, the living room, and the dining room. The utility area is the kitchen, pantry, and laundry (if it is on the first floor), and the back entrance. The family room is in this area because it is the center of noise and activity during the day. The private area comprises the bedrooms and the sitting room, library, or study. This area should be quiet, protected both from exterior and interior noise, and it should be accessible from the private area of the garden.

These areas can be established for every house. There is no such thing as an "impossible" house or an impossible site for a house and landscaping. There are bounds of economic and esthetic feasibility, but with enough time and the proper expenditure of money, any house can be well-organized and pleasant to live in.

The immediate problem is to correct the faults in your home as quickly and as inexpensively as you can. This requires not only good judgment, but insight and talent. The more of these you possess or can hire, the less time it will take, and the greater will be your satisfaction with the end result of the remodeling.

How does your house look from the outside? We tend to judge houses, and the people who live in them, by the way they look when we first see them. You begin to create the atmosphere of your home at the sidewalk.

Just as significant to you is the view you have from your house. If your home does not take advantage of a view or if you can see out only by allowing others to look in, there is something wrong with your house. If, however, there is nothing beautiful to look at, there is something wrong with you. It is possible to create something to look to, from the interior of your home.

Anyone who has ever lived in an apartment or a rented room knows what I mean by lack of view. The view may be only a blank wall, another apartment window, or a hot, bleak roof. One of the many advantages of owning a house is the opportunity to create on the exterior, as well as in the interior, a view of the world as we want to see it.

Redesigning the placement of rooms and storage space to have them working together mechanically, structurally, and decoratively will determine how well your house will "live." Only at great expense can you move the position of the house in relation to its site, but changing the location of rooms within the house can accomplish a lot.

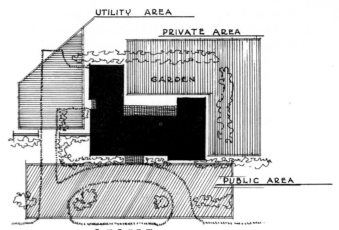

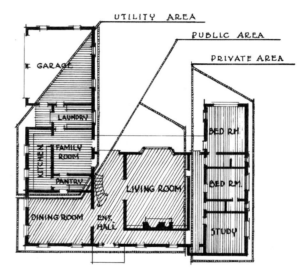

If your living room is at the front and lacks seclusion from the street, additional bedrooms and storage can be built in this area, and you can relocate the new living room at the back of the house. Bedrooms do not need large windows in the same sense as a living room and are easily kept private from the street. The living room at the back can have as much exposure on the garden as you like. This is relatively inexpensive space to work with because no plumbing, and very little heating and electrical work are involved.

Changing the front door and placing the entrance on the side can completely reorient the circulation of a house and can also make use of a limited side yard that serves no other purpose than to space houses equidistantly apart. Too, a side entrance can be advantageous if the house is on a narrow lot.

When a lot slopes up sharply from the street and requires a flight of exposed stairs to the front door, the stairs can be redesigned so that you either enter through the basement or walk up an interior flight of stairs to the main rooms. Besides gaining a new look on the exterior, getting the entrance out of the living room, and having a rain-and-snow-free stair, you open up basement rooms to direct access from the street level, which has obvious advantages for children's playrooms and utility areas and eliminates a lot of normal traffic through the main rooms of the house. A cantilevered balcony or a second-floor porch off the living room will shelter the entrance and screen the living-room windows from the street.

If your site drops away from the street, you can open the basement to a new kitchen and living room with all the glass wall you want. This could give you a whole floor to make into bedrooms. In this arrangement it is quite easy to include a small sitting room on the bedroom floor, saving the remnants of the old kitchen to make a laundry and kitchenette. Think of not having to go all the way downstairs on a cold winter night to get a cup of coffee and a snack. The kitchenette will also be handy when the children get sick or if an elderly member of the family must have meals in his room.

Rather than a bore, a bare, flat lot and a plain house can be the easiest site to maintain because you do not have to cart equipment up and down a hill or get involved with steps and grades and water drainage. The neighbor's windows can be blotted out with fast-growing trees or a trellis and your own private gardens enclosed with walls and hedges. The entrance to a house does not have to be a front door. It can be a garden, a loggia, a courtyard, or a covered walk leading to a terrace.

It will do your house a lot of good if dowdy details are removed from the exterior: shutters that do not fit windows, awkward cornices, window boxes that will not grow flowers, odd columns and miscellaneous bits of decoration that clutter up the façade.

However, if your house has a detail that you like, leave it. What could be nicer than a big, old-fashioned bay window, even if it is in the wrong location, with a comfortable window seat roomy enough for children, books, lunch, drinks, dog, telephone, and radio?

Unless you live in a house of historical architectural merit, do not consider anything about the house as sacred. Every room in the house, every part of the garden can be moved somewhere else, as long as the three principal areas remain and function together as they should.

WILL YOU OVERBUILD
THE NEIGHBORHOOD?

Overbuilding the neighborhood simply means that you put more money into the remodeling of your home than you can get out of it if you should have to sell. It is an important consideration because neither you nor your family will be able to sell it for, or borrow money on, your full capital investment. In essence, overbuilding would be spending twenty thousand dollars on remodeling your home in a neighborhood of ten-thousand-dollar houses.

People are inclined to overestimate the value of their homes and possessions and require the objective eye of an outsider to appraise their property. But keeping a balance between your home and the neighborhood is not difficult if you use common sense.

Take a good look at your house in relation to your neighbors' houses. Look at the street, the block, the whole neighborhood in which you live. Compare your street and your house with the others.

Is the area growing? Good. Is it starting to go to seed? Bad. Are there zoning ordinances that protect the residential quality of the neighborhood, or can someone build a supermarket, a gasoline station, or a rooming house a few doors away from you?

Is a new highway or some other municipal project going to be started in the near future, and will it devaluate private property in the area? Bad. Are taxes stable in your area? Good. Is there convenient transportation; do you have schools, shopping centers, garbage collection, fire and police protection? Good.

How old and how well-kept are the houses around you? Is the neighborhood constant, or do families move in and out? Do most people own their own homes, or do they rent?

All of these factors have a bearing on the amount of money you can prudently put into remodeling your home. They will influence the bank that lends you the money to make improvements, or the bank that may later inspect your home if you sell it, or the amount of mortgage your prospective buyer will be able to get.

Once you have started improving your home, it is hard to stop at the point of dwindling returns in terms of convertible cash. The time to make up your mind on how far you will go and how much you will spend is before you begin. If you do not have a definite plan and budget at the start, you will find almost before you know it that you have invested far too much in one section of the house and not enough in another. Then, to bring the entire house to a uniform level of completion, you will have to spend more than you expected.

If you are not sure of how much your house may be worth on the market, call up a real estate man and ask him how much he can get for it on a quick sale. Have him show you other homes in the area that are for sale, and compare these prices with the price you paid for your house, the mortgage you have, and your interest rates. If there are any building sites for sale, see how much they cost, and compare them with your own lot and the improvements you have made.

Remember, when it comes to resale, a fifteen-thousand-dollar house with three small bedrooms sells faster than a similar fifteen-thousand-dollar house with two big bedrooms, even though the two big bedrooms might be easily divided. Real estate agents write down the number of bedrooms buyers say they must have and simply do not bother to show anything else. A house with two small bathrooms sells faster than the same house with one big, glamorous bath for basically the same reason. Most buyers who want two baths or three bedrooms just do not look at a house without them, regardless of the possibilities of dividing a bedroom or adding a bath. This is true even if the difference in price would more than pay for the alteration.

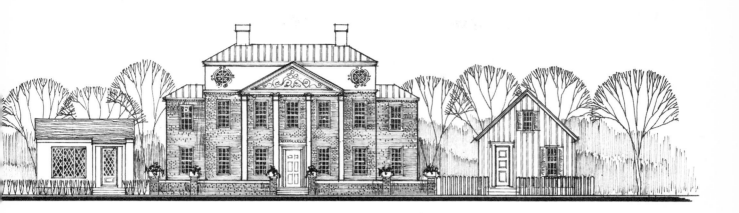

If you have a house that is worth ten thousand dollars in a neighborhood of thirteen-thousand-dollar houses, you might reasonably invest four or five thousand dollars in remodeling. You could easily invest that much on the kitchen alone, but it would not be a wise thing to do. In this case, you would not be overbuilding the neighborhood so much as you would be overbuilding the house. The same five thousand dollars spent on the kitchen of a forty-thousand-dollar house could be a good investment, depending on the condition of the rest of the house.

But let us say you live on a farm, a good farm, with a ten-thousand-dollar house on it. If you and your family spend most of your free time in the kitchen (and a farm kitchen is one of the liveliest, most cheerful places to be in), then five thousand dollars spent on the kitchen, as living space and not just as a food laboratory, might be very well spent. There is no reliable rule of thumb; it is a matter of using your head.

Taking an average house worth twenty thousand dollars in an area of similar houses, five thousand dollars can be well and safely spent, provided that it is not all lumped in one place in the house. It should be applied in an over-all pattern of remodeling, perhaps with one extravagance, such as a fine new front door, an oversize chimney, or a courtyard, or terrace. Even six or eight thousand dollars may not be too much to put into the house, but you cannot depend on getting twenty-eight thousand dollars when you sell; and probably any sum above eight thousand dollars would bring diminishing returns.

Should the twenty-thousand-dollar house be in a neighborhood of twenty-five-to-thirty-thousand-dollar homes, then there will be little question of getting your money back on resale; and provided you invested in good design, you will very likely show a profit.

If you have a twenty-thousand-dollar house in a neighborhood of fifteen-thousand-dollar houses, I would suggest that you proceed very cautiously with any remodeling if you expect to get your money out of it at the time of resale. Because of Americans' inclination to change and relocate, the economics of reselling houses must be considered almost in the same way as automobiles are traded every year or two.

But financial gain is not the only thing to consider in remodeling. It may well happen that by your own good example others in the neighborhood will begin to improve their properties, and this in turn will attract new families who will spend more money on their homes. It is then that so-called "overbuilding" is not only an investment in your own home, but in the neighborhood as well.

It can be profitable to bring neighbors together to discuss the possibilities of building up the whole street. You can begin with something as simple as having each homeowner plant a tree along the street or put a light in front of his house to light the sidewalk. Perhaps each family could contribute to having the street repaved or a new sidewalk built, if you live in a private development outside city maintenance. Once a little enthusiasm is shown and a little personal interest taken, your neighborhood can start to bloom.

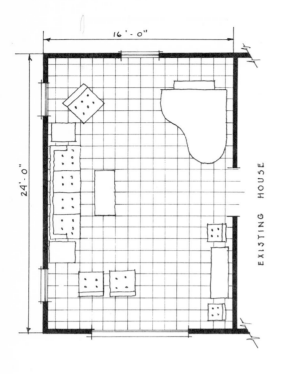

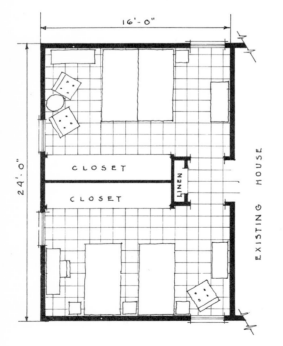

HOW MUCH SHOULD YOU SPEND?

Americans are competitive by nature; all want the prettiest girl in town, the fastest car on the road, and the best house on the block. When remodeling, it is sometimes hard not to pull out all the stops and really do the house up right. How much you should spend—not how much you are willing to spend—ought to be determined by the amount the neighborhood warrants, the time you plan to remain in the house, the present payments, your personal finances, the amount that taxes and insurance will increase by the remodeling, and your age.

If you expect to stay in the house only three or four more years, do not make any changes in it unless you have to. Just stick to maintenance and repair. On the other hand, if you need a new heating system, and it cannot be put off, do not do a patch-work job. Do it right while you are at it. You might be able to save a couple of hundred dollars with a quick, cheap installation, but even for temporary use you will find it is not worth the saving. The first thing a prospective buyer inquires about is heating.

The roof is another item that cannot be put off. A bad roof can ruin the best house in a couple of years with dampness and water marks; replacement or repair must be done at once. If you can get away with patching, do it. A good roof that has been patched looks infinitely better than a new cheap roof.

When you plan to stay in the house another five or six years, you can think about more extensive remodeling, such as a new living room, or more bedrooms and a new bath. With the exception of a fireplace, a new living room is not expensive to build. The wiring and heating are simple, and there is no plumbing to consider.

If you are cramped for bedroom space, a new bedroom is not going to cost you as much as the friction and bad temper you will encounter over the next few years. Bedrooms are no more expensive to build than the living-room area, but proximity to a bathroom and the closets they require can make them more difficult and tricky to add to an existing house. However, lower heat requirements and their smaller size usually balance the cost with that of the living room.

A good-sized bedroom costs little more to add than a minimum-sized bedroom. You cannot estimate the cost by square footage because roof and foundation requirements change for each residence considered.

Bathrooms, in spite of their smaller size, are expensive because of the heating, plumbing, electrical, and fixture requirements. Fitting closet doors, tile work, mirrors, and built-in cabinets can increase the cost enormously in proportion to the size of the room.

If you are desperate for another bathroom but cannot afford it and a bedroom, too, install a built-in wash basin in the bedroom. This at least gets toothbrushing and the "I just want a glass of water" traffic out of the way.

Here again it is false economy to add a minimum-sized bath of 5'x7', when an 8'x8' addition may cost the same or a very little more. A lavatory which can be fitted into existing interior space costs much less. And if you plan to move in a few years it is easier to sell a three-bedroom house with a bath and a half, and you will get more money for it. But if you have a two-bedroom, one bathroom house and spend four thousand dollars to add a new bedroom and a lavatory, you do not necessarily get four thousand dollars more for the house if you sell it. You have more people who are interested, however, because more families want three bedrooms and more than one bathroom. Therefore, you will cover a greater market, and with more exposure, the chances of selling quickly and for more money are increased.

The kitchen is the most expensive room in the house. It requires heating, wiring, plumbing, appliances, built-in counters, closets, special hardware, subfloor and finished floor, and usually some special lighting.

Porches are relatively expensive, too. Although they do not require plumbing or heating, they have to be lighted and need footings, foundations, a roof, flashing, sometimes a railing, steps, painting, and materials that are impervious to weather and changes in climate.

In so far as the time element is concerned, if you plan to live in your present home ten years or longer, you can go into debt for as much as you can afford, without over building your neighborhood, everything else being equal.

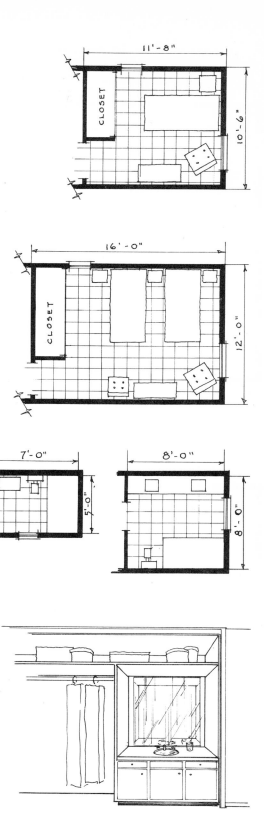

Your personal financial situation is one of the deciding factors in how much you should spend on your house. You can pay for the remodeling in cash and thereby save the money you would have to pay in interest, if you borrow the money or refinance the mortgage. However, this does not mean that over a period of time you will be further ahead financially.

You must weigh the difference in the cost to you between the expense of borrowing and the amount of return you might realize by using the money another way in a sound investment.

Of course, if the additional payments for the new mortgage or loan are increased to such an extent that you are uncomfortably close to the balance in your checkbook, do not remodel. There is nothing so nagging and unpleasant as living in and with a house you cannot afford.

Another thing you should not overlook is the increase in taxes and insurance rates. They may not go up much, but the alterations may so impress the tax assessor that your tax could double. Your insurance increases proportionately with the amount you invest in the house.

If you must get a building permit, this automatically pushes you into a re-examination of the house for tax purposes when the remodeling is completed. Be sure to check with the local building code and avoid having to get a building permit if you want to save money. Since local codes supersedes state codes, it is impossible to generalize, but many codes require a permit only if you add more than four feet in any one direction to your house. Many times porches and loggias do not require a permit and can increase the livable area of your house considerably. The code may call for a permit if the cost of remodeling exceeds a certain level, which can be an advantage in doing a little bit every year. But it also means that you will be living in a constant state of construction.

Your age plays a large role in the amount of money you can borrow and the rate you are charged. A man who is thirty, with a steady job and a good house, has very little trouble getting the money to remodel his home on a twenty- or twenty-five-year mortgage. A man of forty, assuming he has progressed financially, has no difficulty borrowing from a bank an amount that roughly equals his yearly income on twenty-year loan terms to finance a remodeling on his home. However, a man of fifty has trouble getting a twenty-year loan simply because it will not be paid off until he is seventy, which is to say, five or ten years after normal retirement, and he therefore represents a greater financial risk. After fifty, you may get a ten-year loan, but after sixty years of age your chances are slim, unless you have some pretty sound investments and a good reputation to back you up.

I do not think it is wrong for a man of sixty or sixty-five to start remodeling a house if he has the money to do it; he could easily have fifteen or twenty good years left to enjoy it, and it gives him a new interest after he retires and keeps him active physically and mentally.

Buying a House to Remodel

CONSIDER THE NEIGHBORHOOD

There is, of course, the alternative of selling your present home and buying another which will be more suitable to your requirements. Many young families find that in three or four years they may need more bedrooms. Rather than expanding the house to double its size, it may be better to buy a large, old house with the required space. A four- or five-bedroom house with two or three baths may not be a good financial investment in a neighborhood of two-bedroom, one-bath houses, but remodeling existing rooms is usually considerably less expensive than new construction. The answer depends on several personal factors, your own desires, your neighborhood, the convenience, and whether it is worth uprooting your family to move.

Although it is true that we gain the most satisfaction from remodeling our present home, it may not be economically feasible or desirable to alter and improve it beyond a certain point. If the house is half the size you need and cannot be enlarged, you might do better to look for a bigger house. Many people whose families have grown and moved away no longer need or want extra bedrooms or baths and a lot of grass to cut. These houses can often be remodeled to suit your own family less expensively than your present home. On the other hand, if your house is much too large for you because the children have married and live elsewhere, a smaller house with less maintenance and no stairs to climb might suit you better than removing the second floor.

In either case, buying another house to remodel has the distinct advantage of allowing you to have the work done before you move. The remodeling will be finished more quickly, and you do not have to put up with the noise and inconvenience of living in the house while the work is under way. It can also be quite an invigorating experience with none of the sentimental legacies associated with a house that you have lived in for some time.

Finding the right house in a neighborhood you like is a combination of luck and good judgment. You may find the perfect solution in a day or two, but usually it takes a bit of hunting to find what you are looking for.

Pick out a few quiet neighborhoods, and examine them carefully. The neighborhood is going to materially affect the cost of the house, the cost of maintenance, the amount of money you can put into it, the amount you can get out of the house if you sell, your children's social activities and schools, and even the way you live and entertain.

First, explore the neighborhood in general. Look at more than one house in each section, and compare the prices and taxes. Consider several locations. Whether in the country or in the middle of town, go to the town hall and get a copy of the building code and a zoning map showing the areas in which you are interested.

The zoning map indicates whether the area is residential, multifamily residential, two-family residential, or business or industrial; it will also show how close your prospective home is to a factory, school, railroad, dump, or major highway or airport. The zoning ordinance spells out the restrictions on the property. The building code deals directly with construction requirements, new additions, and alterations.

Be extremely cautious about buying a house in undeveloped suburban country without zoning or building restrictions, unless you can afford to buy enough acreage to protect yourself and your view against later buyers who could construct a motel, gas station, or trailer camp next to you.

Examine the utilities. If the neighborhood has no municipal transportation, garbage collection, city water, and sewage disposal, the lack of these facilities increases the cost of maintaining the house. If there is a natural-gas supply line in the street, you have a choice between heating with gas, oil, or electricity, in the event that the house needs a new heating system. If the electric and telephone wires are underground, you are assured of trouble-free service in winter and during wind storms. If there is a fire department and fire hydrants near, your insurance rates are less. Availability of public transportation and the distance from schools, churches, office, and shopping centers bear distinctly on whether you need a second car.

When the house is on a private road, see to it that there is a contract with the developer or

Before

After

owner of the road stating the assessments for repair, snow removal, and general maintenance. Private roads can be turned into public roads, and each property owner can be assessed by the city to pay for the paving of the street and for sidewalk construction. Most public roads are required to be fifty feet wide to accommodate the passage of a fire truck; and if a private road goes public, the required width can be deducted from your front yard.

It is a great advantage to have trees on both sides of the street. Trees keep the street cool in the summer, help hide wires and poles, add to the privacy of both house and garden, and increase the property values on the street. Trees also make the street about 100 per cent more attractive all year round.

Remember the address when you first go to a house with the real estate agent; then drive through the neighborhood during a weekday evening, on a Saturday night, a Sunday morning, to see conditions as they exist at different hours of the day and week.

Try to stay away from developments in which all the houses are the same or all were built at one time, with slightly different façades. These areas are pegged in certain price brackets, and any improvements you make may be lost in a predetermined market.

A composite neighborhood of prices and ages is a better environment in which to live and rear children. Families that have been settled there for some time will have smoothed the way in establishing the character of the section and the atmosphere of the block.

Neighborhood House #9

CONSIDER THE SITE

After you have investigated the neighborhood, you should turn your attention to the site of the house. Consider the size and shape in relation to the set-back regulations (the minimum allowable distance between house and property line) to see if you can add a garage or carport with economy, and without having to get a variance in the zoning ordinance from the city.

Check any easements or right of way that the gas company, water company, or any other utility may have across the property. Have all the water mains and other lines to the house marked so that you do not build or plan an addition across them. Locate the cesspool, drainage field, and any underground springs. Find out whether any subterranean tunnels from mines have been dug under the site or any well shafts sunk into the ground. An abandoned tunnel can collapse at any time from erosion and underground water; in some cases slow fires have been known to smoulder for a generation in an old coal-mine tunnel, creating hazardous conditions and generating dangerous fumes. Having an old well filled with soil or concrete is expensive; you should have an understanding with the present owner on the cost and who is responsible for it. All these factors can have a direct influence on where and whether you can extend the house and even whether you should buy it in the first place.

Is the driveway in good condition? Does it go past the front door; is there a turnaround, or do you have to back out to the street? Consider the length of the driveway from the garage to the street, not only in terms of edging and maintenance, but also with a view to the need for shoveling snow in winter.

Is there a hedge or fence to separate you from the neighbors? A fence can act as a good buffer to keep people out as well as your own children and pets in. It is very aggravating to have all the dogs in the neighborhood running freely across your lawn and damaging shrubbery and the garden. A fence is expensive, and building one after you have moved in can cause resentment, especially if the neighbors do not have fences themselves.

Are there large trees on the site? Trees can turn an otherwise dull house and lot into a real find. Large, slow-growing trees are preferable to fast-growing species, simply because the wood is harder and they do not drop as much bark, twigs and fruit on the lawn and are not as likely to break in a storm. Trees are even worth transplanting to a property, if you must, because they shade the house and windows from the sun in summer, absorb excess moisture, and keep the soil from eroding. They also increase the apparent distance between the house and the street and other houses, and they absorb and deflect sound to make the house quieter.

The drainage of the site should be considered. If the land is low and flat, it can be wet and marshy part of the year. Check the water table with local authorities. If it rises periodically, it can easily flood the basement, wash out the driveway, and cause distressing problems with the sewage-disposal system.

Water draining off the street into the basement and garage can be a problem on property that slopes down from the street level. The driveway for this type of site must be well-engineered, particularly in northern climates where you may find it impossible to get the car out when it snows. A thick hedge or stout fence is also highly recommended for this kind of site; it keeps the lights of passing cars out of the windows at night and serves as an extra protection for children playing on the front lawn. It is desirable to have the street on the north and the view on the south side of the house so large windows that admit the sun and overlook the view do not face the street.

Land that slopes up from the street has the reverse problem. Ice and snow will prevent you from getting into the garage in winter, but this problem is not as serious because the car may be left in the entrance to the drive. If you are elderly or have serious illness in the family, you should consider whether an ambulance can negotiate the drive in winter. Again, it is better for the street to be on the north and the view to the

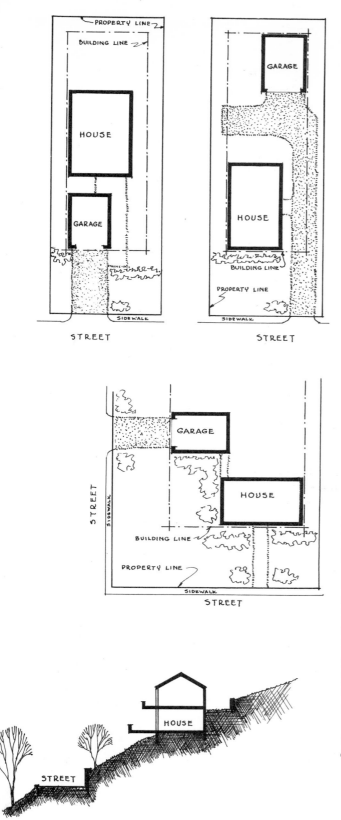

south. However, if the view and the street are on the south, you can mask off the street by careful planning, eliminate most of the noise and still have the view and the sun.

Long, narrow lots can limit the expandable area of the house to the front and back. Too many times the garage must be on the front and is the most conspicuous part of the house, unless you commit yourself to a long, expensive driveway to a garage at the back. The advantage of a narrow site is in less landscaping and grass to cut on the front and a larger private area in the back of the house. Very careful planning is required if you wish to make an addition to the house.

Corner property has the advantage of extra space and light, but the actual available building area can be reduced by set-back regulations, and there is a lack of privacy from two streets. Other drawbacks are the doubled amount of public area to be landscaped and maintained and the limitation of private area of the garden to the far corner. Corner lots provide the advantage of getting the garage and service entrance off to one side. If the neighborhood is crowded and the houses are tightly set on their sites, a corner property can give you additional light and air through three exposures instead of just two. Traditionally, the house on the corner was larger and presumed better than the others on the block, but this is not necessarily true any longer.

Trees, sunlight, a view, and privacy have come to mean much more than they used to, principally because they are getting harder and harder to find. For many people trees and sunlight take precedence and are more valuable than a view. You cannot control a view, and what was once a bucolic scene could sprout Esso and Coca Cola signs almost overnight. And, however spectacular it may be, after living with a view a year or so, its sheer availability soon diminishes its importance. Unless you are living at the bottom of a hole or your house is surrounded by high office buildings, you can get sunlight into it with good planning and design. Privacy can be built in or out, although sometimes at a loss of the view or sunlight.

You have to decide for yourself what you like about the site and what the basic but relative value of one location is over another.

CONSIDER THE LANDSCAPING

Landscaping can make an old house look dignified, a new house seem settled, a small house larger, an awkward house charming . . . or it can do just the opposite. Landscaping can add three thousand dollars to the cost of a twenty-thousand-dollar house, but if done properly, it can make it look like a thirty-thousand-dollar house. The landscaping, as everything else, must be designed and planned. That is why, when you are looking at a house to buy, the planting and grounds should be taken into consideration.

If the so-called foundation planting around the house has grown past the second floor or the roof, it may all have to be removed. The proportions and charm of a house can sometimes be ruined by planting which has grown too high and has obscured the design. Trees this high can sometimes be moved, but it is expensive, hard work, and one side of the tree will have deteriorated from being against the wall of the house. If the foundation planting is only halfway up the first story of the house, it can sometimes be saved with careful pruning. High, rangy planting around the house wall can induce a damp basement. The planting around the foundation should be thick, slow-growing plants. Their foliage should not brush against the house or block the light and air that would otherwise ventilate the basement.

Colonial Williamsburg

Make a mental note of the plants and trees, the types, and their positions. Many times the landscaping has been done lovingly and lavishly but without any sense of plan or design. These trees can be moved and quite a lot of money saved by re-establishing them in a design that complements the house.

The "ivy-covered cottage" can be a bad risk, not romantically, but as real estate. Ivy growing on the walls can grow right through sills and eaves if it is not cut back every year, and it can make a masonry house cold and damp. Ivy growing on the roof can separate shingles, cause leaks, and, if the roof is finished with wood shingles, cause them to rot away.

There is a great difference between growing grass and having a lawn. A good lawn is one of the most expensive and difficult items in landscaping. It takes a lot of time and effort to build a lawn, and if the house you are considering has one, that is a vote in its favor.

Note any large trees on the site. Tall pines drop needles in the fall, and if the branches overhang the roof, the needles will clog the gutters and downspouts. Weeping willows grow well in damp wet soil; so if there are many native willows growing on the property, be prepared for marshy ground part of the year. If soil tends to be dry, a willow finds moisture even if it has to grow into the water main. Lombardy poplars also grow into things like the water main and the cesspool. These trees, and others that grow rapidly, should not be close to the house. They are better as background and a windbreak at the edge of the property.

The surface of the drive is another item of maintenance to keep in mind. Blacktop is the easiest to patch and keep up. Cement lasts the longest, and gravel or brick are the most attractive. A gravel drive has to have new topping every year or two and needs to be weeded and raked.

A garden house for the storage of tools, fertilizer, lawnmower, and other equipment is a big advantage. Too often this equipment ends up in the garage, making the garage harder to keep clean and giving it a messy appearance when the doors are open. If you travel, a garden house also permits someone to take care of your garden and lawn without a key to the house or garage.

Terraces, expensive to build correctly, greatly increase the livable area of the house. Brick and slate are the best materials. Check for loose brick or slate, and check the joints for cracks. Cracks mean that the terrace does not have the proper foundation. If the terrace is against the house, be sure that it drains away from the wall and that there are no cracks, which would allow water from rain and snow to funnel into the basement.

Pools can be very nice, but they can also be a liability. A swimming pool can attract all the children and adults in the neighborhood. You are responsible for all personal safety; so aside from upkeep on the pool, cleaning up after the kids, and the expense of entertaining the neighbors, there is the cost of additional liability insurance. A pool on anything less than ten acres should be fenced to keep tots and animals from falling in, not only in summer, but in winter as well. Shallow reflecting pools and fish ponds tend to attract insects, and unless the water is constantly moving, it gets stagnant in a short time.

Exterior lighting can make the difference between a garden and just a yard. Check to see if an extra circuit has been provided for lighting. If possible, get a plan and mark the lines running to the lights so that someday you do not put a shovel through one of the electric wires.

Garden walls and hedges play the biggest role in the amount of use and pleasure you will get from the outdoors. The smaller the lot, the greater the function of a wall. Nothing is better than stone or brick for garden walls. Concrete-block walls are good, but if used for retaining earth, they should be reinforced with steel.

Fences are good dividers, but most of them require upkeep unless they are steel cyclone fences. If the fence is painted, it may be charming, but remember that it has to be repainted every couple of years. Wood fences that are stained or creosoted require less maintenance. Redwood, locust, and cedar make the best wood fences. Low picket fences keep nothing in or out and are a hazard. Rail fences are not much good either, except for growing roses, which act about the same way as barbed wire in preventing direct access to your garden.

Each thing that is in the garden, whether it is in the correct position or not, reduces your immediate landscaping expense. Statuary, outdoor furniture, and, in many cases, rose gardens and choice bulbs, may be removed by the present owner when he leaves. Be sure that the contract states in writing what outdoor lighting and other effects are to go with the house.

CONSIDER THE HOUSE

Now we get around to the house itself. The job of determining the merits of a structure, finding its defects, and seeing its possibilities is at hand. When you get serious (but before you buy), have an architect or contractor go over the house with you after telling him what you plan to do to it. Theoretically, at least, that is what you should do. In actuality you will probably see one house that you fall in love with, and nothing will talk you out of it.

You will look at many houses, however, and the more you know about what to look for, the fewer surprises you will have after you move in.

If you are looking at a frame house, run your finger over the painted surface of the exterior. It should powder slightly on your finger but leave no mark on the wall. Most paints are designed to do this, so that the wall surface cleans itself and layers and layers of paint do not build up on the surface. Excessive chalking stains lower roofs and terraces and masonry walls below the painted wall, and may lead to a complete paint job. Alligatoring of paint surface requires that all the paint be removed and the surface repainted. If the paint has blistered up a short way from the masonry foundation, it means a damp basement or crawl-space. Blistering of painted walls usually indicates no insulation, or if there is insulation, no vapor barrier. Blistering can also indicate a leak in the roof or around a window. The presence of old, cracked, and chipped paint means that you have to remove a coat of paint before you can repaint the house. If it is very bad, you may have to take the entire exterior down to the original surface of the wood and begin again with a sealer and two or three coats of paint. Check the shutters and the trim, too, because they can cost as much to repaint as the walls.

The shutters should be operable; if nailed to the house, they always look false. Shake them to see that they do not rattle. The putty on the outside of the windows should be firm but not brittle. If it is curling and pieces are missing, a full putty job is indicated. Basement windows should be at least eight to ten inches above the ground; they should be operable and with putty and sills in good condition.

If the house is shingle, the shingles should be firmly nailed. The thicker, the better. Natural-finish shingles are better than painted shingles because they require less maintenance. Once the shingles are painted, you have to keep them painted.

Masonry walls should be closely checked for cracks. Any crack is bad except a hairline crack in a brick, which is not defective as long as the joints are not cracked along with it. Especially serious is a crack running through a masonry wall that you can trace with a pencil point. See that the brick courses run evenly on a horizontal line. If they drop abruptly it could mean that the wall is cracked and the joint patched. Cracked masonry walls are usually the result of uneven settling or insufficient footings.

Mortar should be firm and without cracks, and you should not be able to scrape it out of the joints with a nail or crumble it between your fingers.

Foundation walls should be examined carefully for cracks and termite tubes. Stick an icepick or penknife into sills; if it penetrates easily, you can expect either dry rot, or termites, or both. Pry around all the porches and entrance platforms; check for rot and cracks. If wood porches and platforms are in bad shape, it is best to plan on removing them entirely. Examine steps, and if they are wood, stomp on them to see if they are sturdy. They should not have splinters in them. Wobble the railings, and make sure they are sturdy. Check for splinters, too; children always run their hands along a railing, and if there is a splinter, they will find it. In old wood splinters can be dangerous.

Check all the joints between dissimilar materials. Any joints between wood and masonry should be flashed. Window and door heads should have flashing, as well as all joints and edges of roofs, dormers, chimneys, vents, and intersections between sidewalls and roofs. Copper is still the best flashing material and turns a soft green when aged.

Gutters and downspouts should either be of wood, plastic, or the same material as the flashing. Water from the roof should be drained into a dry well some distance from the foundation. If not, you could end up with a damp basement.

Look at the roof. If it sags in the middle, you will probably need a new roof structure, unless it is an old and well-built house. If the house is fifty years old and has not got a perfectly straight ridge, it could simply have settled down to a nice long life span of a hundred and fifty years, but it may be in bad condition. Look at the structure in the attic before you make up your mind. See that the pitch of the roof is even and does not sag or bow.

Tie a rock to the end of a piece of string to improvise a plumb line. Hold it up and see if the house walls are straight up and down. If they are not, you may encounter expensive and serious structural problems.

Curling roof shingles are bad and indicate the need for a new roof surface. A new-looking but lumpy roof finish usually means that a new, cheap roof has been applied over an old and probably rotten one. Slate, tile, terne metal, and copper are the best roofs. Wood shakes are better than wood shingles, but both have the disadvantage of being able to catch fire, which is something to think about if the house is way out in the country. Asbestos shingles make a good fireproof roof, but most of them are unattractive and without character. Composition and asphalt shingles are sold in various grades from mediocre to poor. Rolled roofing or tarred paper means you will need a new roof immediately.

Locate the fireplace clean-out. It is best outside. A fireplace without one will not do you much good because hauling ashes through the house will discourage you from building a fire in the first place.

Wires and meters often go unnoticed when you first look at a house. The meters should be outside so that meter men do not have to go through the house to read them. Wires can be unsightly, and to move them or have them placed underground is expensive.

See if the windows have screens and storm windows or if they are of insulating glass. All doors and windows should be weather-stripped; having them of insulating glass would be a definite advantage. Storm windows, unless they are built into the windows, seldom work, and it is a chore to take them down and put them up again. Fiber glass or copper screen is preferable to aluminum or plastic; and it is better if the screens (unless built into the windows) fasten to the outside of the window frame instead of the inside. Regardless of what kind they are, screens get dirty or

dusty, and soil the curtains when the breezes blow. If the screens are inside, they get the curtains that much dirtier, and screens look unpleasant at night when the windows are closed.

As you go in the front door, you should note whether it, too, has been weather-stripped.

An entrance hall, which absorbs the wear and tear, drafts, and traffic you want to keep out of the living room, is a big advantage. The hall should have an ample closet. A door to the kitchen from the hall is desirable, but be sure that you cannot see the kitchen sink on the way to the living room or dining room. A guest lavatory off the entrance is another big help, since you can keep it clean and reserved for guests. Check that you cannot see the lavatory door from the living room or dining room . . . or the toilet from any position. A window from the lavatory or a bath beside the front door is unpleasant.

If there are stairs to a second floor, tramp on them to see that they are structurally sound and quiet. Even carpet on the stairs cannot reduce noise sufficiently if the construction underneath is thin and cheap. Wiggle the railing and balustrade to see that it is sturdy and able to prevent someone from falling. Narrow, winding stairs may mean that furniture for the upper stories will either have to be very small or taken in through a window or opening on the second floor. If stairs are steep, they are dangerous. A window directly opposite the end run of the stairs or on a landing opposite the run is a hazard. It is too easy to fall or trip through the glass.

Stand in the middle of the living-room floor, and bring your heels down sharply. If it shakes and rattles, the whole house may be unsound and not well built. This does not mean that it is going to fall down right away, but bracing may be required if you want to keep the needle on the record player from skipping every time someone walks across the room. In addition, it makes for a noisy house.

Look for radiators and registers. They can dictate the location of every piece of furniture. Radiators without covers demand them, and they are very expensive. Radiators and registers are best under windows, but if you have to keep the curtains drawn for privacy, you can also shut out the heat. Behind a sofa they shut out the heat, dry out that particular piece of furniture, and make you uncomfortably warm if you sit there.

A return-air grille to remove smoke and the odor of stale cigarette butts would be helpful in the living room. Check a fireplace for loose bricks, which are a fire menace, and make sure there is a damper and a clean-out.

High windows in the living room, can simplify furniture arrangement, but what is the point of having a view if you can only see it when passing through? French or sliding doors to a terrace or porch double the use of the living room in warm weather.

If you enter directly into the living room, see if it is large enough to be partitioned to make an entrance hall with a closet. Wall-to-wall carpet in the living room (also the hall and stairs) is usually included in the purchase price of a house, but get it in writing. Even if you do not like it, it can be a good base for new carpet.

Look for electrical outlets. Extension cords mean inadequate outlets, cheap construction, and probably a need for new (or at least some new) wiring. Since standard cords on lamps and appliances are six feet long, most codes require electrical outlets every twelve feet along the walls of all rooms. If the house was built before the codes were in effect, you are not required to provide the additional outlets unless you do something . . . anything . . . to the wiring. If you do add outlets, the entire house may have to conform to the new electrical code.

The dining room should be close to the living room, but it is better if you do not go through the living room to get to it. It is also better if you cannot see the kitchen door from the living room. Know how large your dining table is before you go house hunting. At least three feet of clearance on all sides of your table are needed to allow chairs to be drawn up to it comfortably. This clearance should be measured, not only from the walls but from other furniture you plan to have in the dining room.

Not every house needs a dining room, but every house should have a pleasant place to dine. Lack of a dining room limits your entertaining to informal or buffet dinners. Children often behave better and learn better table manners if they are taught in a dining room. Many of the newer houses have omitted the dining room and used the space as a "family room"; this is not the same as a regular dining room.

The kitchen of a house can be a warm, delightful place to relax and dine. The size of the kitchen depends on what you do there besides cook. If there is no dining room, the bigger the kitchen, the better.

Check the cabinets, floor, plumbing, and electrical fixtures to be sure you have something to work with. Cabinet doors and drawers should work smoothly and stay open or shut as you leave them. A wall cabinet that has a door that does not stay closed or that closes when it should stay open indicates improperly hung cabinets or a sagging structure. The latter can be a serious flaw in the construction, and the door itself can cause many bumped heads. Adjustable cabinet shelves that permit you to arrange the space to suit yourself are desirable.

Board marks should not show through finish flooring. Just lean down and look sideways at the floor. Continuous ridges that mark the flooring underneath the linoleum or tile indicate that the floor has not been installed correctly and the covering will wear out quickly.

Ideally, the sink should be between the refrigerator (near the back entrance) and the range (near the dining-room door). There are other quite workable arrangements, but this is a good pattern to begin with because the plumbing and wiring may not have to be changed. To test the pipes, turn on the cold-water tap, slowly at first, then stronger until you have reached full force. Then do the same with the hot-water tap, leaving the cold water on. Suddenly switch the cold water off; if the hot water continues to come out with full pressure in a steady stream, it means that you can have a dishwasher. If it comes out at an angle or with a weak stream, it means either insufficient pressure or pipes clogged with mineral sediment. If it takes the hot water a long time to get hot, either you are going to waste a lot of water or the hot-water tank may be defective. If you turn the hot and cold water off at the same time quickly and there is a clank and a rattling noise, it means that the pipes are in poor condition and you may need a new plumbing system or a pressure-regulating device.

Count the electrical outlets in the kitchen. There should be at least ten single or five double plugs for appliances. If the outlets in the kitchen are inadequate, the house may be underwired and a whole new service may be required.

A house with a cesspool and no public sewer line requires a separate cesspool for a garbage disposer, if you want one. Otherwise the house cesspool has to be emptied every two years or so.

In the bathroom, turn on the water in the tub and then the water in the basin. If the stream in the tub diminishes, you will know that the water is either inadequate or the system is not balanced correctly. Flush the toilet. If the water stream decreases in the tub or the basin, something is wrong with the system. A noise in the tub or in the basin from the water being flushed down the water-closet drain indicates the probable absence of vents on the plumbing system.

If the bathroom is small and cramped, you can expect your blood pressure to rise when you are cleaning it. Take hold of the grab-bars over the tub and shake them. They should be firmly anchored to the wall. If they are glass, plan to replace them immediately. Look for at least two electrical outlets in the bathroom, one for an electric shaver and one for an electric toothbrush.

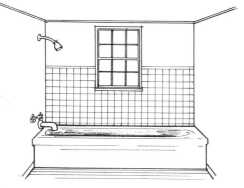

Windows over the tub are bad because you can easily slip and put your arm right through them; they are also an inconvenience because water collects on them from the shower and rots away the sills and the window. Lean on the wash-basin rim. It should support you and not wobble. Check the door to see that it locks and unlocks easily. There should be an emergency key even for a snap lock on the outside of the doorframe to extricate children locked in the bathroom.

If you have children, pay particular attention to the windows in the bedrooms. High windows make the room easier to furnish, but they can also trap children in a fire. The same rule applies for the same reason if you have an elderly person living with you.

Every bedroom should have a light that can be turned on from the door. It should not be a ceiling light, but a light away from the bed so it will not wake someone sleeping if carelessly switched on. The most serious faults in bedroom planning are radiators or registers so placed that there is no room to put a bed on a wall; dangerously high windows; a size so small that the room cannot hold more than one single bed and still have space enough to change the linen.

Most bedrooms can hold a single bed. Fifty per cent can take a double bed without having it over a radiator or register; but only 25 per cent have adequate wall space to take twin beds, without having to place one bed over a register or radiator or under a window. In only a very few of the bedrooms built in the last twenty-five years are you free to place twin beds comfortably and still make up the bed, too. A bed is an awkward, heavy thing to move and hard to reach across. When you are looking at the bedrooms, therefore, make sure there is plenty of room around all three sides of each bed you plan to place in the room.

Closet space is essential. Each bedroom should have a six-foot-wide closet at least twenty-four inches deep for each person using the room. Bi-folding doors are better than sliding doors, and sliding doors are better than no doors, but a hinged door on anything except a walk-in closet can be worse than no door at all because it interferes with furniture placement and is a frequent cause of accidents when left ajar.

The attic should have a good, wide stair (at least three feet) without winders and a good space (four feet) at the top and bottom for landings; lights at top and bottom, too. See that the attic has cross ventilation; if you plan to store anything there, insulation on the rafters is preferable to insulation on the joists.

Check the underside of the roof for leaks, dampness marks, and firmness of structure. If the attic structure on a one-story house is made of wood trusses, it may mean that the partitions below are not load-bearing and you may have complete freedom in moving them. Otherwise, there is usually one partition running the length of the house that is load-bearing and structural, and it must either remain where it is or a steel beam must be substituted when it is removed.

In the basement, look for cracks in the foundation wall. Check the sills and plates for rot, the joists for bridging, the floor for dampness and drains, and the windows for operability and cross ventilation.

Every basement should have two exits; high windows do not count. Although many codes now require it, older homes may not have an outside exit in the basement. It is essential, not only for safety, but also for convenience. A basement garage should have an insulated and fireproof ceiling, and preferably should not be located under bedrooms.

While you are in the basement, look over the furnace. You may not know anything about it, but see that it runs, regardless of the season. It is better if the oil storage tank is buried outside the basement underground. If the tank is outside, it is probably a large one, at least bigger than the 275-gallon tanks used in cheap construction. The larger the tank, the less expensive the oil because you can have it delivered in quantity in an off-season.

Find out the capacity of the hot-water heater. For a family of five you need at least a forty-gallon tank. An oil-fired hot-water heater, if you have an oil-fired furnace, is usually less expensive to run than an electric one.

If there is a well instead of city water, get a sample of the water and send it to the county center to be analyzed for mineral content and purity. Do not take the owner's word that it is as pure as crystal. It is best if the well has a sealed, submersible pump. The diameter of the well will determine the flow and capacity of the water. Look for a hose bib in the basement, one in the garage, and one on each side of the exterior of the house.

A laundry in the basement with a fairly new washer and dryer is a good sign, even though the basement is a poor place for the laundry. If the owner is willing to place good laundry equipment in the basement, it usually indicates that it is a warm, dry place to work.

Look into the fuse boxes. Each major appliance, range, oven, oil burner, water heater, furnace, and any appliance rated over 1,400 watts, should have its own circuit. Each circuit should be labeled so that you know how many there are and which fuse controls which circuit. There should be a separate circuit for exterior and garden lighting.

To help you remember the houses you look at, take snapshots as you go through each. Even if they are not too clear, they will tell you enough to spark your memory. Usually you will be welcomed for a second look if you make an appointment in advance.

SECTION TWO

The Value of an Architect

IS IT IMPORTANT TO HAVE AN ARCHITECT?

Although it is basically true that only you can decide where and what is most important to you to remodel, you may still need the professional services of an architect. When you go to the dentist, only you can tell him which tooth hurts; then he decides how to fix it. If your whole house "hurts all over," it is not just a matter of preference; only an architect can tell you both what is wrong and how to fix it.

Whether you require an architect's services depends on your house and what you would like to do with it. Actually, the best way to find out if you need an architect is to ask one. An architect, unlike members of some other professions, does not charge you to come to his office to examine your problem and help you decide whether employment of his talents is indicated. Not one architect in ten thousand takes you on as a client to remodel your house if he does not think you really need him.

The line between "to have or not to have" an architect is not too fine. If you are handy and need a new bedroom closet, I do not think that you need an architect, or a contractor either. But if you need a new bedroom closet and do not **know** where to put it, then you may need an architect, whether you have a contractor or not. If the scope of the remodeling is such that you need a contractor, it is wise to get both the design and the contractor through the architect.

Price alone does not dictate the need for an architect. A new closet may cost only a hundred dollars, but it can easily be misplaced, with the result that you are constantly bumping into doors, the room seems small and cramped, and there is no proper space for beds. Or it can be designed so that the room is quieter than before, there is more wall space, and the doors and hardware are an asset to the room.

You could be planning to spend two or three thousand dollars to make your basement into a game room without needing an architect. If there are no structural problems or changes, chances are that you and the decorator (if you decide to have one) or you and your contractor can settle on the layout and the finish materials you want for the floor, walls, and ceiling. Some contractors specialize in basements and have standard designs you can choose from. They are uninspired, and the workmen have used the same elements many times. Because they are standardized, however, you are often able to get a lot for your money.

The same thing often applies to kitchen remodeling. You can visit the showrooms of competent kitchen specialists, and simply pick one of their standard designs. They fit a reasonable replica into your available space. It is not going to be a very unusual kitchen, and it may or may not function well for you, but it is a new kitchen and usually better than the one you had before. An architect, using the same budget, could possibly get you an outstanding kitchen.

Any change of openings, addition of a room, porch, or garage, or change of interior partitions, calls for the advice of an architect. For anything that changes the façade or roof line, it is best to get professional help. Windows and doors are most important elements in the façade; they are the eyes and ears of the face of the house. Any inept tampering with them can change the entire effect from the successful to the ridiculous. The roof line is important because it establishes the outline and shape of the body of the house.

For those who have no knowledge of design or especially of construction, the decision is not much of a problem. You know you need help and are intelligent enough to get it. It is the people with a little knowledge who most often get into trouble. The results of their inept design and remodeling can be seen from coast to coast in the sheets of glass on the front of a Cape Cod cottage, the shutters on picture windows, the Victorian front porch on the Colonial house, the shed dormer on the Georgian, the sun parlor on the Spanish.

For the architect, remodeling is more time-consuming and in many ways more difficult than designing new buildings from the ground up. I even know architects who employ other architects for their own homes. The remodeling architect must design not only around the family, view, climate, zoning, and orientation but also around the present style of the house, correcting the structural and design discrepancies that already exist. Before anything can be done, the faults must be analyzed to determine exactly how serious they are. Flaws in design and bad design are more difficult to correct than no design at all because a balance must be kept between the old and new parts of a house. It is like a seesaw; too much emphasis on one side or the other throws the whole thing off balance. Changes and additions must be compatible with the old house, using the good elements of the existing structure and blending in the new work to emphasize the good points and negate the bad. The architect creates the equilibrium required in every successful remodeling, and he plans it within your budget.

If the floor is unsound, if the roof sags, if the sills are rotted, or if the foundations are crumbling, these structural elements must be corrected before or during the remodeling. The architect can put to work the design of the circulation and placement of the rooms in repairing or replacing structural elements. Adroit placement of a partition can shore up a sagging floor and eliminate the expense of new joists or a beam. If the roof structure is in poor shape, it may be less expensive to replace it than to patch up the old one. It may also cost only a little more to gain attic space or a second floor while you are putting on a new roof and roof structure. The architect evaluates the pros and cons from a structural, design, and financial point of view.

Removing a partition to enlarge a room requires in most cases the addition of a beam to take the place of the original support. Foundations under walls at the end of the new beam must be increased in order to carry the additional concentrated loads. Will the beam be big enough? Will there be headroom under the beam? How is it going to look? How much heavier should the foundation be? The contractor or carpenter cannot answer these questions; only the architect can.

You can hardly expect to keep up on all the new materials and new methods of construction, and it is a rare contractor who can determine the basic esthetic qualities of one type of wood against another. New metals, plastics, finishes, and paints are appearing on the market in ever-increasing abundance. Many of them are excellent time and labor savers; others are a complete waste of money. The architect knows these products, their proper application, and, most important, their suitability for your home.

If you are only going to put up storm windows and repaint the house white, it is fairly safe to say that you do not need an architect. Nevertheless, you may want one. See the chapter "Remodeling with Paint" before you decide.

Again, a sick house, like a sick mind or body, needs a proper physician to treat its ills. The architect's function is to provide the best therapy for your home. Because of professional ethics and strict standards of the American Institute of Architects, he cannot come to you. You must go to him and ask for his help.

Another thing to keep in mind when working with an architect and a contractor is that the contractor will try to please the architect; it is good business for him to do so. The architect builds and remodels many houses, whereas you will probably only remodel one, at least in your present area.

WHAT DOES AN ARCHITECT DO?

The architect redesigns your house around you and your family, tailor-making the environment around your personal, social, and financial requirements and, at the same time, trying to satisfy the physical and psychological needs of each member of the family. He selects materials and fixtures for a safe and attractive home, advises you on matters of insurance and payments to the contractor, and keeps you free of legal entanglements.

He begins by interviewing you in his office. At the first meeting he wants to know your general requirements, the size and makeup of your family, the amount you plan to spend on the remodeling, and your hopes in undertaking it.

Generally, you are given the standard AIA Owner-Architect contract to take home and read, sign, and send back. The architect does not ask you to sign it in his office; there is a lot of print, and most people want to (and should) read every word and ask questions if something is not clear. Alternatively, he may simply ask you to send a confirming letter mentioning the standard conditions and fees required. At the first meeting he explains the fee for his services and the method of payment. This is as much for your own protection as for the architect's; the standard AIA form of contract, especially, has been worked out over years of practical application.

The architect may ask you for the names of your bank, business, and social associations. You, in turn, should ask him for references and the names of former clients with whom he has done business.

At a second interview in your home, the architect measures the house in detail, takes photographs, and tries to find out all the things you believe are wrong with the house. He attempts to discover—which is not as easy as you might suppose—what you really want in a home and what you actually need. He studies you, your family, your house, and its construction.

From his notes and photographs the architect reconstructs a plan and elevation of the house as it now stands, making careful note of the location in regard to zoning and set-back regulations, trees, driveway, location of neighboring houses, main views, and prevailing breezes. With these in mind, he analyzes your requirements to see whether all the things you want are possible. If they are not, he designs substitutions and replacements so that you can get as much as is feasible within the budget you have established.

The architect may make fifty to a hundred sketches of the plans in his preliminary exploratory work, discarding some and refining others that he thinks have better possibilities. The first plans are quite rough, and are usually scaled at one-eighth inch to the foot. At your first design meeting, he shows you three or four of the more developed sketches. You go over them together and decide in which direction you want to work. There is never only one solution to a problem. Several elements in each scheme may combine to make a completely new concept of the remodeling.

The most successful sketch, or the best elements in several, form the basis for the architect's continued study of your house. At the next meeting he has refined the drawings somewhat and may have a rough perspective or elevations showing how the house would look if you agree on that particular scheme. He explains in detail the refined scheme, which by now is identified by a letter or number. His presentation of Scheme "A," however, does not mean that the architect has made only one set of rough drawings by this stage. The letter "A" usually identifies the plan he thinks is going to please you best. It may be followed by Scheme "B," on to Scheme "H," or however many are necessary. A slight variation may be identified as Scheme "A-1."

After several weeks or a month, the architect has worked up the sketches to a point where you can both agree on the course to pursue. Usually these sketches, too, are at a scale of one-eighth inch to the foot, drawn rather roughly, with approximate room sizes indicated and very foggy elevations shown. With these the schematic phase of the drawings is finished.

After the sketches are approved, the architect begins a further study of each room and the placement of windows and doors in relation to furniture arrangements and views. General areas of terraces and porches are discussed. Kitchen counters and the location of the range, sink, and refrigerator take rough form. Bathrooms begin to take shape, and fixture placement is decided. You are asked to choose between a rectangular or square tub and to decide whether you want a separate shower stall and toilet enclosure.

Exterior treatments and elevations are studied to tie the new parts of the house to the existing structure. Redesigning and co-ordination occupy the major portion of the architect's time.

Another hundred to hundred and fifty drawings may be made and discarded through this phase of the architect's study of your house. You may see only several, but for every drawing an architect shows you, at least ten have been made in study . . . sometimes many more, depending on the complexity of the house and the alterations.

At the end of two or three months, a preliminary study of the entire project has been completed. These drawings can be at one-eighth inch to the foot, but sometimes architects prefer to work at a larger scale on remodeling to be sure of sizes and the proper meshing together of old and new elements. As many as five preliminary schemes for a remodeling may be made before you and your architect are satisfied that the house is just the way you want it.

Heating, plumbing, and electrical systems are studied, and a rough preliminary set of specifications made to assure inclusion of everything that has to be considered.

At this stage of the design the architect gets a preliminary estimate of the cost from a contractor. This indicates whether or not the design is progressing within your budget. If it is not, the architect sits down with you, and together you eliminate or substitute elements you can live without or add later. It is not unusual for the preliminary bid to come back "on the high side." The contractor does not have firm specifications and drawings that show the entire scope of the work, and so, to protect himself, he estimates on the outside. The client usually has added things from time to time that were not part of the initial conception and were not considered in the original budgeting. It is up to the client to decide, with the help of the architect, whether the additional elements are essential or whether they can be omitted in preference to other requirements or in deference to the budget.

When the preliminary drawings have been approved, the architect begins his working drawings and final specifications. Details of the kind of molding you want around the doors, the width and height of the stairs, the size of the shower stall and the bedroom closets, all are decided at this stage. Materials for the floors and walls are chosen. Window sizes become exact, doors are designed, and kitchen counters and cabinets are decided upon. Equipment and fixtures are chosen, and their placement in the room is drawn to the fraction of an inch. Heating and electrical outlets are designed around the furniture and window placement already determined in the preliminary drawings.

The completed working drawings and specifications are sent to three or four contractors for signed bids. The contractor who gave the preliminary bid is always asked to participate in the final bidding, although he does not receive preferential treatment.

The architect checks the contractors' reputations and looks at completed houses and alterations they have done. He talks to homeowners to see whether the contractor's men were clean, honest, and prompt. He of course checks the bank, credit rating, outstanding bills, and general reliability of each man and his subcontractors. If he has no personal experience with a contractor under consideration, he calls his fellow architects to get a line on him.

Getting the bids back takes two or three weeks. Then you and your architect compare the various bids against the contractors' reputations and performance. The estimates must be examined carefully to be sure that the contractors are all bidding on the same thing and not omitting or substituting from the specifications.

All the estimates may be higher than your original budget. If they are, you, the architect, and the contractor with the best reputation and the lowest bid get together and discuss the best way of getting a revised and lower bid by substituting

materials, another method of construction, or other details that the contractor may know to bring down the cost. These changes and substitutions are noted and explained in a revised specification and are subtracted from the signed estimate submitted by the contractor.

After the contract has been signed and the remodeling started, the architect still has to make additional drawings and details. All the little things in a remodeling cannot be anticipated, especially in a house where you are not sure what you will find, say, when you remove a wall. One small thing can change the design or the location of kitchen or bathroom fixtures. As the construction progresses, the architect makes further drawings to accommodate the changes and to explain to the contractor exactly how the work is to advance.

Every week as the work goes along, the architect comes by to answer questions the contractor may have and to see that the remodeling proceeds according to his drawings and specifications. He settles any controversies between you and the contractor. He checks the payments you make to the contractor, verifying that you do not overpay or pay for work that is not yet in place. He makes sure that finished work is of first quality and if it is not, he requires that the contractor remove it and do it again.

Some people, especially contractors, minimize the importance of the architect during the construction period, but they are wrong. It is the architect who sees that his plans are carried out the way they were drawn and that the client actually gets what he is paying for.

When the work is completed, the architect sees that the client gets a complete release from the contractor and his subcontractors for any and all liens against the house or construction. He makes sure that the contractor has completed the job to the satisfaction of the owner, and he keeps in abeyance 10 per cent, or so, of the contract price for a period of thirty days, so that if anything goes wrong in that time, he can notify the contractor to return and repair it.

Architects generally carry their responsibility for the remodeling and the client's satisfaction for a year after the work is completed. Since an architect cannot advertise or actively seek out prospective clientele, his best inducement for additional business is a happy client in a handsome home.

THE COST OF AN ARCHITECT

Each architect establishes his own fees, and you should not hesitate to ask him what they are. You can obtain a list of recommended minimum fees for architects in your area through the local chapter of the American Institute of Architects.

As I pointed out before, an architect does not charge you for discussing your remodeling problem with him at his office. He does, however, submit a bill for a visit to your house, even though it does not result in your becoming a client, if in his estimation, the scope of the work you want done does not require an architect's services over and above the advice he has given you. But the time, effort, and skill consumed in making the trip, conducting an investigation of your situation, and giving you on-the-spot advice merits a fee.

If you want a bedroom closet and have a plan of the house to give the architect, he may sketch several suggestions for you in his office. Ask him how much his fee is for everything from a quick sketch to working drawings, specifications, and supervision. Do not expect free sketches. If you want some good, elementary advice on what to do with your house, ask the architect to come over and make a few quick sketches. It is well worth the hour or two of his time; this, plus the time he has spent with you in your first trip to his office, can make an ordinary alteration in your house into a distinctive contribution to your property.

An architect's preliminary fee is only a small percentage of the remodeling. In each case the amount of money you plan to spend determines the scope of the architect's work. His aim is not primarily to save you money (although in many cases he does), but to see that the money you have budgeted for the house is spent in the best way, so that you get the most out of your home in comfort, convenience, and attractiveness.

Other than the small lump sum an architect charges for a preliminary sketch of your remodeling, there are four basic methods of charging:

1. A percentage of the remodeling cost is the most customary charge. This percentage may vary from 15 to 20 per cent. In some cases, when the job is a large one, the percentage is less. A usual figure is 18 per cent.

The percentage fee is collected not only on the cost of the general contracting, but also on the cost of hardware, light fixtures, and everything encompassed by the remodeling that the architect has designed, specified, or helped you to select. Most architects get a professional discount of 20 to 50 per cent on such items as hardware and light fixtures. One method is for the architect to buy these for the client, give him the discount, and include the wholesale price as part of the construction figure on which the standard percentage of fee is based.

Kitchen appliances and equipment are not usually included in the architect's fee, although he must plan the kitchen. Ovens, ranges, refrigerators, and freezers are left to the owner to purchase. If the architect can get these items at a discount, he usually does and turns the entire saving over to the client.

2. The architect may charge you a professional fee plus expenses. This method of payment is sometimes used when the client wants to know for banking purposes exactly the amount he must pay, or when his budget is very limited, or when the house is a considerable distance away from the architect's office. In this form of compensation you pay the architect a lump sum for the design and supervision of the remodeling, plus his expenses for traveling, hotels, meals, and any other items of expense he encounters in his work for you.

The fee for remodeling a medium-sized house might be three thousand dollars, but in addition you would have to pay travel and gasoline expenses, telephone bills, paper, and blueprinting costs. (Blueprinting runs about ten cents a square foot.)

Most architects, especially those who do not have large offices, do not like to use the fee-plus-expenses contract because of the extra bookkeeping and paper work involved. Also, if the scope of the remodeling increases by a substantial degree, the contract has to be renegotiated, which sometimes causes hard feelings.

3. The architect can charge on a multiple of his direct personnel expense, but this system is rarely used in residential work. It is a method whereby the client pays the architect three or four times the cost of his draftsmen and other employees who are working on the job.

4. You can also hire an architect on salary by the week, day, or hour. This type of contract is used when the scope of the work is large and undetermined. The cost of the architect may vary from one to two hundred dollars a day, perhaps

more. Or, if the client prefers, the architect may charge by the hour on smaller work. An hourly rate may be from twenty-five to fifty dollars on most remodeling.

In sum, by far the most logical and equitable method for both client and architect is the percentage-of-cost remodeling contract on most domestic work.

HOW TO WORK WITH AN ARCHITECT

To be able to work well with an architect, you must first find one with whom you have an easy rapport and in whom you have complete confidence. How will you find him?

A good way to start is by calling the nearest office of the American Institute of Architects, which has on file a list of all the registered architects in your area who do residential and remodeling work. Make appointments to see several. You do not have to hire the first one you talk to. Get an impression of each man's work; look at his office; get the names of a few former clients for whom he has done work similar to what you have in mind. Call the clients, and ask them about their experience with the architect. Drive out and look at some of his completed work. Remember, though, that these projects were designed to suit particular clients, who were deciding factors in the form the remodeling was to take.

Another approach is to ask local and near-by architectural firms for recommendations. Even if the firm is principally engaged in large commercial work, a member may consider designing your remodeling. The pleasure of working on something intimate may intrigue him. And some architects simply like to remodel houses.

If these efforts fail, you might try calling a couple of contracting firms. Look out, however, if they say the son or the wife of the contractor will be glad to draw something up for you, unless you know they are qualified architects. You are looking for professional help, and it will not cost you any more (actually not as much) by the time you are finished.

After you have talked to several former clients and weighed all you have been able to find out about the architects, choose the one you and your wife get along with best, the one whose tastes most resemble yours.

You may wish to consider a young architect or designer just out of architectural school. Often they have the freshest approach, and they know the latest materials and building methods.

When the choice has been settled upon, sit down with the architect in your home and explain again what you would like to have him design. *What,* that is, not *how.* Tell him what you think is wrong with the house and how much additional space you need. Tell him, too, how you want to live and the kind of atmosphere you would like your home to have. Discuss the furniture arrangements you need, the location of the piano, sofa, large chests, and the size and number of beds. The design must accommodate these.

You should be able to give him a survey like the one you got with the deed, showing the location of the house in relation to the lot boundaries and trees. A set of plans of the house is helpful but not essential. Your architect will want to measure the house himself, not only to become familiar with it, but also to check on room sizes and door and window locations. Very often a house has not been built precisely the way it was originally drawn, and a few inches one way or the other can make a big difference.

Be frank with your architect about your budget and your financial situation. Do not pose unnecessary problems by saying that you will only spend "X" dollars, when you are actually thinking of spending more. Tell him how much you have to spend, including his fee. Then let him take the ball and run with it.

It is not unusual for the architect to request a retainer on the signing of the contract. The amount is usually 5 per cent of his fee.

It is advisable to use the standard AIA contract between owner and architect. This fully protects you as well as the architect and saves the time and cost of getting a lawyer to draw up a contract which, however sufficient, is not likely to be as good or as inclusive. The AIA contract has been developed over a period of many years to protect the interests of both the client and the architect.

You can sign a letter of agreement instead, but it should include the standard provisions and general conditions of the AIA contract.

Do not push your architect any more than you can help. If you forgot to tell him something pertinent to the design or to your requirements, by all means communicate with him. You should telephone and then send a letter confirming your conversation. But try to give him the time he requires to formulate design sketches for you.

When the day does come and you are invited to go over the first sketches, do not be shy about criticizing things you do not like. That is why he is asking . . . to find out what you do and do not like about what he has done. If you do like something, say so. It tells him he is headed in the right direction. From your choices he will be able to develop a design using the best elements of each.

When the rough or sketch work is completed and approved, you are expected to pay the architect an additional sum. Usually this amount, plus the original retainer comes to about 15 per cent of his total fee. For example, if the remodeling is budgeted to cost ten thousand dollars, exclusive of the architect's fee, you owe him (on a fee of 20 per cent) two thousand dollars over-all. Assuming that you paid him a retainer of 5 per cent (one hundred dollars) when you signed the contract, you owe him two hundred dollars more when the sketches are finished, in all, three hundred dollars or 15 per cent of his total fee at this stage.

You may be asked to sign the sketches as evidence that you approve the work thus far. When you do, the architect can then proceed further to perfect the design. As the architect works up the preliminary drawings, you are asked to state preferences for materials, equipment, and fixtures, so that he has some idea of what you are getting into in the way of installation. During this time you are free to make all the corrections and changes you like. Keep a list of all the questions that occur to you, and ask your architect about them. Do not call him every time you think of something. Wait until you have a batch of questions, and then ask him to answer them all at once.

Do not request sketches of the interior. These take a lot of time, and perspective sketches are not part of the contract unless they are written into the agreement. Most architects make one or two pictures of the exterior if you and your wife find the regular scale drawing difficult to read, but any more than this is an imposition.

When the preliminary drawings are finished, you are given a copy. These are customarily printed on white paper so that notes can readily be made on them. Blueprints are used on the job because they do not get as dirty or fade as quickly as the whiteprints.

Take the preliminaries home, and study them for at least a week. If there is anything that does not suit you, write it down and bring it to the architect's attention when you return the preliminaries. He makes the changes you want and gives you a corrected copy. It is not unusual for an architect to have to make two or more preliminaries to satisfy you.

When you reach agreement with the architect on the preliminary, you owe him an additional 35 to 50 per cent of his fee, and he can now proceed to the third phase of the remodeling of your house.

After the working drawings have been started, try to avoid making any changes in the design or specifications. All changes should have been made on the preliminary.

You now have to decide exactly what models and colors you want in appliances and equipment, choose the hardware you prefer, and select the light fixtures, finishes, and special fixtures you want in the kitchen and bathrooms. Of course your architect helps you and suggests what he thinks is suitable within your price range.

If you plan to buy any new furniture, now is the time to decide on what you will have so that space can be arranged for it. If a sofa is to fit between two windows, the size is important in determining the placement of the windows. Wall space must be allowed for beds and bedside tables. Telephone outlets should be settled on, so that the telephone men can install them through the wall without having to run wires all around the baseboard.

After the working drawings and specifications are finished comes selection of the contractor. When this is done and the contract is let to begin the construction, you owe the architect 80 per cent of his total fee. The remainder can be paid in monthly installments during the construction. Some architects wait until the close of the job and then submit a final bill for settlement.

During the construction, keep out of the way as much as you can. Do not complain to the contractor or his workmen. Call the architect directly, and have all orders issued through him; otherwise the work becomes hopelessly confused, and the contractor has an excellent excuse to charge you for extras.

THE STANDARD FORM OF AGREEMENT
BETWEEN OWNER AND ARCHITECT

ON A BASIS OF A
PERCENTAGE OF CONSTRUCTION COST

THIS AGREEMENT

made this   day of   in the year Nineteen Hundred and

BY AND BETWEEN

hereinafter called the Owner, and

hereinafter called the Architect

WITNESSETH,

that whereas the Owner intends to

hereinafter called the Project,

NOW, THEREFORE,

the Owner and the Architect, for the considerations hereinafter set forth agree as follows:

ARTICLE 1. THE ARCHITECT AGREES TO PROVIDE PROFESSIONAL SERVICES FOR THE PROJECT AS HEREINAFTER SET FORTH.

ARTICLE 2. THE OWNER AGREES TO PAY THE ARCHITECT AS COMPENSATION FOR HIS SERVICES:

2.1 For his basic services   (%) of the project construction cost, hereinafter referred to as the Basic Rate, the work to be let under a single lump sum contract.

2.2 For work let on a cost-plus-fee basis, increase the Basic rate to   per cent (%).

2.3 For work let under separate contracts, increase the Basic Rate to   per cent (%).

2.4 For Additional Services defined in Article 4 hereinafter,   (   ) times the Direct Personnel Expense as defined in Article 7.1 hereinafter.

In computing Direct Personnel Expense principal's time shall be computed at $ per hour, and employees' time shall be at their regular rate of pay plus normal benefits.

2.5 Reimbursable expense as defined in Article 7.2 hereinafter to the amount expended.

TERMS AND CONDITIONS OF AGREEMENT BETWEEN OWNER AND ARCHITECT

ARTICLE 3. ARCHITECT'S BASIC SERVICES

3.1 *Schematic Design Phase.*

3.1.1 The Architect shall consult with the Owner to ascertain the requirements of the Project and shall confirm such requirements to the Owner.

3.1.2 He shall prepare schematic design studies leading to a recommended solution together with a general description of the Project for approval by the Owner.

3.1.3 He shall submit to the Owner a Statement of Probable Project Construction Cost based on current area, volume or other unit costs.

3.2 *Design Development Phase.*

3.2.1 The Architect shall prepare from the approved Schematic Design Studies, the Design Development Documents consisting of plans, elevations and other drawings, and outline specifications, to fix and illustrate the size and character of the entire Project in its essentials as to kinds of materials, type of structure, mechanical and electrical systems and such other work as may be required.

3.2.2 He shall submit to the Owner a further Statement of Probable Project Construction cost.

3.3 *Construction Documents Phase.*

3.3.1 The Architect shall prepare from the approved Design Development Documents, Working Drawings and Specifications setting forth in detail the work required for the architectural, structural, mechanical, electrical, service-connected equipment, and site work, and the necessary bidding information, General Conditions of the Contract, and Supplementary General Conditions of the Contract, and shall assist in the drafting of Proposal and Contract Forms.

3.3.2 He shall keep the Owner informed of any adjustments to previous Statements of Probable Project Construction Cost indicated by changes in scope, requirements or market conditions.

3.3.3 He shall be responsible for filing the required documents to secure approval of governmental authorities having jurisdiction over the design of the Project.

3.4 *Construction Phase—General Administration of Construction Contracts.*

3.4.1 The Architect shall assist the Owner in obtaining proposals from Contractors and in awarding and preparing construction contracts.

3.4.2 To the extent provided by the contract between the Owner and the Contractor, he shall make decisions on all claims of the Owner and Contractor and on all other matters relating to the execution and progress of the work or the interpretation of the Contract Documents. He shall check and approve samples, schedules, shop drawings and other submissions only for conformance with the design concept of the Project and for compliance with the information given by the Contract Documents, prepare change orders and assemble written guarantees required of the Contractors.

3.4.3 He will make periodic visits to the site to familiarize himself generally with the progress and quality of the work and to determine in general if the work is proceeding in accordance with the Contract Documents. He will not be required to make exhaustive or continuous on-site inspections to check the quality or quantity of the work and he will not be responsible for the Contractors' failure to carry out the construction work in accordance with the Contract Documents. During such visits and on the basis of his observations while at the site, he will keep the Owner informed of the progress of the work, will endeavor to guard the Owner against defects and deficiencies in the work of Contractors, and he may condemn work as failing to conform to the Contract Documents. Based on such observations and the Contractors' Applications for Payment, he will determine the amount owing to the Contractor and will issue Certificates for Payment in such amounts. These Certificates will constitute a representation to the Owner, based on such observations and the data comprising the Application for Payment, that the work has progressed to the point indicated.

By issuing a Certificate for Payment, the Architect will also represent to the Owner that, to the best of his knowledge, information and belief based on what his observations have revealed, the quality of the work is in accordance with the Contract Documents. He will conduct inspections to determine the dates of substantial and final completion and issue a final Certificate for Payment.

3.4.4 If more extensive representation at the site is required, the conditions under which such representation shall be furnished and a Project Representative selected, employed and directed, shall be agreed to by the Owner and the Architect and set forth in an exhibit to this Agreement.

ARTICLE 4. ARCHITECT'S ADDITIONAL SERVICES

The following services cause the Architect extra expense. If any of these services are authorized by the Owner they shall be paid for by the Owner as a Multiple of Direct Personnel Expense:

4.1 Making planning surveys and special analyses of the Owner's needs to clarify requirements of the Project.

4.2 Making measured drawings of existing construction when required for planning additions or alterations thereto.

4.3 Revising previously approved drawings or specifications to accomplish changes.

4.4 Providing Semi-Detailed or Detailed Cost Estimates.

4.5 Preparing documents for Alternate Bids and Change Orders, or for supplemental work initiated after commencement of the construction phase.

4.6 Consultation concerning replacement of any work damaged by fire or other cause during construction and furnishing professional services of the types set forth in Article 3 above as may be required in connection with the replacement of such work.

4.7 Arranging for the work to proceed should the contractor default due to delinquency or insolvency.

4.8 Providing prolonged contract administration and observation of construction should the construction contract time be exceeded by more than 25% due to no fault of the Architect.

4.9 Preparing as-built drawings showing construction changes in the work and final locations of mechanical service lines and outlets on the basis of data furnished by the Contractor.

4.10 Making an inspection of the Project prior to expiration of the guarantee period and reporting observed discrepancies under guarantees provided by the construction contracts.

ARTICLE 5. THE OWNER'S RESPONSIBILITIES

5.1 The Owner shall provide full information as to his requirements for the Project.

5.2 He shall designate, when necessary, representatives authorized to act in his behalf. He shall examine documents submitted by the Architect and render decisions pertaining thereto promptly, to avoid unreasonable delay in the the progress of the Architect's work. He shall observe the procedure of issuing orders to contractors only through the Architect.

5.3 He shall furnish or direct the Architect to obtain at the Owner's expense, a certified survey of the site, giving, as required, grades and lines of streets, alleys, pavements, and adjoining property; rights of way, restrictions, easements, encroachments, zoning, deed restrictions, boundaries, and contours of the building site; locations, dimensions, and complete data pertaining to existing buildings, other improvements and trees; full information as to available service and utility lines both public and private; and test borings and pits necessary for determining subsoil conditions.

5.4 He shall pay for structural, chemical, mechanical, soil mechanics or other tests and reports if required.

5.5 He shall arrange and pay for such legal, auditing, and insurance counselling services as may be required for the Project.

5.6 If the Owner observes or otherwise becomes aware of any defect in the Project, he shall give prompt written notice thereof to the Architect.

ARTICLE 6. PROJECT CONSTRUCTION COST

6.1 Project Construction Cost as herein referred to means the total cost of all work designed or specified by the Architect, but does not include any payments made to the Architect or consultants.

6.2 Project Construction Cost shall be based upon one of the following sources with precedence in the order listed:

6.2.1 Lowest acceptable bona fide Contractor's proposal received for any or all portions of the Project.

6.2.2 Semi-Detailed or Detailed Estimate of Project Construction Cost as defined in paragraph 6.4 below.

6.2.3 The Architect's latest Statement of Probable Project Construction Cost based on current area, volume or other unit costs.

6.3 When labor or material is furnished by the Owner, the Project Construction Cost shall include such labor and material at current market cost.

6.4 If a fixed limit of Project Construction Cost is stated herein, or if otherwise authorized by the Owner, Estimates of the Probable Project Construction Cost prepared in Semi-Detailed or Detailed form by an experienced estimator will be secured by the Architect during the Design Development or Construction Documents Phase.

6.5 If the Statement of Probable Project Construction Cost, or the Semi-Detailed or Detailed Cost Estimate, or the lowest bona fide proposal is in excess of any limit stated herein, the Owner shall give written approval of an increase in the limit, or he shall cooperate in revising the project scope or quality, or both, to reduce the cost as required.

6.6 Since the Architect has no control over the cost of labor and materials, or competitive bidding, he does not guarantee the accuracy of any Statements of Probable Construction Cost, or any Semi-Detailed or Detailed Cost Estimates.

ARTICLE 7. DIRECT & REIMBURSABLE EXPENSE

7.1 Direct Personnel Expense includes that of principals and employees engaged on the Project including architects, engineers, designers, job captains, draftsmen, specification writers, typists and Project Representatives, in consultation, research, designing, producing drawing, specifications and other documents pertaining to the Project, and services during construction at the Project site.

7.2 Reimbursable Expense includes actual expenditures made by the Architect in the interest of the Project for the following incidental expenses:

7.2.1 Expense of transportation and living of principals and employees when traveling in connection with the Project; long distance calls and telegrams; reproduction of drawings and specifications, excluding copies for Architect's office use and duplicate sets at each phase for the Owner's review and approval; and fees paid for securing approval of authorities having jurisdiction over the Project.

7.2.2 If authorized in advance by the Owner, the expense of Project Representative, overtime work requiring higher than regular rates, perspectives or models for the Owner's use.

7.2.3 If their employment is authorized in advance by the Owner, fees of special consultants, for other than the normal structural, mechanical and electrical engineering services.

ARTICLE 8. PAYMENTS TO THE ARCHITECT

8.1 Payments on account of the Architect's basic services shall be as follows:

8.1.1 A minimum primary payment of 5 per cent of the compensation for basic services, payable upon the execution of the Agreement, is the minimum payment under the Agreement.

8.1.2 Subsequent payments shall be made monthly in proportion to services performed to increase the compensation for basic services to the following percentages at the completion of each phase of the work:

Schematic Design Phase	15%
Design Development Phase	35%
Construction Documents Phase	75%
Receipt of Bids	80%
Construction Phase	100%

8.2 Payments for Additional Services of the Architect as defined in Article 4 above, and for Reimbursable Expense as defined in Article 7.2, shall be made monthly upon presentation of Architect's detailed invoice.

8.3 No deduction shall be made from the Architect's compensation on account of penalty, liquidated damages, or other sums withheld from payments to contractors.

8.4 If any work designed or specified by the Architect during any phase of service is abandoned or suspended in whole or in part, the Architect is to be paid for the service performed on account of it prior to receipt of written notice from the Owner of such abandonment or suspension, together with reimbursements then due and any terminal expense resulting from abandonment or suspension for more than three months.

ARTICLE 9. ARCHITECT'S ACCOUNTING RECORDS

Records of the Architect's Direct Personnel, Consultant, and Reimbursable Expense pertaining to this Project and records of accounts between the Owner and Contractor shall be kept on a generally recognized accounting basis and shall be available to the Owner or his authorized representative at mutually convenient times.

ARTICLE 10. TERMINATION OF AGREEMENT

This Agreement may be terminated by either party upon seven day's written notice should the other party fail substantially to perform in accordance with its terms through no fault of the other. In the event of termination, due to the fault of others than the Architect, the Architect shall be paid for services performed to termination date, including reimbursements then due, plus terminal expense.

ARTICLE 11. OWNERSHIP OF DOCUMENTS

Drawings and Specifications as instruments of service are the property of the Architect whether the Project for which they are made be executed or not. They are not to be used on other projects except by agreement in writing.

ARTICLE 12. SUCCESSORS AND ASSIGNS

The Owner and the Architect each binds himself, his partners, successors, assigns and legal representatives to the other party to this Agreement and to the partners, successors, assigns and legal representatives of such other party in respect of all covenants of this Agreement. Neither the Owner nor the Architect shall assign, sublet or transfer his interest in this Agreement without the written consent of the other.

ARTICLE 13. ARBITRATION

Arbitration of all questions in dispute under this Agreement shall be at the choice of either party and shall be in accordance with the provisions, then obtaining, of the Standard Form of Arbitration Procedure of The American Institute of Architects. This Agreement shall be specifically enforceable under the prevailing arbitration law and judgment upon the award rendered may be entered in the court of the forum, state or federal, having jurisdiction. The decisions of the arbitrators shall be a condition precedent to the right of any legal action.

IN WITNESS WHEREOF the parties hereto have executed this agreement the day and year first above written.

Owner _____   Architect _____

The Contractor

HOW TO CHOOSE A CONTRACTOR

Finding a good contractor is not too much of a problem, if you have retained an architect to design and supervise your remodeling. Let him verify the qualifications of local contractors, and if you wish to do a little cross checking, ask him for the names he is researching and the work they have recently done. Previous personal experience with the contractors and references from other architects are, of course, the architect's most reliable sources, but all other investigative channels are as accessible to you as to him. Call the homeowners and inquire about the character of the contractor and the quality of the work he did for them. Then combine your information with your architect's. Together you can determine which ones to ask to bid on your work.

If you do not have an architect, it takes several weeks of effort to find a competent, responsible contractor. You can call an architect, and he will be glad to suggest a contractor. But this in no way obligates the architect; you have to rely on your own investigations.

Make a list of the contractors in your area from the classified section of your telephone book. Avoid those that are too far away; distance increases the cost of transporting men and materials, increases the contractor's expense, and decreases his enthusiasm.

Visit first those contractors who specialize in remodeling. Talk to the contractor, and find out if he is interested in doing the work and when he can get started. Ask for the names of people for whom he has completed recent remodeling projects and the names and addresses of his subcontractors. It is much better if he has a more or less established crew of labor and subcontractors that work as a team. If you wish to hire the man, make an appointment for him to come to your house so that you can explain what you want done. Set a definite time and date for the following week, and see how promptly he keeps the appointment. If he is not punctual for the interview to get a job, you can expect endless procrastination and delay once he gets it.

Have your bank investigate his financial situation. Ask the local Better Business Bureau if there are any complaints against him.

Do not hesitate to telephone the people for whom he has worked before. Ask them if he and his workmen were neat, if they arrived on time and did a good job without bickering, and if they finished on schedule. Ask what complaints, if any, they had about the contractor and whether they would hire him again.

Sound out the subcontractors, asking each if he ever had any trouble getting his money from the contractor, if the jobs were well organized, and if they would work for him again. This may seem like a lot of trouble, but it may save you a lawsuit and a number of headaches.

Without an architect, his drawings, and specifications, it is difficult to show a contractor what you want. However, give exact copies of whatever you do have to each contractor, so that each gives you an estimate on the same thing. If you can have your thoughts and requirements put into sketch form by a draftsman, so much the better. Itemize everything, room by room, giving as much detail as you possibly can, stating the height, width, depth, color, finish, brand name, and location, north, south, east, west wall. Write everything down, even simple things that seem obvious. Give each contractor a copy, and have him return it with his signature when he gives you his final estimate for the work. Do not accept verbal bids, regardless of how small the job.

The contractors should sign and return all the original material you gave them, together with an estimate of the total cost of the work, the starting date, and the completion date. If you have any doubts about the contractor, ask him to furnish a Bid Bond, which is a letter from an insurance company stating that he is capable of undertaking the job. At the time of signing your contract, request a Performance Bond. The Performance Bond should be incorporated with a Labor and Material Payment Bond. This assures you of being able to have the work completed at the contractor's expense if he cannot or will not go on with the remodeling. It also prevents your being sued by subcontractors and suppliers for work and materials already installed.

The contractor with the lowest bid is not necessarily the one to select for the job. Go over all the estimates carefully to see that nothing has been left out or substituted. Be wary about engaging a contractor who has not been in business in your area very long or one who works "out of his hat." A contractor who is just getting started may be so anxious for the work that he puts in a bid too low to allow him a profit and winds up either doing a poor job or quitting and leaving you with a half-finished job.

The contractor with the highest bid is not always the best one either. He may have purposely made the bid high so that he would not have to be bothered with the job. Some contractors do not like remodeling work, and you do well to avoid them.

Go over the intermediate bids. Weigh each contractor's estimate of the work against what you have been able to find out about him, his work, and his business. If all other things are equal, choose the one whose personality you like the best. The man is, after all, going to spend a month or more in your house.

Bids on remodeling work are usually good for thirty days. If a longer period elapses before acceptance, the contractor may not be able to get the same subcontractors, and his schedule, as well as the prices and climatic conditions, may have changed so that a new estimate has to be submitted.

HOW TO WORK WITH A CONTRACTOR

How you work with your contractor is implicit in the terms of his contract, whether it states a lump sum or cost plus. Because no one can be absolutely sure of what will be uncovered under the walls of an older house, some contractors do remodeling only on a cost-plus basis; in such a case you must be very sure of your contractor and keep at least 10 per cent of what you think you are going to spend in an emergency fund to meet unexpected bills. (This can be a good idea, regardless of the kind of contract you have in remodeling.)

Most contracts are let from competitive bidding, and after the bids are in, one general contractor is chosen. Then, to bring the cost down, you, the architect, and the contractor eliminate some of the less important, but expensive items and substitute less expensive, but still good materials. If you do not have an architect, you must deal directly with the contractor in cutting down the cost of remodeling.

You then have your lawyer draw up a contract that follows the form of the Standard AIA contract between Owner and Contractor, as reproduced at the end of this chapter. If you have an architect, you simply use a standard contract and do not need a lawyer to set forth the terms. Be sure that your working contract specifies the duties and responsibilities of the contractor, the fee and how it is to be paid, the starting and finishing dates, and the responsibility of the contractor for liens against the property, as well as for insurance for the workmen and general public on the property during construction.

If the contract is a large one and the work is to take several months, the contractor usually submits a bill at the beginning of each month, to be paid by the tenth of that same month. If you have an architect, he checks and signs it before you pay, stating that 10 per cent is being withheld until thirty days after completion of the project. This is to guarantee that the contractor is not overpaid for any work or materials and that if there is anything wrong with the job, he will correct it.

Often the contractor charges more if you and your family are living in the house while it is being remodeled. This is not unreasonable, there are so many things and people to work around. Even if you can take only a two-week vacation, it is better to do so. Ask the contractor for a work schedule to determine when would be the best time for you to be away. In any case, the work schedule lets you know when the electricity and water will be turned off.

Do not follow the contractor around asking questions, changing your mind, and giving him confusing directions. If he asks you a question, refer him to your architect or to your written instructions and contract before you answer. If you do not have an architect, make a note of his question and your answer, together with the date. Under no circumstances should you give instructions to the subcontractors or any of the workmen.

Remove as much of the furniture and bric-a-brac as you can from the rooms in which men will be working . . . all of it if possible. The contractor is not a moving company and does not take kindly to having his men hustle carpets and sofas around or waste time carrying small items of glassware and pottery from room to room. Also, the contractor is not responsible for breakage of that sort; if his men smash something accidentally, forget it.

Never ask the contractor's workmen to baby-sit or answer the telephone while you run in to town. A regular baby-sitter charges only a fraction of the cost of a plumber, and the kids may break or lose tools. They might also pick up some pretty lusty conversation to shock Grandma. Just to answer the telephone, a workman may have to climb down off a ladder and walk through a couple of rooms, and he does not know what to say when he gets there.

Also, be sure to keep your pets out of the way, whether or not they are the type that scratch or bite; they can distract a workman so that even if the animal does not injure him, he may cut himself on a nail or take a finger off with a saw.

Do not complain about the noise. No one can keep a saw quiet or hammer softly. Noise, confusion, and a certain amount of dirt are part of remodeling. Do not be a pest with the vacuum cleaner either, if you expect workmen to work. There is bound to be some mess, and if it bothers you, clean it up when they leave.

If the workmen store any tools or equipment overnight, keep the children away from them, and do not borrow any tools, no matter how good a craftsman you may think you are. A carpenter's or mason's tools are as personal to him as your toothbrush is to you.

Have a place for the workmen to eat, and invite them to keep their lunches in the refrigerator. Do not eat with them. They think it is rude to refuse, but you are only wasting their time. Besides, they cannot relax and swap stories while the owner's wife is around. Their usual lunch time is one-half hour; so do not encourage stretching it out. Keep a pot of coffee on if you want to, although they usually prefer their own.

Be up and dressed each morning when they arrive, and do your best to stay clear of them during the day. All complaints, instructions, and directions should go directly to your architect, if you have one, or to the general contractor, not to the workmen on the job.

If you have not yet moved into the house you are remodeling, make sure that the water and electricity have been turned on. In winter there should be some heat in the house. It need not be kept at 70 degrees, but the temperature should not go below fifty degrees. The telephone should be connected, usually in the contractor's name, so that he can call you or the architect to ask questions, order supplies, or, if the need arises, get an ambulance for an injured workman. Stay away from the remodeling job during the day unless the contractor asks you to come over. Make your inspections in the evening and on week ends, and keep lists so that your questions can be asked and answered at one time.

HOW TO WORK WITH A SUBCONTRACTOR

There are instances when you can do without a general contractor; that is, if the job is small and uncomplicated and if you have the time and patience to act as your own general contractor. The most important thing about working with subcontractors – electrician, plumber, carpenter, and mason – is the scheduling of jobs; getting them in and out with a minimum of confusion, waste time, and duplication. If you are not very careful, you find one man being held up by another and the plumber ripping out work the carpenter has just finished.

You must go through the same procedure for each subcontractor as you do in finding a general contractor, checking references and asking for estimates of the work. It takes longer to do the same amount of remodeling if you use only subcontractors, and in most cases the cost is proportionately more for what is accomplished. Have a separate signed contract with each contractor. These should be drawn up by your lawyer.

Be doubly sure that your insurance is checked; it should cover all workmen against accidents that may occur in your home and should be increased to the maximum until the remodeling is finished. Even if an accident is the result of their own unaccountable negligence, you are liable. The cost of this extra insurance should be figured in the total cost of your remodeling.

In doing your own contracting it is absolutely essential to have an established plan and a firm work schedule. So many things may inadvertently go wrong that you should do everything possible to steer clear of the obvious mistakes. In other words, have a definite, well-drawn plan, a minutely detailed work schedule, and the ability to make quick decisions that affect the entire structure and design of the remodeling.

Without an architect or a general contractor, you are responsible for getting the building permits and for seeing that the construction is in line with zoning ordinances and the building code. It is best, too, if you plan to work only with the help of subcontractors, to have the cash in hand for your remodeling. Many banks and lending agencies do not lend any sizable amount of money under these conditions.

Do not try to rush anything through. The subcontractors who are willing to work for you on a small project are only using the job to fill in while they wait for bigger work. For this reason they may want to work at odd times or on Saturdays, when the large projects are closed down. You should expect this and other delays. A plumber is reluctant to leave a large job to install a sink, an hour's work, and then have nothing more to do until the bath tub arrives or until the carpenter builds the countertops in the bathroom.

You probably need a carpenter and his helper full time. Very often the carpenter knows the other subcontractors and is able to act almost as a general contractor and co-ordinator. But since this is not really his job and he may not have much experience at it, you can expect mistakes. Have a written contract with the carpenter, and do not hire him as an employee. If you act as his employer, you are responsible for state and federal withholding taxes, unemployment benefits, and workman's compensation, for which there are endless forms to fill out.

Masonry is tricky, and you are well-advised to get the best-qualified mason you can find to lay concrete block and pour the concrete for you. If the mix is not right or if the blocks are not laid properly, the whole works can collapse, leaving you far worse off than before you started.

The advantage of dealing directly with the subcontractors you hire is that you have a choice. When you have a general contractor, he picks the subs. There may be a carpenter or mason you know and want to hire for work on your house. He may not want to associate with a general contractor because he likes being his own boss.

Dealing directly with the subcontractors also allows you to go ahead at your own speed, which may be slower than that of a general contractor. If you subcontract in stages, you have to pay only for as much as you have done. If you are working in the kitchen, for instance, you can have the range and refrigerator installed where you want them and wait to have the counters built next year. Restoration work is often done this way, especially when the right paneling, door, or mantle is not available at the moment and you have to wait until it turns up at your favorite junkyard or auction.

You may be able to do some of the work yourself on week ends or vacations. Working with subcontractors can save you money, and the money you do spend will be on a go-as-you-can-pay basis.

THE STANDARD FORM OF AGREEMENT
BETWEEN OWNER AND CONTRACTOR

THE AIA SHORT FORM CONTRACT FOR

SMALL CONSTRUCTION CONTRACTS

WHERE THE BASIS OF PAYMENT IS A

STIPULATED SUM

FOR OTHER CONTRACTS THE AIA ISSUES THE STANDARD FORMS OF OWNER-CONTRACTOR AGREEMENTS AND THE
STANDARD GENERAL CONDITIONS FOR THE CONSTRUCTION OF BUILDINGS FOR USE IN CONNECTION THEREWITH

THIS AGREEMENT

made the   day of   in the year Nineteen Hundred and

BY AND BETWEEN

hereinafter called the Owner, and

hereinafter called the Contractor.

WITNESSETH,

That the Owner and the Contractor, for the considerations hereinafter named agree as follows:

ARTICLE 1. SCOPE OF THE WORK—
The Contractor shall furnish all of the material and perform all of the work for

as shown on the Drawings and described in the Specifications entitled

prepared by   Architect
all in accordance with the terms of the Contract Documents.

ARTICLE 2. TIME OF COMPLETION—The work shall be commenced and completed as follows:

ARTICLE 3. CONTRACT SUM—The Owner shall pay the Contractor for the performance of the Contract
subject to the additions and deductions provided therein in current funds, the sum of

dollars. ($)

ARTICLE 4. PROGRESS PAYMENTS—The Owner shall make payments on account of the contract, upon requisition by the Contractor, as follows:

ARTICLE 5. ACCEPTANCE AND FINAL PAYMENT—Final payment shall be due   days after completion of the work, provided the contract be then fully performed, subject to the provisions of Article 16 of the General Conditions.

ARTICLE 6. CONTRACT DOCUMENTS—Contract Documents are as noted in Article 1 of the General Conditions. The following is an enumeration of the drawings and specifications:

GENERAL CONDITIONS

ARTICLE 1.   CONTRACT DOCUMENTS

The contract includes the AGREEMENT and its GENERAL CONDITIONS, the DRAWINGS, and the SPECIFICATIONS. Two or more copies of each, as required, shall be signed by both parties and one signed copy of each retained by each party.

The intent of these documents is to include all labor, materials, appliances and services of every kind necessary for the proper execution of the work, and the terms and conditions of payment therefor.

The documents are to be considered as one, and whatever is called for by any one of the documents shall be as binding as if called for by all.

ARTICLE 2.   SAMPLES

The Contractor shall furnish for approval all samples as directed. The work shall be in accordance with approved samples.

ARTICLE 3.   MATERIALS, APPLIANCES, EMPLOYEES

Except as otherwise noted, the Contractor shall provide and pay for all materials, labor, tools, water, power and other items necessary to complete the work.

Unless otherwise specified, all materials shall be new, and both workmanship and materials shall be of good quality.

All workmen and sub-contractors shall be skilled in their trades.

ARTICLE 4.   ROYALTIES AND PATENTS

The Contractor shall pay all royalties and license fees. He shall defend all suits or claims for infringement of any patent rights and shall save the Owner harmless from loss on account thereof.

ARTICLE 5.   SURVEYS, PERMITS, AND REGULATIONS

The Owner shall furnish all surveys unless otherwise specified. Permits and licenses necessary for the prosecution of the work shall be secured and paid for by the Contractor. Easements for permanent structures or permanent changes in existing facilities shall be secured and paid for by the Owner, unless otherwise specified. The Contractor shall comply with all laws and regulations bearing on the conduct of the work and shall notify the Owner if the drawings and specifications are at variance therewith.

ARTICLE 6.   PROTECTION OF WORK, PROPERTY, AND PERSONS

The Contractor shall adequately protect the work, adjacent property and the public and shall be responsible for any damage or injury due to his act or neglect.

ARTICLE 7.   ACCESS TO WORK

The Contractor shall permit and facilitate observation of the work by the Owner and his agents and public authorities at all times.

ARTICLE 8.   CHANGES IN THE WORK

The Owner may order changes in the work, the Contract Sum being adjusted accordingly. All such orders and adjustments shall be in writing. Claims by the Contractor for extra cost must be made in writing before executing the work involved.

ARTICLE 9.   CORRECTION OF WORK

The Contractor shall re-execute any work that fails to conform to the requirements of the contract and that appears during the progress of the work, and shall remedy any defects due to faulty materials or workmanship which appear within a period of one year from the date of completion of the contract. The provisions of this article apply to work done by subcontractors as well as to work done by direct employees of the Contractor.

ARTICLE 10.   OWNER'S RIGHT TO TERMINATE THE CONTRACT

Should the Contractor neglect to prosecute the work properly, or fail to perform any provision of the contract, the Owner, after seven days' written notice to the Contractor, and his surety if any may, without prejudice to any other remedy he may have, make good the deficiencies and may deduct the cost thereof from the payment then or thereafter due the contractor or, at his option, may terminate the contract and take possession of all materials, tools, and appliances and finish the work by such means as he sees fit, and if the unpaid balance of the contract price exceeds the expense of finishing the work, such excess shall be paid to the Contractor, but if such expense exceeds such unpaid balance, the Contractor shall pay the difference to the Owner.

ARTICLE 11.   CONTRACTOR'S RIGHT TO TERMINATE CONTRACT

Should the work be stopped by any public authority for a period of thirty days or more, through no fault of the Contractor, or should the work be stopped through act or neglect of the Owner for a period of seven days, or should the Owner fail to pay the Contractor any payment within seven days after it is due, then the Contractor upon seven days' written notice to the Owner, may stop work or terminate the contract and recover from the Owner payment for all work executed and any loss sustained and reasonable profit and damages.

ARTICLE 12.   PAYMENTS

Payments shall be made as provided in the Agreement. The making and acceptance of the final payment shall constitute a waiver of all claims by the Owner, other than those arising from unsettled liens or from faulty work appearing thereafter, as provided for in Article 9, and of all claims by the Contractor except any previously made and still unsettled. Payments otherwise due may be withheld on account of defective work not remedied, liens filed, damage by the Contractor to others not adjusted, or failure to make payments properly to subcontractors or for material or labor.

ARTICLE 13.   CONTRACTOR'S LIABILITY INSURANCE

The Contractor shall maintain such insurance as will protect him from claims under workmen's compensation acts and other employee benefits acts, from claims for damages because of bodily injury, including death, and from claims for damages to property which may arise both out of and during operations under this contract, whether such operations be by himself or by any subcontractor or anyone directly or indirectly employed by either of them. This insurance shall be written for not less than any limits of liability specified as part of this contract. Certificates of such insurance shall be filed with the Owner and architect.

ARTICLE 14.   OWNER'S LIABILITY INSURANCE

The Owner shall be responsible for and at his option may maintain such insurance as will protect him from his contingent liability to others for damages because of bodily injury, including death, which may arise from operations under this contract, and any other liability for damages which the Contractor is required to insure under any provision of this contract.

ARTICLE 15.   FIRE-INSURANCE WITH EXTENDED COVERAGE

The Owner shall effect and maintain fire insurance with extended coverage upon the entire structure on which the work of this contract is to be done to one hundred per cent of the insurable value thereof, including items of labor and materials connected therewith whether in or adjacent to the structure insured, materials in place or to be used as part of the permanent construction including surplus materials, shanties, protective fences, bridges, temporary structures, miscellaneous materials and supplies incident to the work, and such scaffoldings, stagings, towers, forms, and equipment as are not owned or rented by the contractor, the cost of which is included in the cost of the work. EXCLUSIONS: The insurance does not cover any tools owned by mechanics, any tools, equipment, scaffolding, staging, towers, and forms owned or rented by the Contractor, the capital value of which is not included in the cost of the work, or any cook shanties, bunk houses or other structures erected for housing the workmen. The loss, if any, is to be made adjustable with and payable to the Owner as Trustee for the insureds and contractors and subcontractors as their interests may appear, except in such cases as may require payment of all or a proportion of said insurance to be made to a mortgagee as his interests may appear.

Certificates of such insurance shall be filed with the Contractor if he so requires. If the Owner fails to effect or maintain insurance as above and so notifies the Contractor, the Contractor may insure his own interests and that of the subcontractors and charge the cost thereof to the Owner. If the Contractor is damaged by failure of the Owner to maintain such insurance or to so notify the Contractor, he may recover as stipulated in the contract for recovery of damages. If other special insurance not herein provided for is required by the Contractor, the Owner shall effect such insurance at the Contractor's expense by appropriate riders to his fire insurance policy. The Owner, Contractor, and all subcontractors waive all rights, each against the others, for damages caused by fire or other perils covered by insurance provided for under the terms of this article except such rights as they may have to the proceeds of insurance held by the Owner as Trustee.

The Owner shall be responsible for and at his option may insure against loss of use of his existing property, due to fire or otherwise, however caused.

If required in writing by any party in interest, the Owner as Trustee shall, upon the occurrence of loss, give bond for the proper performance of his duties. He shall deposit any money received from insurance in an account separate from all his other funds and he shall distribute it in accordance with such agreement as the parties in interest may reach or under an award of arbitrators appointed, one by the Owner, another by joint action of the other parties in interest, all other procedure being as provided elsewhere in the contract for arbitration. If after loss no special agreement is made, replacement of injured work shall be ordered and executed as provided for changes in the work.

The Trustee shall have power to adjust and settle any loss with the insurers unless one of the Contractors interested shall object in writing within three working days of the occurrence of loss, and thereupon arbitrators shall be chosen as above. The Trustee shall in that case make settlement with the insurers in accordance with the directions of such arbitrators, who shall also, if distribution by arbitration is required, direct such distribution.

ARTICLE 16.   LIENS

The final payment shall not be due until the Contractor has delivered to the Owner a complete release of all liens arising out of this contract, or receipts in full covering all labor and materials for which a lien could be filed, or a bond satisfactory to the Owner indemnifying him against any lien.

ARTICLE 17.   SEPARATE CONTRACTS

The Owner has the right to let other contracts in connection with the work and the Contractor shall properly cooperate with any such other contractors.

ARTICLE 18.   THE ARCHITECT'S STATUS

The Architect shall be the Owner's representative during the construction period. He has authority to stop the work if necessary to insure its proper execution. He shall certify to the Owner when payments under the contract are due and the amounts to be paid. He shall make decisions on all claims of the Owner or Contractor. All his decisions are subject to arbitration.

ARTICLE 19.   ARBITRATION

Any disagreement arising out of this contract or from the breach thereof shall be submitted to arbitration, and judgment upon the award rendered may be entered in the court of the forum, state or federal, having jurisdiction. It is mutually agreed that the decision of the arbitrators shall be a condition precedent to any right of legal action that either party may have against the other. The arbitration shall be held under the Standard Form of Arbitration Procedure of The American Institute of Architects or under the Rules of the American Arbitration Association.

ARTICLE 20.   CLEANING UP

The Contractor shall keep the premises free from accumulation of waste material and rubbish and at the completion of the work he shall remove from the premises all rubbish, implements and surplus materials and leave the building broom-clean.

IN WITNESS WHEREOF the parties hereto executed this Agreement, the day and year first above written.

Owner _____   Contractor _____

SECTION THREE

The House

THE LANDSCAPING

You can bring about one of the biggest changes in the appearance of your house by remodeling the landscaping. Have you ever noticed how much better a print or a painting looks after it has been framed? Sometimes the roughest sketch takes on new power and significance. Landscaping is the frame for your home; it sets it apart and completes the picture. But, just as the picture frame must be suitable—imagine a Mondrian in a baroque frame—so should your landscaping be designed in a style that complements and emphasizes your house.

A Colonial house, for instance, should not be smothered in planting and have two tall evergreens on either side of the front door. The early colonists kept the trees down and the doors clear so that unfriendly Indians would have no place to hide and shoot arrows into them when they went out to the barn. Later, as more formal styles were built, they had splendid gardens . . . but away from the house. The carefully designed and executed architectural detail was not covered by shrubbery.

Modern and contemporary architecture, on the other hand, usually needs luxuriant planting to integrate it with the land, to soften the sometimes hard lines, and to provide shadows and color.

Landscaping should have a foreground, a middleground, and a background. The foreground begins at the street or road and is the fence, hedge, or planting there. If the house is symmetrical and formal, you can use a tightly clipped hedge, a masonry wall, or shaped evergreens. But if you have a sprawling shingle house that tends to be rustic, do not use evergreens that are trimmed into little round balls or rigid shafts standing at attention. For an informal house use graceful, loose trees that bend in the wind, a split-rail fence covered with roses, or a low stone wall with ivy or moss in the chinks.

A fence or wall makes any lot seem larger and is almost indispensable in locations where a definite boundary line is needed or the house is close to the street. A brick or stone wall implies a formal house, as do board-and-batten and some picket fences. Never use a low metal or wood picket fence with sharp edges on the street. People may trip and fall over them or children tumble from their bikes and be impaled. Gates and entrances should anticipate the character of the house and be neither too grandiose nor too modest. Avoid the monumental overhead construction that is traditionally reserved for cemeteries.

You can minimize street and traffic sounds with correct planting, walls, and grass. Landscaping can also absorb heat and glare and keep your house cooler in the summer. Most codes limit the height of a wall on the street to four feet, but even a wall that high can help deflect a lot of noise and heat. Except on street and highway intersections, there is no limit to the height of trees and shrubbery you may plant inside the wall. Large trees and plants should be grouped to frame a view of the house. Strategic planting can block off automobile lights and prevent passers-by from looking into the house.

The middleground of your landscaping comprises the house, lawn, and trees immediately in front of and beside it. Big trees should shade the house and the entrance, or be grouped with shrubbery to balance and frame the house or hide unattractive views. Do not ever interrupt the flow of lawn and space with small, isolated trees, flower beds, roadside sculpture, or ornaments which are distracting and make mowing the grass doubly difficult. Any statuary worth having should have a special setting of its own.

Your middleground planting should stress the good points of the house and lead the eye away from any undesirable details. The accent on every house front should be the entrance and the front door.

Foundation planting should be just that. It should hide the foundation in winter and summer, nestle the house to the ground, and make it seem to belong there and no place else on the site. A spike-type tree at each corner is not the answer. Plants should be almost the size you want them when they are placed. Get slow-growing ones and prune them every year; do not let them get high or rangy.

The background of your landscaping should, ideally, be trees and sky, not other houses or buildings. You can establish a good background by planting fast-growing trees, such as poplars or willows. The cost of large-size trees may be double that of smaller ones, but weigh the initial cost against the rate of growth and the question of whether you are going to live long enough to enjoy the full-grown trees; if not, the initial investment on small trees may be a waste.

The back of the house should be just as well planted and landscaped as the front. This is the part you and your family use the most; so make the living side of your property as attractive as the part you present to the public.

Your back yard or the private area of your garden does not need to be large in order for you to raise a few vegetables and have a cutting garden, terrace, pool, fountain, and path winding through the trees. In fact, a small area is usually easier to work with and develop than acreage. Almost no space is too small; the Japanese make veritable forests out of tiny interior courtyards no bigger than our bathrooms.

You can incorporate the cutting garden and the

Colonial Williamsburg

vegetables with the foundation planting. Have a tub of tomatoes growing on the terrace; edge the walk or borders with parsley; and perhaps let beans, squash, and eggplant grow over an arbor or cover the side of the garage. Even corn makes a passing-fancy hedge; your garden is much easier to care for and more pleasant if you do not get too utilitarian about it.

If your garden is large, you probably want vistas of lawn and flowers. Flower beds that are outlined with little rocks, bricks, or logs are hard to mow around, and the scraggy grass makes them look untidy; the logs rot and harbor insects. Edge

the beds simply with a straight cut or metal edging that the lawn mower skips over.

Have an area to walk to, no matter how small, that has some nooks and crannies in it. Here is the place for a bench, a piece of sculpture or a little pool. Have it in a quiet, secluded corner. Make it private enough so that you can stroll through it at night in your robe. That is one of the things a garden is for.

Children should have a play area where you can see them from the kitchen or family room. Use grass, and have a concrete section that can be covered (for small children) with an outdoor plastic carpet so that they do not get hurt if they fall. Avoid thorny plants, gravel, and pebble walks. Most children love to dig in dirt, and some like to plant things and watch them grow. A child's idea of a garden and beauty is not the same as an adult's. If you respect his concept of beauty, even though it is a tired old petunia struggling in the mud, he will be inclined to respect yours. Keep all fertilizers and sprays out of harm's way.

If the care and feeding of grass discourages you, plan your landscaping and gardens without it. Grass is not a must. Use hardy groundcovers, with islands of brick, slate, or stone; or combine these materials with raised areas that spill over with colorful annuals against backgrounds of evergreens.

The sound of gently splashing water is always welcome and relaxing. Fountains with small electric motors are inexpensive and recirculate the water in a small pool, keeping it from becoming stagnant and attracting insects. Regardless of how much you like music, repress the impulse to put a loudspeaker in the garden unless you have considerable acreage. The neighbors may not complain, but you have no right to fill their ears with your choice of music any time you feel like it.

Lighting should be an integral part of every landscaping plan. Do not light up the garden like a filling station and see that no lights shine into a neighbor's windows or onto his terrace or porch. The subdued light of gas flame or candles flickering through the garden is very appealing. Several lights can be portable so that you can further enjoy seasonal blooms at their peak. One or two spots aimed up in the trees can cast a lovely green glow, but do not make this too stagey. Conceal the source of such lights, and keep spotlights off the house itself.

THE DRIVEWAY

Although we have been living in the automotive age for many decades, we still seem not to recognize that a driveway's primary function is to get us comfortably to the entrance door. The drive should not be ten feet away, or five feet, but one step away. Nothing else makes any sense at all. Why ask your family or guests to run for it in bad weather? The old-fashioned porte-cochere, used extensively in the more enlightened horse-and-buggy days, deserves an unqualified come-back.

The driveway should also connect the utility area and garage with the street. These things are all possible, even on the smallest site, with correct planning. Sometimes it takes a bit of juggling, a new entrance, a porch removed, or the front door changed to a new location.

In the North it is well to keep the drive short in order to minimize the work of snow removal. This is often difficult in remodeling because we are working with existing conditions and must make the most of what we have. On a narrow site it may not be possible to have a short drive-way without moving the garage, but even on a narrow lot, the drive should go past the entrance and provide parking and turnaround space. The hazards involved in a poorly designed drive that forces you to back out onto the street, especially if children play in that area, are too great in contrast to the saving you may gain by such an economy. Determining the minimum spaces for parking and turning your car around helps in planning the best driveway for your site.

If your site is wide but shallow, create a buffer between the street and the drive to get away from a commercial look. This is not difficult if you have ten feet or more. In most cases driveways may extend to the lot line, but you should leave enough space for a fence and planting. The minimum width of a drive is eight feet; turns must be wider.

For a house on a hill, turn the driveway to slow the descent of your car and build low walls. A wider drive is recommended on hills so that delivery trucks can navigate without going over the edge of the paved area and mashing down plants and borders.

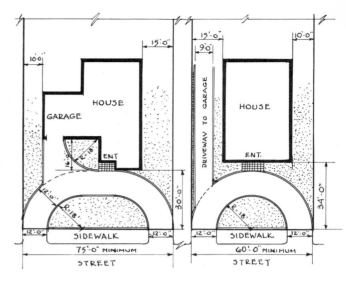

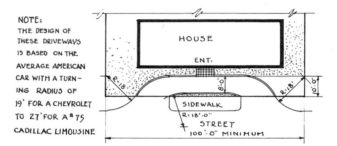

NOTE:
THE DESIGN OF THESE DRIVEWAYS IS BASED ON THE AVERAGE AMERICAN CAR WITH A TURNING RADIUS OF 19' FOR A CHEVROLET TO 27' FOR A #75 CADILLAC LIMOUSINE

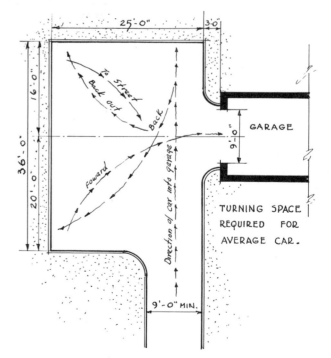

TURNING SPACE REQUIRED FOR AVERAGE CAR.

To save a good tree and make the drive more interesting, spend the extra it costs to create an island in the roadway, if you have the space. This is especially effective on a sloping site. The island takes up differences in levels and absorbs some of the blankness of the drive. You also have less water standing in the drive after a heavy rain.

Keep the crown in the middle of the road to drain water off to the sides. Edging the drive cleanly makes grass and drive easier to care for. Have trees to mark the way at turns and entrances, turnarounds and parking places so that you do not have to resort to excessive exterior lighting.

Have one or two small lights at the entrance gate on the street. Low lights in the plantings on either side of the drive are helpful but should be used sparingly; a white line painted along each edge is almost as effective in keeping cars off the lawn. Inconspicuous lights should be placed at the parking area, and a good-sized one should light the drive where your guests get out of the car. Be careful that no lights shine directly in the driver's eyes.

Driveways are contracted for, by the foot, usually in nine-foot-wide sections, since that is the average width. For long driveways, blacktop, concrete, and gravel are the better materials.

Blacktop is subject to considerable deterioration and is unattractive unless kept in excellent repair. It lacks the residential quality of gravel, but children love it for bicycling, basketball, and other games.

Concrete makes a rather dull driveway. It does not require much upkeep, but it shows dirt, tire tracks, and oil marks. It is fine for roller skating and reflects less heat in summer than blacktop. The tar joints required for contraction and expansion, unless designed with the landscaping, tend to give it a public highway look.

Gravel makes the softest, nicest, friendliest driveway. Everyone likes the sound of gravel under the wheels and the pleasant way it announces arrivals. This type of drive requires raking now and then and a new load of gravel every other year or so. It is not good on steep grades; the gravel runs off. While fair for bicycles, it is not too good for tricycles or for very young children who like to nibble on it.

Brick is by far the most attractive and the most expensive driveway surface. It needs a little weeding and an occasional scrubbing. Incorporated with a brick entrance and terrace on a small site, it can make the approach seem much larger.

Both brick and concrete drives can have snow-melting coils placed just under the surface; this is very convenient in hard climates.

A cobblestone drive is excellent in character and appearance, but it is expensive unless you can buy old cobbles when the town repaves a street.

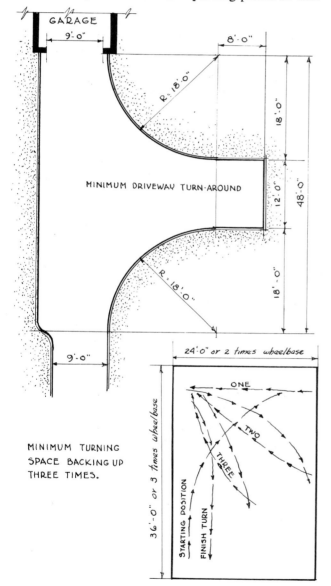

MINIMUM DRIVEWAY TURN-AROUND

MINIMUM TURNING SPACE BACKING UP THREE TIMES.

THE ENTRANCE

The entrance is the introduction to your home. Do not make people search for it or work to get there. It should be the most prominent element of the façade, conspicuous from the street or drive. By this I do not mean that the front door must be on the front of the house or on the side facing the street, but simply that your entrance should be on the drive and lead you to the front door.

Basically the entrance should provide a broad, covered platform not more than two or three steps up from the driveway. You should be able to pause there, out of the weather, to find your latchkey, fold your umbrella, or remove your galoshes. The roof should shelter your guests, protect the door and fixtures, and keep rain and snow out of the entry. A doormat or scraper should be set into the floor so mud and snow are not tracked inside the house.

Entrance lighting is a safety factor, and should not be confused with door lighting. A ceiling light is usually sufficient. But if there are more than three steps up to the door, you should place another light just above ground level in or on the steps. For a really warm welcome in the North, you might put a combination illuminating and heating light in the ceiling of the entrance. A light at the driveway is a good idea if it is any distance from the entrance; you can see who is getting out of the car before you open the door. But do not spotlight the entrance.

Entrance steps and a path (if you have one) should be wide enough for three people to walk together easily without brushing the shrubbery. This width gives an open greeting and is an advantage when you are helping people to their cars.

Materials of the entrance will be dictated by the design and materials used in the house, but for the floor of the platform and the path, brick or stone is best, both for foothold and appearance. Slate, if it is rough, is also very good. Thin, smooth slate freezes over quickly and is very hard to keep clean. Plain old concrete is all right, and can be made to look better if painted or scored in a good design. Any of these materials can have snow-melting coils placed undernearth, which is worth doing if you live in a cold climate.

Wood is the poorest material for the entrance floor. It splinters, rots, encourages termites, and

must be kept painted, which makes it slippery when wet and a matter of yearly maintenance and expense. A wood railing on the stair or platform, however, can be quite serviceable; but be sure it is sturdy enough to lean and sit on. Many wood railings are better in design than the best metal ones and require no more upkeep. Wrought-iron columns call for matching or similar hand-rails; but you may combine wood columns with metal railing, if you stick to simple lines and classic proportions.

Try to avoid aluminum or plastic awnings over the entrance. These are rarely attractive. Canvas can be good-looking, but use real canvas. Note, however, that it does not usually last more than a couple of years and should be taken down in northern climates unless commercial and very expensive construction is used.

The type of roof you have over the entrance depends on the house. A flat roof tends to disappear and assimilate into the architecture of almost any house; a pitched or gable roof sometimes adds needed detail and character to the façade.

Some houses simply do not look well with any cover projected over the entrance. In many instances you can make an exterior entrance by indenting the walls of the house three or four feet. If the house is small and you do not want to lose

this interior space, the paving and decoration around the door become your primary concern. In any event, no cover over the entrance is better than the wrong one.

The entrance does not have to be directly in front of the main door. It can be an enclosed courtyard with a covered walk on one side. Or the entrance could be an arcade or loggia beginning at the drive and leading to a front door at the side or around to the back of the house.

If you build a new living room on the back of the house, you may want to move the main door to a new and perhaps isolated location. The courtyard or loggia can conduct you to this door, no matter where it is. Build some big plank gates with massive hardware at the driveway leading to an enclosed garden. Put the doorbell at the drive, and have an intercom and latch release so that just anybody cannot walk through.

On a narrow lot it is often possible to move the entrance to the side and use the small setback yard to good advantage. Planting and a fence can separate it from the side wall of the neighboring house.

If your house is on a hill, eliminate dangerous and difficult stairs by planning a new entrance through the basement with an interior stair up to the main floor. Interior stairs cost less than the all-weather construction required outside, and by opening up the basement, you can achieve a new sense of spatial expansion on the interior and exterior.

The back entrance should be in a rear court or other space separated from the lawn and garden. It may be visible from the drive, but not from the front door and public side of the house. Here, all the utilitarian and service facilities of the house should be concentrated and dealt with, out of sight of both the public area in the front of the house and your private living area in the back. Have the garbage cans, meters, bike rack, drying yard, cordwood, and so on shielded from view by a garden house and a hedge or fence. Do not try to grow grass here if the area is too small. Put down a concrete slab or a gravel bed.

The "back" entrance should not be treated like the proverbial stepchild. There is no reason for not having it just as inviting, in its own way, as the main entrance. Materials and lighting should be similar, although of secondary importance, to the "front" entrance.

THE FRONT DOOR

Changing your front door can be one of the easiest, least expensive, and most gratifying steps in remodeling.

You may try painting or staining the old door yourself. There are instances where years of coats of paint with the inevitable checks and cracks improve the looks of a door with a subtle blending and translucence of colors, as in many old doors in Europe and the Orient. A simple rubbing and coat of clear varnish may be all that is needed to bring it out beautifully.

If you paint the door, stay away from the common shades of red, blue, and green. Anything straight out of the can is liable to be prosaic. Mix your own shade of eggplant, moss green, vermilion, or cobalt or cerulean blue. You can change your mind and the color of your door every year; it only takes an hour's time and a couple of dollars worth of paint.

Staining requires taking the door down to the original wood, but if yours is a solid door with well-designed panels, it is worth the effort. You may discover detail and beautiful wood you never knew existed under the old layers of paint. There are excellent ready-made stains that seem to transform even crate wood into walnut or mahogany. You do not have to make the door an even stain. Go about it as though it were an oil painting, mixing your own stains from several tubes of artist's oils; bring out highlights and details with a slightly different color. Old wood absorbs the stain like a sponge; so you will find it hard to make a mistake you cannot correct.

The design of some doors is so poor that only covering or replacing them is satisfactory. Try covering it before you throw it away. Get some planking, or plywood with a design in walnut or teak, and glue it to both sides of the door. Leave a small space at the edges so the door will close tight on its existing stops and against the weather-stripping. Use elegant hardware in a pewter or bronze finish. If you want it more casual, use big black iron hinges, with a latch and escutcheon plate to match. Your front door should be distinctive all the time, not just dressed up at Christmas.

If you buy a new door, you can spend anywhere from twenty-four dollars to twenty-five hundred dollars, plus the cost of installation and weather-stripping. This is one place where I believe you should forget economy in deference to fine design and the best hardware. A good design costs no more than a poor one. Check the junkyards, wrecking companies, and antique dealers for doors. An old door has dried out, probably done all the warping and shrinking it is going to do, and the craftsmanship on most of them is far superior to the machine-made doors that are turned out today. Even the best brand-new doors may warp, and the guarantee only replaces the door, not the labor for hanging it or the weather-stripping, which can cost another fifty to seventy-five dollars for the average front door.

All front doors swing in, which keeps them from blowing out of your hand in a wind, and is cordially inviting as well. Double doors take up twice the interior space, but they have an air of being especially welcoming. They also cost twice as much as a single door, and the weather-stripping again is more; however, they can be a handsome addition to your house.

There is little point in buying a new door or trying to make the old one more attractive if you are going to hide it behind a tacky aluminum storm door. If you have one, take it down and throw it away. It might be able to keep out a draft or two in the winter and convert to a screen door in the summer, but it only assures you of having an ugly door all year round. Properly weather-stripped, the front door itself will keep out cold drafts. If you need a screen door in the summer, get a good wood one in a panel design that goes with the house door.

Doors with obscure glass panes can be very handsome and help light the entrance hall. If the panes are small enough, one pane can be glazed with clear glass so that you can see the face of the caller. Avoid the Papa Bear, Mama Bear, Baby Bear peephole designs. If you already have one, you can relieve the design somewhat by placing picture molding on the door to draw the peepholes into an over-all pattern. Or, block out two of the windows. Better still, put a little shutter or door in one and cover the others. The condition of the door may be perfectly good; it is only the design that is so cloying.

Before

After

OLD FRENCH DOORWAY

Light fixtures

Door height 6'-8" - 7'-0"

Center of fixture 5'-0"

Before

After

After

Regular molding can also transform a blank-faced slab door into something interesting. Almost any millwork shop or hardware store can supply you with intricate wood details and molding usually used for furniture. Look through an architectural history book at the library and copy down details of a door you like. Your door will not be an exact reproduction, but it will be better than it was before. If you do not want to go this far, you can hammer a design into the door with upholstery studs.

Do not have a big window at one or each side of the door. It destroys the feeling of security a front door should impart. You should be able to see who is at the door without being seen yourself. Big windows only have to be curtained and are apt to crack if the door is slammed. Side lights with front doors have been standard for several hundred years, but these too should either be curtained or paned with obscure glass. A peep-through or small window in the door is sufficient to let you see who is there.

Light fixtures on the exterior of the door should be at eye level to light the face of the caller. Exterior lights should be bright in comparison with the light just inside so that you are not silhouetted in the doorway.

It never pays to buy cheap builder hardware. The difference between a cheap doorknob and a first-rate one may be ten or twenty dollars but the good one will last a lifetime and improve with age, while the cheap one will look worse and finally fall apart in your hand. The door knocker, the hinges, the latch, and the side lights should all be of the same material and feeling. Often you can mix periods and origins of style if the materials are the same and the character is similar. For instance, you may be able to combine Colonial with Spanish or some French Provincial. In these matters it is better to follow the advice of an architect or a decorator before you get too far off the track.

You may not want a door buzzer if you have a knocker, but be sure a child can reach one or the other if you have both. The buzzer on the back door should have a slightly different tone from the one on the front door so that you can quickly distinguish them. Door chimes had some vogue twenty-five years ago, but they can become tiresome.

THE ENTRANCE HALL AND STAIRS

The entrance hall, whether formal or informal, sets the stage for the rest of the house. It should be inviting, but its basic utilitarian function must never be overlooked. The hall stops drafts, wind, cold, and heat from entering the main rooms. It insulates against sound as well and gets coat closet, powder room, and telephone off in a corner where they belong.

A small entrance hall is better than none at all, but it should have space for a chest to hold mittens, gloves, sunglasses, and keys, with a mirror above it for last-minute checks on makeup and hairdo. There should also be space for a coat closet, which should be ventilated if you keep overshoes and galoshes in it.

A few steps up from the entry to the entrance hall can cut drafts and reduce the number of exterior steps to the front door. Never have one step; have two or more, or none.

Wood is not a good choice for the entrance hall floor. Carpet is better, and is easily vacuumed. Slate, brick, stone, and terrazzo are good, sturdy materials. Sometimes a small space with masonry on the floor just inside the door will work well for stamping snow off shoes; or, if you live in the country, use another built-in mud mat similar to the one on the outside of the door.

Lighting should be adequate but not excessively bright; it should provide a comfortable transition from the darkness outside to the more brightly lighted living rooms.

Extra heat in the entrance hall by the front door tends to equalize the temperature in winter as the door is opened and closed. But do not place an uncovered radiator where you are apt to back into it. All radiators and hot pipes should be covered; guests can easily run into them, and that is not the sort of warm welcome they expect.

When you come into the entrance hall, you should not be able to look into a bathroom door or down a bedroom hallway. It takes only a little expert planning to overcome this. A door to the pantry or kitchen is a great convenience, but if the door is left open, make sure you cannot see the kitchen sink. It is rather pleasant to be able to see into the living room from the entrance hall, but not directly into the dining room.

The most convenient and efficient location of

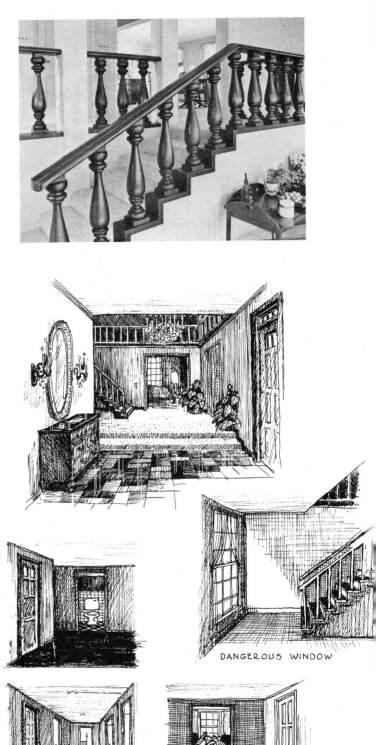

DANGEROUS WINDOW

stairs to a second floor should either be here or in a stair hall just off the entrance. There should be lights at the top and bottom of the stairs controlled by a three-way switch.

Nothing is more dangerous than a badly designed or rickety staircase. The rise of the step (the vertical part) should never be more than seven and a half inches, the run (the tread or horizontal part) not less than ten inches. This "rise over run," as it is called, establishes the rhythm of your footsteps and can make a stair easy or difficult to climb, safe or treacherous to descend. Your stride should be even and steady, and landings should have the same pace as the treads. Any break in the stride by even slight changes in the proportion of rise over run tends to trip you and can make you lose balance.

Your stairs should be at least three feet wide. Four feet is better, because it allows one person to walk beside another and help him up and down. Winders in stairs are a hazard and should be eliminated.

There is no stair made that is not improved with carpeting, not only for safety but for quietness as well. The carpet should have an underpadding, and be fastened securely.

Railings and balustrades should be heavy enough to be leaned on, thrown against, and slid down. A stair wider than three feet needs a handrail on the wall side too. Headroom should be considered carefully, especially if you have youngsters who jump down the last few steps.

Everyone loves a curved staircase. They cost more than a straight stair, but in remodeling you can sometimes save space with a curved or circular stair.

Do not have a window directly in front of the bottom run of a stair or on a landing facing the run. If you fall on the stairs, you can go right through the glass.

Another thing to correct immediately—and this is found in many of the newer split-level houses—is the "down" run of stairs just opposite the front door. You could come in at night and fall down them or open the door for guests and thoughtlessly fall backward down the steps. Should a hail-fellow-well-met type burst through the door when a child is coming up the stair, it could knock him right back down. These stairs were designed for a Marx Brothers comedy and not for homes.

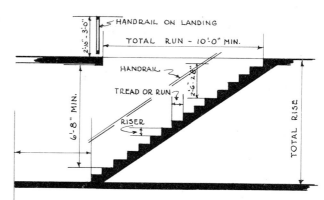

RUN (TREAD) PLUS TWICE THE RISER SHOULD EQUAL 25
or RUN MULTIPLIED BY THE RISE SHOULD EQUAL 75

CLOSED STAIR   OPEN STAIR

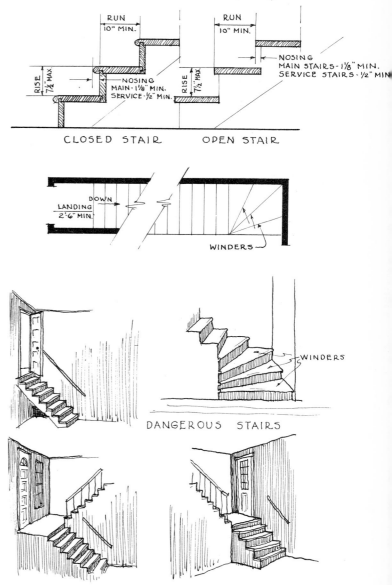

DANGEROUS STAIRS

THE LIVING ROOM

Before you remodel your living room or build a new one, decide how you are going to use it. Is it to be the center of family activity, or will it be more like a drawing room, only for adults and for children on their best behavior?

There is no maximum or minimum size for a living room. Average sizes are 16'x24', and 14'x20'. The smaller your living room, the more carefully it must be designed and furnished. Even a 16'x24' room cannot be furnished easily if it is all doors, windows, radiators, and fireplace.

A sunken living room can be a most refreshing change, and the steps down increase the height of the room. If you are adding a living room, it is not difficult to lower it a few steps from the rest of the house. But lowering an existing space can be troublesome. If you have a crawl-space underneath the floor, it is relatively simple as long as you maintain the three-foot crawl-space most codes require. You can either drop the floor, settling it to its new level on jacks, or build a new one, using what material you can salvage out of the old floor. Remember, never have just one step up or down into a room, always have two or more. People do not notice one step and frequently trip over it.

If the living room is to be used by the family all through the day, you probably want it to face south for the sunlight. You want lots of windows, doors to a terrace, a big masonry fireplace, and easy-to-care-for materials. You may want vinyl or tile floors or wide plank boards finished with plastic varnish and a few tough rugs that can be rolled up for dancing. You need bookshelves, the hi-fi, a place for records, the television set, and wood storage. The furniture should be rugged and adaptable so that you can arrange it for a Cub Scout meeting or a cocktail party. Lighting is not too complicated. You need lots of outlets for table lamps and perhaps a big wrought-iron chandelier toward the fireplace end of the room. Heating requirements are less than for the average living room. Radiators or registers may have to go between the doors and windows or, in the case of registers, in the floor in front of the doors. You should have a vent to remove smoke and odors usually on the end opposite the hearth, because a large fireplace draws out some of the air. Put the

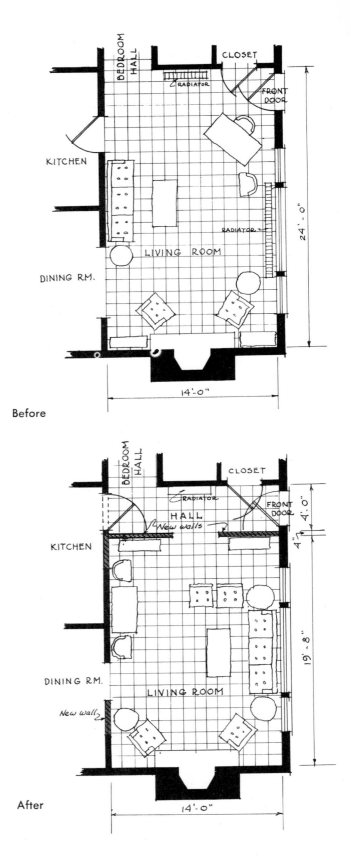

Before

After

return-air grille behind a table or by the floor where it does not show, rather than in the middle of a wall.

If you plan a more elegant room, the furniture may be on a smaller scale, and you can use more delicate materials. This living room probably is used mostly in the evenings. It is better opened to the west than the south; you can block out the bright afternoon sun, then enjoy the slanting rays of evening light. Carpet is the easiest floor to maintain, though certainly an oriental rug on a parquet or marble floor is far finer. The smaller fireplace may have marble around the opening, with a marble or granite hearth and perhaps an antique mantel. You may want detailed cabinets and wainscot paneling for the walls.

The wiring for this room need not be so flexible because, for the most part, the furniture is going to stay put. You might have rheostat valance lighting over the windows and draperies, ceiling spots for paintings, wall sconces on either side of a mirror. The heating requirements are higher because the fireplace is smaller, and you use the room in the evenings.

Always make a furniture plan for any room before designing the heating and lighting. Do not have registers or radiators behind a sofa or piano. Locate chairs that are used for reading, and have electric outlets nearby. When furniture is to be placed in the middle of the room or around the fireplace, put outlets in the floor. Wires running across the floor or under a rug are unsightly and dangerous.

If there is a view from your living room, be sure your windows are low enough so that you can see it comfortably from a sitting position on the sofa or from your chair beside the fire. Mullions and rails on windows should be well above your line of vision when you are seated.

Of course you do not have to have a sofa. They are expensive, often awkward, and no one sits in the middle unless he is having his picture taken. If your living room looks better and is more easily furnished without a sofa, do not invest in one.

The picture window, as such, is so far out of favor that I hardly feel it needs mentioning. But if you want a picture window for your living room or any other room, place the heating either well to the sides, or in the floor about eight inches in

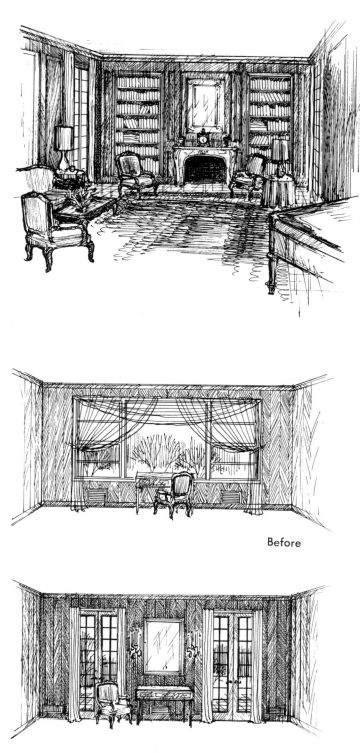

Before

After

front of the window to avoid interference from the draperies.

If you need additional wall space or privacy in your present living room and have a big picture window, close it up, and put in two or three floor-to-ceiling windows or French doors with furniture space between them. If the front door is in the living room, partition it off into an entry. If the dining room is off the living room with a large opening, make the opening smaller and put on doors that can be closed. Close off the extra door to the kitchen if it is in the living room.

However, if your living room is a hallway and you are stuck with it, make it into a real hall, and build a new living room or a sitting room. The expense of a new living room is not excessive and may be less than trying to get an adequate living room out of the existing chopped-up space. Furnish the original area with a library table, some upholstered benches, and occasional chairs, and put down some hard-surface flooring that needs little care.

You can use this space for entertaining; the children can play or study there. Many of the magnificent old houses and castles of Europe were built around this conception of a hall and even got their names from it. Hardwick Hall, Haddon Hall, Arbury Hall, and Little Wenham Hall (which dates from the thirteenth century) are English examples. The Italians had their palazzos, the French their chateaux, the Spanish their palacios, all designed around a great room or courtyard.

Small living rooms can be charming, and if your family is large, perhaps two small sitting rooms would be better than one big room. One can be set aside for general wear and tear and the children's use. The other can be a tidy place where adults can escape for quiet entertaining and relaxation. Ideally the first would face southeast; younger children can play there before their naps, and older ones do their homework and watch TV in the late afternoon and early evening. The second room might open to the southwest.

Too many times a fireplace is planned only as a picture without considering how it is going to be used. The location of the fireplace requires much more thought than the placement of the television or it can be a waste of money.

People and furniture tend to gather around a hearth. The fireplace should never be adjacent to

Before

After

the entrance or placed where it is in the path of circulation. A living room functions better if the fireplace draws people away from the entrance so that the whole room is used. Do not put the fireplace in an exposed corner or in cross drafts.

If you plan to have the fireplace against an exterior wall with a lot of glass, you should get the best professional help and advice. Glass around the fireplace usually destroys the intimate cavelike atmosphere that is the special attribute of a fire on the hearth, and there is the obvious danger of the curtains catching on fire or the window glass breaking with too much heat.

Every house does not have to have a fireplace, but most are better with a well-planned one in a real living room.

House #38 Informal Living Room

House #37 Formal Living Room

THE DINING ROOM

The dining room can be well worth the space it takes if you are going to use it; if you are not, it is a waste. A formal dining room is a separate dining room; an informal one is a part of some other room. Most women want a dining room, but too few make much use of them after they have them because it is easier to feed the family in the kitchen.

The size of your dining room depends on how many there are in your family and how much you entertain at sit-down dinners. There should be a minimum of three feet from the edge of the table to the wall or another piece of furniture; this is just enough space to pull a chair up to the table. A rectangular table that seats six is 3'x5', so that the smallest clear space you could call a dining room would be 9'x11'. Add two feet of length to the table for each additional pair of settings. Buffets, sideboards, china cupboards, tea carts, and other furniture, must be planned outside this space.

Some typical furniture dimensions may help you plan your dining room.

Round dining-room tables are happier and more convivial than rectangular tables. The conversation around a circular table is more animated, friendlier, and more relaxed. The symbolism and empathy of the ring and the circle go back thousands of years and have always been important in oriental as well as western cultures. A round table often takes up less space, too. You should allow two feet of perimeter for each person to be comfortably seated. Four people can dine at a table 3' in diameter, five at a table 3'6" in diameter.

If your dining area is an opening off the living room, it is likely to be used less than a separate dining room, simply to avoid messing up that part of the living room two or three times a day. If the dining room is one end of the living room, you may have neither a dining room nor a living room, but just a room.

If you have breakfast in your dining room, try to open it to the east to catch the morning sun. Your whole day will seem brighter. Never put a

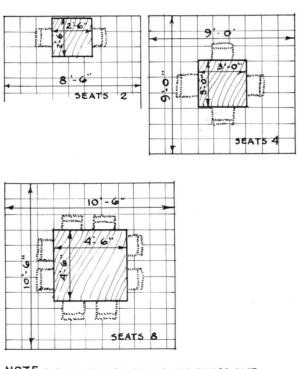

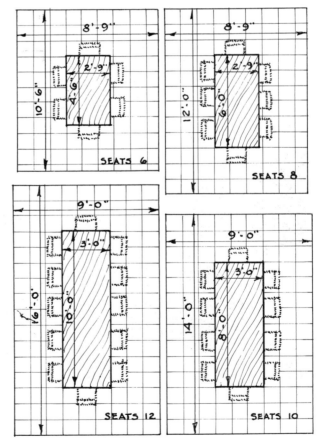

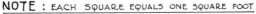

NOTE : EACH SQUARE EQUALS ONE SQUARE FOOT

big picture window in a dining room that faces the street; you have to keep the curtains drawn or be on display all through dinner.

Lighting in the dining room plays a considerable part in the enjoyment of the meal. Candlelight is best, especially when you are entertaining. All electric lighting should be of low wattage and either pink or yellow in tone. These warm tints make the food look more appetizing, relax your nerves, slow you down, and contribute to your over-all enjoyment and contentment. Lighting with cool blue or green tones grays the meat and makes it seem tough, turns mashed potatoes into concrete and gravy into lard.

If there is a sideboard or buffet, place several double outlets on each side for hot plates, food warmers, and a grille for buffet dinners. A down-spot over the buffet and one over the table highlight flower arrangements. Additional convenience outlets should be placed for other furniture and for the vacuum and the waxer-polisher. A double plug in the floor at the customary position of the hostess enables you to connect the waffle iron, toaster, and coffee pot at the table where you want them.

There are two schools of thought concerning the floor. On a hard waxed surface spills are quickly wiped up, and chairs push back easily from the table. With a soft covering, a carpet, noise is deadened, and glassware that may be dropped is not so apt to break; a quick going over with a carpet sweeper or vacuum is easier than scrubbing, waxing, buffing, and polishing.

Heating in the dining room should be slightly lower than in the living room. The radiators or registers should be some distance from the table and directed away from it. Never put the heat under the table.

If you like to cook over charcoal, plan a fireplace for your dining room. Place it well away from the table, at least eight feet. The fireplace should be small, however, so that nearby furniture does not get blistered from the heat.

House #37 Dining Room

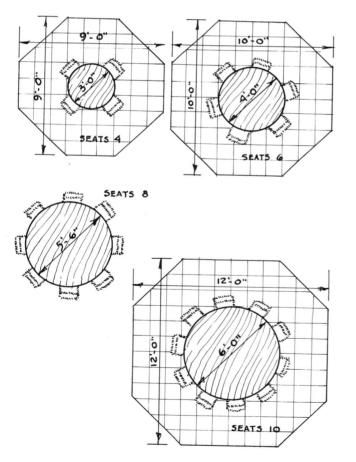

THE FAMILY ROOM

The family room, popularly thought of as a recent American innovation, is neither recent nor American in origin. It has its antecedents in the "keeping room" of our early settlers, who brought their ideas of houses and architecture with them from Elizabethan England, and before that in the "keep" of the Normans. In the United States the family room was a large room, usually on the back of the house, where the daily cooking, eating, sewing, and living went on. Those who could afford it had a "parlor" for formal occasions like weddings, funerals, and Sunday afternoon visits from the preacher; the big room at the back was kept for family use.

Today's family room can be a part of the kitchen or a separate room for everyday use. Do not be deluded by the "family room" misnomer that some builders apply to space off the kitchen that is only large enough for a table and a few chairs; this is just the old breakfast room with another name.

The family room does not have to be large, but there should be space for a sofa and comfortable chairs, a desk, telephone, books, television, and the baby's playpen at least. It should be in the middle of the house, preferably facing south, with lots of light and access to the garden. It can also be used partially as a hall, with doors to the dining room, living room, and the front entrance. Even a hall to the children's bedrooms can open off the family room if it is a separate room and not part of the kitchen. I rather like the idea of the family room's being a big open space very much like the old farm kitchen, where the family can work, relax, play, and study, with the kitchen at one end. If you are going to have it at all, it should be much more than just a room filled with the old living-room furniture, even though this is probably where the old furniture will end up.

It should be filled with the smell of cooking, baking bread, and logs burning in the fireplace. One of the best "family rooms" I've ever seen was my Aunt Bessie's big old kitchen. It had a cold-water pump over a copper sink that drained through a hole in the floor, and a giant iron stove that burned logs and sometimes great black lumps of coal. Geraniums in unadorned coffee cans bloomed their heads off in the windows overlooking the vegetable garden. There were rocking

Norman Keep

chairs, pictures of horses, seed catalogs, and the Sears, Roebuck "wish-books." In the middle of the big round table was a huge oil lamp, and in the air was the smell of kerosene, pipe tobacco, fresh bread, wood smoke, flowers, and of course Aunt Bessie, who was a combination of lilac and apple pie. That was a happy room.

You cannot have my Aunt Bessie, bless her, but you can have a happy, warm family room if you do not go in too much for frozen foods and an antiseptic atmosphere. A glass of water does not taste nearly as good as a cold tin cupful from the old pump; but a drinking fountain can be fun, and most children cannot pass one without taking a sip.

If you plan your family room so that it opens onto a porch, you can move some of the furniture outside in the summer and have breakfast there. Screen the porch and leave the family-room doors open in summer; children can make as many trips between the porch and the family room as they like without letting in a fly.

Furniture and materials should be sturdy and easy to keep clean. The floor could be tile, brick, linoleum, or wide wood planks, not little strips of hardwood. You may want a rug under the coffee table. Panel the walls with wood or cork, so that you can tack things up where you want them. Heating in the family room should be a little higher than in other rooms if children play on the floor.

NEW ENGLAND SALTBOX

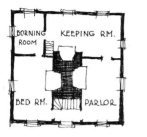

BORNING ROOM
KEEPING RM.
BED RM.
PARLOR

FIRST FLOOR PLAN

House #38 Family Room
House #37 Family Room

THE KITCHEN

The kitchen is the hub of your home, and the bigger it is, the better. The working area itself, however, should be organized and concentrated in one place. There is a logical progression of food from the back door to the dining table. For example: you buy a chicken at the market and bring it in the back door to be refrigerated until cooking time; so the refrigerator should be near the back door. When you start to prepare dinner, you take the chicken out and clean it; this indicates that the sink should be between the refrigerator and the range. When the chicken is cooked, out of the oven and into the dining room, which means that the stove is best placed near the dining-room door. Store, clean, cook, serve. With minor variations, it should be as simple a pattern as that for all meats and vegetables.

In remodeling we must work with the existing kitchen, which does not always allow us to follow the ideal pattern. The closer you can stick to this basic design, however, the easier and more convenient your kitchen will be.

For example, do not sprain your budget trying to create the much-touted "work triangle" between sink, refrigerator, and stove. This is a pseudo-scientific time and step saver. Relax and plan your kitchen the way you want it. Better still, have it designed by an architect who can combine imagination with common sense. If you cannot put the sink under a window, build a window over it. Never put a range under or within three feet of a window because the curtains or shades may dry out and catch fire and the condensation of cooking vapors will eventually rot away the sill and woodwork.

There are four designs for the basic working area: the one-wall kitchen, the galley or parallel kitchen, the L-shaped kitchen, and the U-shaped kitchen.

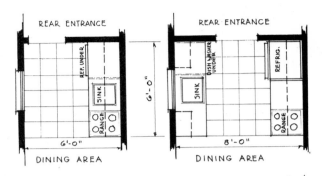

NOTE: F.H.A. minimum kitchen area is 60 square feet.

The one-wall kitchen usually works out best in a small area where not too much counter and storage space is required. The minimum space is about six by six feet. If you have an additional ten or more inches on the opposite wall, you can provide pretty good storage in shallow shelves. If the length is over three times the width, the room will look like a bowling alley. You will also have quite a hike, regardless of the width, if the distance between the refrigerator and the sink gets to be more than twelve feet. Good space and appliance distribution can be created within a relatively narrow room, however, and windows and skylights can be used to offset the tunnel effect.

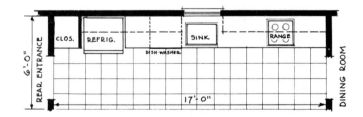

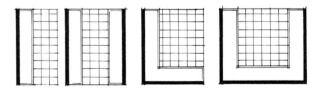

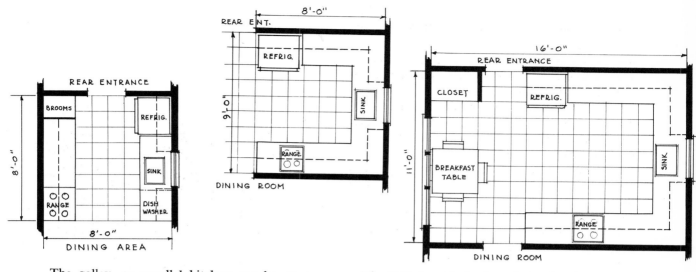

The galley, or parallel kitchen can be an expanded version of the one-wall kitchen. The entire opposite wall can be cabinets and counter, or it can contain one or more of the appliances. The minimum width is eight feet, allowing a four-foot aisle between counters. If you can get a table and chairs in this space, it is too wide; the furniture will constantly be in the way.

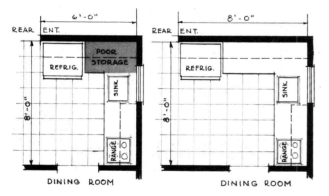

An L-shaped kitchen works out very well in a medium-sized room because you then have the other half of the room for a breakfast table. But it is no good trying to force an "L" shape if one leg is less than eight feet; you lose two feet of storage in the corner, and the range or refrigerator eats up most of the remaining space. If you can have an uninterrupted counter and the wall is six feet or more, you gain two feet of good storage and more countertop. Anything less than six feet is a waste of money; you would be far better off stopping at the corner.

The "U" shape is the best design for the average kitchen in so far as ease of working and step saving are concerned. The minimum width is nine feet, allowing a clear space of five feet between the counters. Seven feet clear is recommended if someone works with you or if a dishwasher is beside the sink at the bottom of the "U." On widths less than nine feet, the corner cabinets (which offer poor storage at best) use up an increasing percentage of available space. You can store seldom-used things there conveniently enough, but it is awkward if you have to use that dead space for everyday storage.

The U-shaped kitchen loses its convenience if the space becomes so large that you can place a table and chairs in the center. You only increase the steps and inconvenience by having to walk around the furniture.

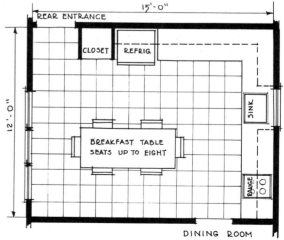

In remodeling, unless you add a whole new room, the kitchen may not work out precisely into an "L" or "U" shape or any standard concept. This is solved by compensating in one area for deficiencies in another.

You may use the range or the sink and dishwasher in an island pattern, with or without hanging cabinets over it. You can make the entire kitchen center an island, leaving the walls to windows. If you are very crowded for space, you can sometimes cantilever a few feet over the existing foundation for additional cabinets, roofing the new space with glass or plastic for more light.

Floor counters are usually twenty-four inches deep and thirty-six inches high. But if you are a tall person, have them built higher; if you are short, have them lower. The four-inch toe space at the base of the cabinets serves advantageously in remodeling to take up any uneven floor spaces. Countertops should be level, even if the floor is not.

A plastic such as 'Formica' is about the best commercial countertop. This is a trade name that has become standard for other good plastic laminates. They do not stain, fade, chip, or rot; they are easily wiped clean, and have some heat resistance. A burning-hot pan can mar a plastic-laminate surface, and a knife can cut it, but ordinary caution should preclude such mishaps. These countertops should be self-edged with square corners; metal edging wears thin as a razor and can cause a bad cut. Sheet vinyl may look like Formica to start with, but it does not hold up. Stainless steel makes an exceptionally durable countertop, but it is noisy, needs constant polishing, and reminds one of a hospital lab. Tile countertops look great, are nearly indestructible, and break things faster than you can set them down; also, the joints eventually disintegrate here and there, making little potholes. An all-wood countertop of maple makes a chopping block; it cannot be kept spotless and needs to be scrubbed down once a week with a wire brush. If an immaculate looking countertop is desired, it would be best to have the chopping block in one small area.

Wall cabinets are usually twelve inches deep; and they are placed eighteen inches above the countertop, twenty-two inches over the sink, and thirty inches over the stove. If you are short or if the ceiling is low, by all means have yours lowered

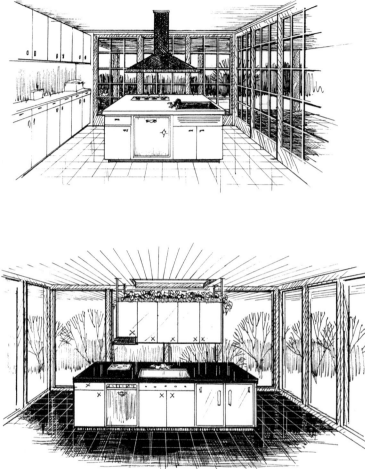

to where you can reach the top shelf. The maximum height of the top shelf should be only six feet off the floor. In remodeling, the top of the wall cabinets can be dropped about a foot below the ceiling; this gets you away from the problem of having to cut and patch cabinets under an existing ceiling that may not be even. Except in special wall cabinets, keep the doors small so that they do not project over the edge of the countertop when open.

Cabinets with a plastic finish are the easiest to keep clean. There are some good strong colors, or you can have a natural-wood finish, but be careful not to take the rough, woodsy look too far. Ordinary plywood simply varnished is probably the ugliest kitchen cabinet conceived. Plywood prefinished in the same material as the counter-tops is handsome, durable, and easy to work with. Cabinets made on the job are less expensive than the store-bought variety, but may not function as well, and the finishes are not as perfect as shopwork. Because of the cutting and fitting involved in remodeling, however, they usually work out better. Metal cabinets, except for extremely costly models, are not as good as wood; they are flimsy and noisy. All metal cabinets rust, and the cheaper varieties have rough edges that are a constant source of irritation.

Each family has somewhat different requirements for china storage. In general, allow about one-fourth more than the minimum you need for odd bits and pieces that do not match but are either too useful or too good to throw away. The average family has two and a half sets of dishes, one for "good," one for everyday, and a half set of miscellaneous china and crockery.

Hardware is as varied as kitchens themselves, but avoid little knobs and hardware with small or sharp projections; things are always getting caught on them, especially if they extend in front of the small overhang of the countertop.

Cabinet latches should be of the best because they get so much wear; the best cost only pennies more. There are three types: the friction catch, the magnetic catch, and the touch latch.

The friction catch works very simply and is easy to install. A metal piece on the door is caught and held by a metal clasp in the cabinet; these tend to be noisy, but they are inexpensive and they do work. The magnetic catch is quiet and without question superior. It works the same way a magnet picks up and holds a nail. The magnetized metal on the door attracts a piece of metal on the cabinet; doors open and close gently, and the catch never wears out. The touch latch is a variation of the friction latch, as are all the latches that work with balls, rollers, or nylon prongs. It has an alternating device that is supposed to release or hold on contact; press in, the door opens; close, the door stays closed. That is the theory, but

in practice it does not always work, and you find yourself pounding on the door or giving up and using a substitute from another cabinet.

Doors and cabinets in the kitchen should all have metal pulls and not tricky touch-plates or concealed and recessed pulls; otherwise the doors are soon spotted with grease and flour from your hands.

Main storage areas in the kitchen include all the obvious places related to the main function, but near the back door you should also have a closet for coats, brooms, and buckets. If you store rubber or plastic boots and galoshes or volatile cleaning fluids in the back closet, be sure the closet is vented to the exterior.

If space allows, it is better to have the refrigerator and freezer together near the back door, rather than have the freezer in the basement or garage. Many times, however, there is not enough room. Plan to have a countertop on the sink side of the refrigerator, and see that the door is hung away from the sink. Double-door refrigerators should have countertop space on both sides. Vegetable bins should be directly under this countertop, canned-goods storage adjacent or opposite. A chopping block of hard maple set into the counter-top between the refrigerator and the sink is a great convenience. Do not worry about getting a refrigerator with all the latest gadgets; the only worth-while innovation is the frost-free machine that defrosts itself.

If you have a dishwasher, your sink need only be a single well, large enough to accommodate big platters and cooking pots. Too often a double well, though convenient for soaking things, makes both sides too small for washing a roasting pan or getting the grease off oven shelves.

The sink can be porcelain-on-steel, enameled cast iron, or stainless steel. Porcelain-on-steel is the cheapest, the hardest to keep clean, and the least durable . . . and it chips. Enameled cast iron is a little better, but it shows all the pot marks and breaks the dishes just as easy. (It comes in colors, if this matters to you.) Stainless steel sinks, though they can be noisy, are better; they are cleaned in a third of the time, you do not break as many dishes, and the designs are excellent. They are offered in many combinations of designs and sizes. You are going to use the sink constantly; so get the best you can. It costs little more than a cheap one by the time you have it installed. Do not get one that has a projecting soapdish under the faucet; the soap disintegrates, and you will always be hitting your hands or knocking dishes against the receptacle.

A bar sink with an under-the-counter refrigerator in another part of the kitchen keeps the host out from under your feet while he is mixing drinks for guests. A cold-water faucet on a gooseneck connection is all you need. The children's soft drinks can be kept on an easily accessible lower shelf, and cocktail glasses and trays can be stored there.

Automatic disposers are wonderfully functional, and the new ones chew up just about everything but paper, foil, and tin cans. For this reason the control switch ought to be a bit inconvenient, out of the way where it cannot be confused with another, where children cannot reach it, and where you, yourself, have to reach far enough so that your free hand cannot possibly be in the drain.

If you have a cesspool, you may not be able to drain food waste into it, and some cities will not permit you to drain into the city main. This necessitates a separate septic tank for the disposer, which raises the cost of installation.

Dishwashers should be installed on rubber or plastic cushions to cut down on the noise and vibration. Some of them make a terrible racket and use many gallons of hot water; so investigate thoroughly before you buy one. Keep in mind that any dishwasher sounds a lot louder in your kitchen than it does in the big showroom.

A range top, separate from the oven, considerably extends the design possibilities of the kitchen. You can place the cooking units where you want them. The oven need not be in the middle of things; you can put something up to roast or bake and forget about it until dinnertime. Range tops also free the space under the counter for the storage of pots and pans. Set three or four burners at the back of the counter away from children, and free the front of the counter; place the controls in front or at the side of burners so that you do not have to reach over. This is a lot safer, and it also lets the vent hood catch all the unwanted odors and steam, heat, and grease. Another unit can be placed next to the dining-room door for sauces or for warming the coffee.

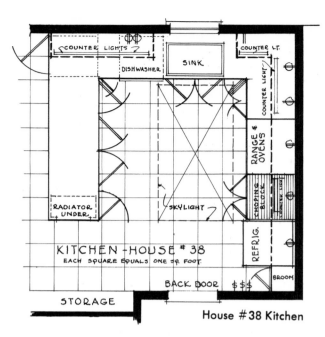

House #38 Kitchen

Several years ago manufacturers came out with a range having an eye-level oven on top. Aside from being too high for convenience, you have to reach over hot burners to get to the oven, and the hoods and vents are not adequate. This sort of stove concentrates all the heat right in your face. Another model slides the burners five or six inches in front of the edge of the counter. These are silly and inconvenient, and can be dangerous.

Wall ovens took the kitchen planners by storm ten years ago, but they proved expensive to buy and to operate and were just as difficult to clean as any others. With that window staring you in the face, you also had to clean them more often. They are less expensive now, and they do have distinct advantages; the oven is raised so that you do not have to stoop with hot, heavy loads, and they can be removed from the main circulation area of the kitchen.

A countertop right beside the oven gives you a place to set things when the bell rings. Big ovens are expensive to buy and to heat; two smaller ones may be much more useful.

Despite all the cooking that goes on in the kitchen, it is still a difficult room to heat. This is mainly because the walls are covered with cabinets and cannot hold registers or radiators. If you have hot-water heating, you can get around this by using the end of a base cabinet to hold a radiator

or by running coils of copper pipe under the floor to form a radiant-heating system. You could also run a heat pipe around the ceiling to radiate heat and warm the room, but this requires very hot water, and dirt and grease inevitably collect around the pipe.

If you have warm-air heating, registers are often placed in the floor, but this is difficult in the kitchen. Either they are where people trip over them, or they are directed toward the sink, stove, breakfast table, or other locations where you do not want direct heat. However, if you have no wall space for registers, you can create an area in the toe space under the base cabinets with grilles all along the way. With warm-air heat you can also place registers in the ceiling, although this does not solve the problem of a cold floor.

Highly efficient electric units can be placed in the ceiling. Combining heat, light, vent, and fan, they are excellent for taking the chill out of the kitchen on a cold morning. The best location is over the rear door or in the center of the ceiling, not directly over the sink or range. The light in the unit can be used for general illumination.

Lighting can make the difference between a good and a mediocre kitchen. The vital light is the one over the sink; so begin with it. Some sinks have a built-in light, but usually this is only a gimmick; it is in the way, and needs constant cleaning; also the wiring can be dangerous. And, you still need a ceiling light.

Counter lights under the wall cabinets are good and give you illumination where you need it. Spot several more lights over the counters to expose wall-cabinet interiors, and have a light over the back door. You need a light over the range top; if you have a hood, be sure a light is incorporated with the hood and fan. Electric outlets can be provided with the counter lights placed on the underside of the hanging wall cabinets, or you can install additional outlets in the wall over the counter. These can be separate or in a continuous strip with a plug every six inches or so.

Kitchen light fixtures should not be of clear glass or contain a fine grille in front of them, because these collect dirt and grease and are difficult to clean. Simple down-spots are effective; they do not collect dirt, and it is easy to change

the bulbs in them. One thing to be very cautious about when buying light fixtures for the kitchen and elsewhere is the ease with which the bulbs are replaced. Cheap fixtures are an initial saving, but some of them have to be completely dismantled before you can replace a bulb. Make the salesmen show you how the bulb is changed before you buy the fixture.

Never put a larger bulb in a fixture than the manufacturer recommends. The fixture is designed, ventilated, wired, and insulated for a bulb of the prescribed wattage. If too much heat is generated, you can blow a fuse or set the house on fire. The least it will do is to shorten the life of the bulb.

For the floor of the kitchen you can choose anything from stone to carpet. Stone, brick, or slate are fine if the structure can support the weight, and if you do not mind a hard and noisy surface. They are more tiring to work on than one of the softer finishes, and slate shows every scratch and spot of grease. Asphalt tile, although the least expensive, is not a good choice; it is the most difficult to maintain, is very brittle, shows stains and scuff marks, and is not grease resistant.

Linoleum, either in rolls or sheets, is the usual kitchen flooring. Inlaid linoleum is more expensive; the color and design go all the way through, and it is tough, greaseproof, durable, and easy to clean. Dampness and water deteriorate linoleum; it should not be used on top of concrete nor have the life washed out of it.

Vinyl-asbestos tile is resistant to grease, easy to clean, and holds up reasonably well. It is a good choice for an economical kitchen floor of long life and low maintenance.

Rubber tile requires a great deal of attention and is very slippery when wet. Available colors are limited compared to other flooring materials. It should never be used below grade or on a concrete slab.

Cork tile is soft, quiet, and comfortable underfoot; with the new plastic finishes it is a fine selection for the kitchen floor. It is rather expensive, needs some attention, and is not as durable as vinyl, but it is such a handsome material that you can always make a case for it.

Vinyl tile is resistant to practically everything except fire and is the best, toughest, easiest to care for, and most expensive floor for the kitchen. Its fine appearance and satisfactory service over the years may well compensate for the higher cost.

The kitchen is no place for a wood floor. However, if, for one reason or another, you want to use or refinish an existing wood floor because it is of hundred-year-old wide planks, you can stain and coat it with a clear plastic finish that will make it almost like vinyl. It is slippery and shiny, but it cleans easily, does not need waxing, and wears pretty well. But most old wood, waxed or unwaxed, needs constant care. Water stains it and raises the grain, causing splinters; moisture and changes in temperature make the wood swell and shrink, leaving cracks for dirt to collect and make its own dust.

Carpet is fine for a town house or for a bachelor's city apartment, but it is not feasible for the average family kitchen. If you are buying a new kitchen floor, pick up the best one you can afford, and keep it up as well as you can.

Most people prefer to paint kitchen walls. It is the most suitable wall surface, easily cleaned and/or changed. Wallpapers (even the coated plastics) have a tendency to come off the wall, roll, or blister. With the new paints it is almost easier to repaint than to clean, and you can change the color every year or two. Considering the amount of time one spends in the kitchen, it is not a bad idea to relieve the scene with a change of color. Enamel paints are easy to clean but are difficult to repaint, and the shine is hard on the eyes and unattractive. Cabinet interiors give you a chance to brighten things up with a splash of color. Use a striking color. You do not get bored with it because the doors are not open that much.

The exposure of your kitchen, whether east for the morning sun, south, west, or north—has something to do with the color you paint the walls. If you face north, paint the kitchen a warm color, such as yellow to simulate sunshine. A kitchen that faces southwest is hot in the late afternoons of summer; so paint the walls a cool color, blue or green.

You can get east light into your kitchen in most cases by projecting a wall or by building a dormer or skylight. Morning sun is the best light by which to start your day, especially for the breakfast-getting routine. And whatever the space, there should be a place to eat in the kitchen, even if it is only large enough for two people.

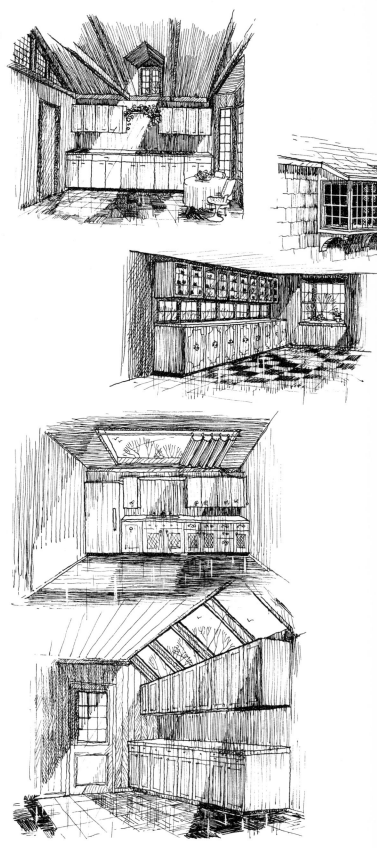

THE BEDROOM AND DRESSING ROOM

We spend about one-third of our lives sleeping. The best bed in the world is not going to improve our sleep or help us rest better if the bedroom is noisy, cold, hot, bright, or an otherwise unpleasant place in which to wake up.

Most bedrooms are too small. The windows, heating, and lights are in the wrong place, and as a result we have to put the bed in the wrong place. Often the bedroom itself is in the wrong location.

If you are adding a bedroom, try to place it on the northeast side of the house. North rooms are the coolest and best for sleeping. If the bedroom also has an eastern exposure, the early sun can lift your spirits for the whole day ahead.

Bedrooms facing south may be very good for the ill or bedridden, but they get very warm in summer and retain the heat until late in the evening. West bedrooms are usually hot in summer and cold in winter because of the prevailing winds. They are also too light for children who must retire early.

Do not blithely place a window in the middle of each outside wall of your bedroom addition. Let the furniture determine the placement of windows, and, in so far as you can, the location of doors and closets. Often you can greatly improve an existing small bedroom by rearranging the windows and heating to provide proper space for the beds.

It is no trick at all to make a bed if you can move around it, but if it is pushed against a wall or wedged into a corner, you have a real chore hustling the sheets and blankets and moving the clumsy bed. Two feet of clearance from the edge of the bed to the wall is recommended as the minimum; you can get by with eighteen inches but at the price of bumped elbows and shins every time you make up the bed.

The Federal Housing Administration (FHA) allows a minimum bedroom of eighty square feet, with the smallest dimension 8'0". This is adequate for a single bed and very little other furniture. But it is the way space is used, not so much the space itself, that is important.

Do not place a bed under a window. There are drafts, even when the window is closed, and a child can fall out or cut himself on the glass if it is low. If the window is open, sudden rains come right in on the counterpane. High windows in the bedroom are particularly dangerous because they are difficult to escape through in case of fire; they also have the drawbacks of being harder to open and close and to curtain and clean.

Arrange the furniture so that windows can be low to the floor with nothing placed in front of them. Even a lamp on a night table should not be in front of the window; breeze-blown curtains can knock it over and give you quite a start in the middle of the night, plus broken glass and perhaps a bare wire to step on.

Cross ventilation in bedrooms is a major asset, but it should not be gained by the forced use of high windows. If you can have only one small window in the bedroom, a double-hung sash reaching nearly to the floor will draw the warm air from the top of the room and filter in fresh air at the bottom. This solution provides much better and safer ventilation than two high windows.

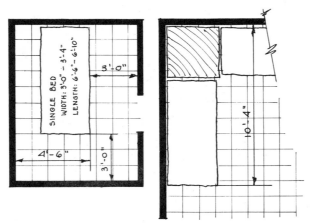

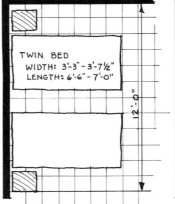

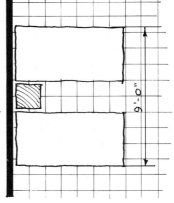

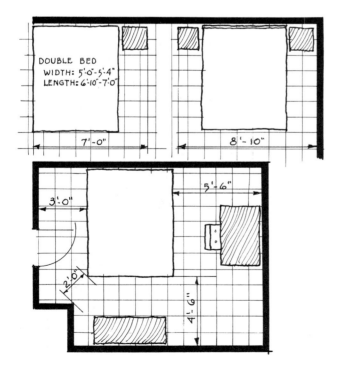

DOUBLE BED
WIDTH: 5'-0"-5'-4"
LENGTH: 6'-10"-7'-0"

7'-0"

8'-10"

5'-6"

3'-0"

12'-0"

4'-6"

Lighting in the bedroom is simple. The old-fashioned ceiling light right in the middle is a faulty conception and poor design and gives sleepers a rude awakening. Have a good-sized table lamp, controlled from the door, on a dresser or desk. Lamps on bedside tables are a necessity. Have them at reading height, or provide special reading lights over beds. Install several double outlets for electric blankets, heating pads, radio, television, hairdryer, and other equipment. Never have extension cords running over the floor or under rugs or behind beds; these can be very dangerous, especially when you are half-asleep.

The bedroom should be carpeted. It is warmer, easier to take care of than any other floor, and much safer in case of a fall. You may not want carpet in the children's rooms; cork tile or vinyl are the next best floor coverings, and wood the worst because of splinters. Carpet makes rooms quieter, deadens sounds, and helps blanket noises from other rooms.

Closets between rooms are effective in reducing sound transmission. The double-wall thickness and the clothing itself cut sound considerably.

Bedroom closets should be about six feet in length for each person using the room. Children using the same closet can have two clothes rods at different heights. It is convenient to have closets lighted, and you may also find that they are kept neater as a result. You should be able to lock bedroom doors, but never closet doors. Each closet door should have a knob or other unlatching device on the inside so that no one can get shut in.

Hinged doors are fine if you have space for a walk-in closet and room for the doors to swing. Full-length mirrors are easily attached to them. Sliding closet doors are apt to be a noisy nuisance; whatever you want always seems to be in the closed half. Bifolding doors, which work better than any of the others, are by far the best for average closets. They are the most expensive, but worth it. You should not economize on things you use every day.

If your bedrooms are small and lack closet space, you can add closets inexpensively by cantilevering out over the foundation.

Extensive built-in storage in bedrooms is not too good an investment because needs change and wardrobes with them. Built-in drawers are quite expensive as compared to some of the values you can find in antique stores or second-hand furniture shops. Antiques increase in value, and you can take them with you if you move.

A dressing room can often get closets out of the way so that the bedroom can be enlarged without extensive remodeling. Built-in storage is good here and adds to your convenience and to the value of the house.

If you are planning to add a bathroom, make the addition large enough to contain a dressing room; the bathroom can be small if you place the lavatories in the dressing area. At least one wash basin should be in the dressing room, possibly at table height as part of the lady's vanity. The vanity should have both natural and artificial light for applying cosmetics in the daytime and at night. Flooring should be carpet, usually the same as in the bedroom or bath. Walls can be either closet doors or mirrors, or both, but there should be at least one full-length mirror.

If you do not want to spend money to add another full bath, you can cut down on the bathroom traffic and economize with a built-in wash basin in a bedroom.

The heating required in bedrooms is lower than for other rooms, but have it adjustable to suit various conditions. Decide where to place the beds; then plan the registers or radiators. Never put a bed in front of a heat outlet. Place the heat on outside walls under windows if you can, but be sure that curtains do not cover it.

A vent, fan, heater, and light combination in the ceiling is a good idea. It warms the room quickly on cold winter days and, depending on the location and number of windows, may be all the heat that is needed. If the dressing room is between a well-heated bedroom and bath, electric ceiling heat may be sufficient.

House #37 Dressing Room and Master-Bath

THE BATHROOM

If you have a big bathroom that merely needs modern fixtures and equipment, you do not have much of a remodeling problem because you have space to work with and it is just a matter of redesigning to get the best use out of the existing space. The real headache and expense are in remodeling the little 5'x7' cubicle with tub, wash basin, and toilet jammed against one wall without adequate light or ventilation. These minimal bathrooms cost more to remodel, unless you only want to replace the fixtures, because you must usually build additional structural space. Sometimes you have an interior problem that can be solved by rearranging existing walls. But more often than not, you have to add new exterior walls to gain any kind of elbow room.

Adding a bathroom from scratch involves the question of where to add it conveniently and economically. Because of the standard sizes of fixtures, bath sizes are more or less set, and their economics are predictable. The cost is less if you use existing interior space, and adding a bath over, under, or next to an existing one is more economical than building it a distance away from the plumbing lines. But if you do effect small economies and the bathroom ends up being inconvenient or not where it is really needed, the saving you made on a few lengths of pipe has cost you too much.

How is the new bath to be used? Is it for the exclusive use of the owner and to be entered only through the master bedroom? Is it primarily for the master bedroom, but also for the occasional use of guests because the children's bath is always such a mess? In the latter case you have to position it so that guests can get to it without going through the bedroom or winding through a long corridor past the children's rooms. Is it to be a new bath for the children? Then it should be at their end of the house, contain two wash basins and be partitioned so that two can use it at once. If it is to be a big bathroom for the whole family and if you do not incorporate the old bathroom into the new facilities, design a good new use for the present one by making it into a powder room or laundry. If the addition you need is just a powder room, place it off the main hall on the first floor.

You should plan a bathroom so that you do not look directly into it from other rooms. In particular, do not place the toilet where you get a direct view of it from the open door. This is a matter of esthetics more than anything else. There are more attractive things to see, such as a sweep of lavatory countertop with a big mirror over it.

Important aspects in the design can make the difference between a safe and agreeable bathroom and a hazardous cell that is merely functional. Every bathroom should be large enough to faint in without going through a piece of glass. This means a good space, at least 6' by 6', that is free of fixtures and furniture. It should be big enough so that an elderly or sick person can be assisted. A larger bathroom is also much easier to clean without aggravating your blood pressure.

Most accidents in the bathroom occur in or at the tub. Never plan window openings lower than six feet above the tub or they can be dangerous. Any window at all over the conventional tub is a poor idea; it is drafty, and steam and condensation soon deteriorate the sill and framing. Glass towel racks and soapdishes do not belong in the bathroom and certainly should not be near the tub. Any towel bar over or near the tub should be anchored securely to studs and should be capable of supporting your weight if you grab it to prevent a fall.

Similarly, bathroom dividers and shower stalls should not be of ordinary glass. Unbreakable, shatterproof glass or plastic is the only acceptable transparent or translucent partition.

Bath tubs are rectangular or square, made of enameled cast iron or enameled steel. The rectangular tub comes in standard sizes of 4'6" to 7'0" in length; 2'4" to 3' wide; and 12" to 16" high. The larger ones are better for bathing children and for relaxing yourself, but the bigger the tub, the more hot water you use. Square tubs with corner seats come in sizes from 3'3" to 4' square, and 12" to 16" high; the corner seating is sometimes helpful for the elderly or lame, provided you have good grab-bars. But the only way to clean these tubs is to climb in and scrub.

Sunken tubs can be inviting, relaxing, glamorous, and expensive. Avoid the manufactured 3'x5' sunken tub; it can be dangerous in the average bathroom. If you want a sunken tub, it should be custom-designed and have a safe bathroom built around it. Design it like a tiny swimming pool at one end of the bathroom; or place it in a room of

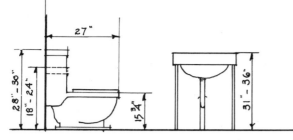

its own, with tile sides, walls, and slip-proof tile floors, with wide easy steps down into it.

Whether you choose an enameled cast-iron or steel tub, get an acid-resistant finish. The enameled cast-iron tubs are the best, but also the heaviest; a 5′ tub, 16″ high and 30″ wide, weighs about 365 pounds. A steel tub is not as good, but the same size weighs only 140 pounds. So if you are adding a new tub in an old house where the combined weight of tub, water, and bather is going to be a problem, get the lighter-weight tub. Any tub exerts less strain on the structure if placed with one side on an exterior wall. If this is not possible, place it over or near an inside partition.

A shower in the bath tub is not the best solution for either the tub or the shower. Tubs are primarily designed for sitting, not standing. Square tubs are especially poor and skiddy for a shower, and the shower curtain is always reaching in after you. However, the tub-shower has become something of a convention because it saves space and caters to different bathing preferences.

If you plan such a combination, consider these ways to improve it. Take the tile or waterproofing material to the ceiling, and provide adequate grab-bars at proper standing height. Be sure to have the shower-head installed well over your head height. Have separate controls for the shower. If, for some reason or other, you cannot have separate controls, get an automatic diverter; when the shower is turned off, the valve adjusts itself and allows water to come out again only through the tub spigots. This at least keeps you from getting a headful of water when you think you are turning on the tub. An excellent shower device is a valve that allows you to dial the temperature of the water. If your water pressure is low, an automatic temperature control on the shower protects you from getting doused with cold water or scalded with hot when others are using the water supply elsewhere in the house.

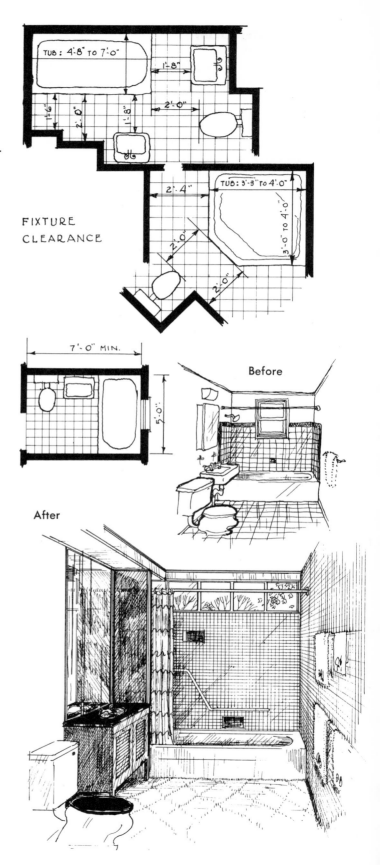

FIXTURE CLEARANCE

Before

After

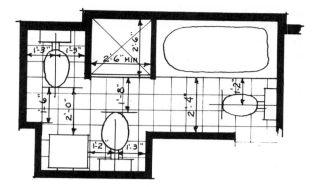

FIXTURE
CLEARANCE

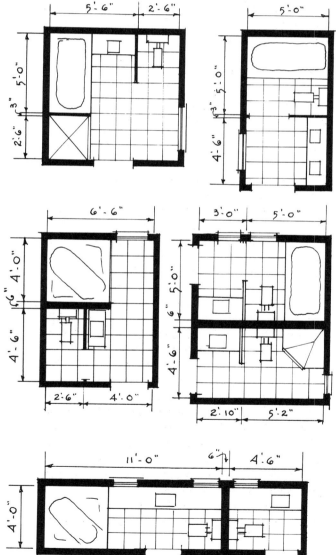

When there is a problem with tub weight or space, a shower stall is a good solution. It should be 36″ by 36″ if you do not want to hit your elbows on the walls . . . larger if possible. The best ones are tiled floor to ceiling, with a translucent plastic door set in metal, usually aluminum, nickel-plated brass, or chrome, to prevent rusting. The floor can be slip-proof tile on a lead pan, which is best, or a precast base of terrazzo.

One-piece plastic shower stalls are lightweight, impervious to solvents, mold, and fungus; they are inexpensive and look it. Metal shower enclosures are also lightweight and inexpensive, but they rust away and are terribly noisy. Safety in the shower is just as essential as it is in the tub; so install good strong grab-bars. A combination light and vent can be placed in the ceiling; it should be vapor-proof, and the switch should be on the outside of the stall.

Wash basins should easily support your weight when you happen to lean on them. They can be wall-hung, free-standing, or built into the counter-top, but all should be firmly anchored to the wall or floor. They are made of vitreous china, enameled cast iron, porcelain-enameled steel, or stainless steel. All come in various shapes and finishes and in wide price ranges, but the determining factor should principally be how good the design is and how well it fits into your bathroom. The countertop ones are the most satisfactory. The wide shelf allows you to place toilet articles within easy reach. You do not have to juggle soap, shaving cream, razor, toothpaste, toothbrush, hair tonic, hair spray, comb, and brush on a little bitty edge that invites you to knock the whole kit and caboodle onto the floor or into the toilet. The space under the countertop hides the pipes and stores extra towels and bathroom supplies. If you only have minimum space to work with, you can still manage an almost generous countertop with a stainless steel wash basin. These are available in a good range of sizes and shapes, are highly practical, easy to clean, and quite good-looking.

Try not to have a window directly over the wash basin. This may be suitable for a woman, but it is difficult for a man to shave if he has to shift position down the line to see in a mirror.

Medicine cabinets are usually over the lavatory; but they should not contain strong medicines. It is much too easy for a child to crawl up, open the cabinet, and start to play doctor. Cotton, adhesive, dental floss, and other toilet articles may be stored in the cabinet; but medicines, especially the familiar aspirin, should be kept in a locked closet if you have small children. And even if you do not have little children around, sleeping pills and other potent medicines should not be kept in the same place as the aspirin and other nostrums; you might bumble around in the middle of the night and get the wrong bottle.

The medicine cabinet does not need to be over the wash basin, however; instead put in a wide mirror over the whole wall. It doubles the apparent size of the bathroom. In the guest bath or powder room, use a mirror with a slight tint of pink, peach, or gold. These mirrors are good for the ego and make your guests think your house and your company do wonders for them.

You have a choice of four types of toilet: the washdown, the blow-out, the reverse-trap or siphon-jet, and the siphon-vortex action. Wall-hung closets must have a reinforced and sturdy wall to support the weight, but they are easier to clean under.

The washdown is distinguished by a round bowl, front drain, low water level, a lot of noise, constant scrubbing, and a cheap price. It overflows readily, has to be scrubbed every other day, and always needs attention.

The blow-out action is the noisiest. It should be used only with a flush valve, which is very economical of water.

The reverse-trap and siphon-jet are the same type, except that the siphon-jet is larger. Both are reasonably efficient, sanitary, and quieter than the washdown type.

The siphon-vortex is the best, the most sanitary, efficient, and expensive; it also cleans itself with a minimum of noise and upkeep.

Any of these types may be had with a flush valve, which eliminates the water tank if you have enough pressure. These valves are generally used in hotels and office buildings that have a house tank on the roof.

Additionally, there is the silent-flush, which is expensive but a good choice for a location where you want to cut down on noise.

There is a big difference in the cost of toilets not only from one manufacturer to another but within each manufacturer's line as well. However,

it does not matter whether you get a mail-order one for twenty dollars or a showroom model for a hundred dollars, all are beset with the same troubles. The expensive one does not last any longer than the cheap one. None functions too well, and all have the same gurgles, gulps, and leaks because the basic engineering has not changed since the early 1900's. The chain does not dangle from the ceiling any more, but it is still the same old ball and plunger.

The fixture itself is best made of vitrified china, not enameled cast iron. Get an insulated tank, or have insulation added so that it does not drip moisture as the cold water fills it and condenses the warm humid air of the bathroom. Another way of preventing condensation is a hot-water mixing valve; just enough warm water is added to the tank to avoid the problem. Insulated and oversize drainage lines for an upstairs toilet minimize the sound of rushing water in rooms below.

Bathroom fittings, principally faucets, spigots, and shower heads, are at their lowest design ebb in two thousand years. The Romans had much better (and certainly more handsome) fittings than are available in most places today. The fittings we have are poorly designed and ugly. They are not made for wet, soapy fingers; many have rough sharp edges, offer poor control, and are either too large or too small. If you wash your hands under a standard fitting recommended for a standard wash basin, you must bump your knuckles on the back of the basin just trying to get them wet. The cheapest are usually the worst. Some hardware manufacturers supply fittings in the shape of pineapples, swans, and other devices that vary from the "cute" to the grotesque. Few come up to what bathroom fittings should be; handsome, plain, smoothly fit to the hand, good to the touch. Some of the old-fashioned fittings are much better. Get the most functional and best-looking ones you can.

Bathroom doors should be able to be snap-locked from the inside, but there should be a lock release or a key on the doorframe outside. A narrow door is bad. Try to have it at least 2′ 6″ wide. This is the minimum width through which a wheelchair can pass; it may not be an important consideration now, or even enter your head, but the possibility may arise later on.

Natural light and ventilation in the bathroom are preferable, but not absolutely essential. If the only place for a window is over the tub, make it a high horizontal window. Ventilation by means of fans and vents can be arranged and are entirely satisfactory. A skylight is an excellent means of providing light, ventilation, and privacy for your remodeled bathroom.

Finishing materials in the bathroom can be tile, painted plaster, wallpaper of coated plastic, or coated wallboard. If you use tile on the walls, cover the entire wall from floor to ceiling. Do not stop the tile part way up. Stopping the tile three or four feet over the tub and some distance back of the wash basin makes the room look smaller. If you cannot afford tile over the whole wall, do not start with it. There are other suitable materials.

I am a firm believer in wall-to-wall carpet with underpadding for the bathroom floor, even if the household includes little children. Good carpet costs less than tile, is easier to maintain, quieter, warmer, much safer, and infinitely more comfortable. If you drop your glasses, they do not break, and your chances of slipping and falling are 75 per cent less.

Do not be afraid of color in the bathroom. The area is comparatively small, and with paint or paper you can redo it in a day. Doors and trim painted the same color as the walls with flat paint, make the room seem larger.

Fixture colors are a matter of taste. The darker the fixtures are, however, the more they show the dust, powder, and dirt.

General lighting should include several ceiling lights. A small bathroom seems larger if there are pin spots lighting only the floor. In lighting the wash basin area, remember that you must light the person looking into the mirror; lights directed at the mirror do no good at all. A small light above the mirror, probably the most common situation, is the least effective. The best lighting is patterned after the theatrical makeup mirror. Circle the mirror with bare, low-wattage incandescent bulbs. Another inexpensive way of lighting this area is a dropped ceiling with warm-toned and covered fluorescent lights reflecting light back up from a white countertop. The usual fluorescent lighting is harsh in the bathroom.

Heating in the bathroom is usually easy because of the small area, but placement of the heat source must be carefully studied. One register or radiator is usually enough. It should not be beside or in front of the toilet and radiators and hot pipes should be covered to prevent burns. If you have warm-air heating, a duct into the area below the bath tub and a register in the wall seven feet over the tub circulate heat throughout the room and pleasantly warm the surface of the tub. A combination heater-fan-vent in the ceiling is helpful and warms the room quickly. There should be a red warning light on the switch to indicate when the heater is on.

A bathroom can be soundproofed to some extent by using certain construction methods. The door can be made less of a sound conductor by installation of standard weather-stripping. Soundproofing dictates that you place a buzzer low enough on the bathroom wall for a child or anyone else to reach in case of emergency.

House #38

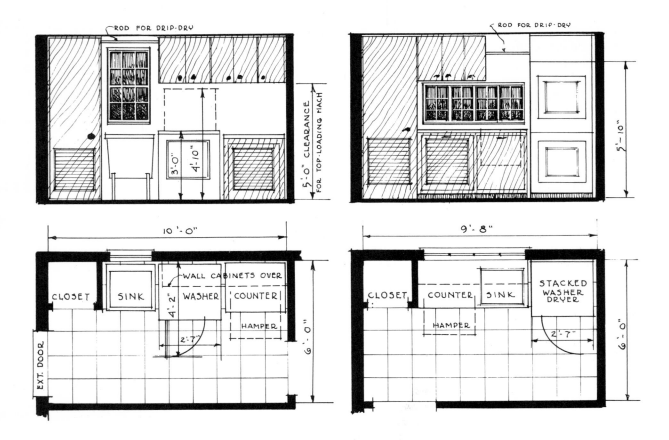

THE LAUNDRY

Several hundred, perhaps a thousand years ago, the great houses and estates of Europe set aside a week or two each springtime to do the laundry. Lines would be strung across the lawns and parks to dry the sheets, pillow cases, blankets, linens, and the rest of the year's wash. There would be a flurry of sewing, mending, folding, and then everything would be returned to the linen rooms, to be used up and washed again the next year.

Washdays are still with us, but they have lost some of their ritual and most of their drudgery. With today's automatic washers and dryers, washday can be any day, and in a big family it is just about every day.

If you are adding a laundry room, size need not be much of a consideration. The laundry can be quite small; its actual convenience depends on its location. Laundries used to be in the basement. Then they moved up to the kitchen. Neither location was or is really suitable. Basements are not generally pleasant places to work in. They tend to

be damp normally, and a laundry there adds to the moisture. Unless you have a laundry chute, everything has to be trundled down, and there is only one way to get it back up.

Although the housewife spends a lot of time in the kitchen, it is not a good location for the laundry. Installing a washer and dryer does not automatically create a laundry because you also need room to sort, soak, fold, and store. You may not be cooking when you are doing the wash, but who wants socks and sheets piled up in the kitchen? Just the lint and dust are reason enough to keep laundry away from food, and you still have to tote the hamper back and forth.

Put the laundry near the point where most of it originates, the bedrooms. This is where soiled clothing piles up, where sheets, blankets, clothing, towels, and other items are used and stored. If you have a two-story house, put the laundry on the second floor near the bedrooms. With a one-story house, try to place it off the bedroom hall.

If you have to have the laundry in the base-

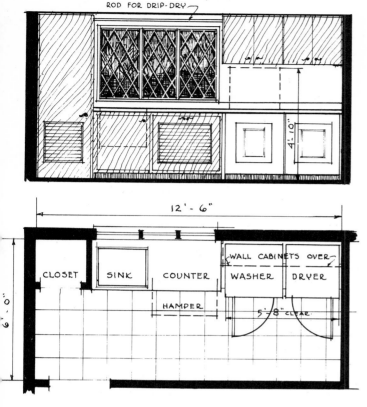

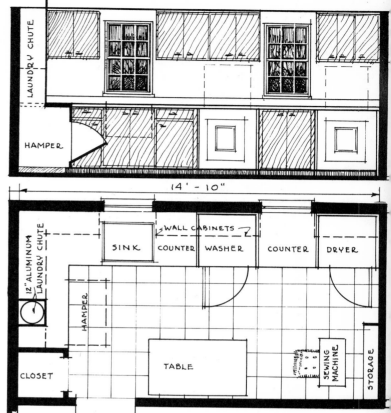

ment, open it up to the sky and sunlight so that it is an agreeable place to iron and mend.

When you are remodeling your kitchen and want to include a laundry because there simply is no other space for it, place it in the rear entrance to the kitchen. Create a separate room for the back entry and the laundry. If your house has a back stair, it should exit in this general area. The room can be small but pleasant, with a small sink and closet adjacent to the back door. This sort of laundry is particularly good if you have someone come in once a week to help with the washing and cleaning; this keeps the service area in one place.

A separate washer and dryer are generally preferable to a single washer-dryer combination. They are faster, and only half the things can go wrong at one time. Place the dryer on an exterior wall if it has an outside vent. You need a hamper with three divisions (white things, colored fabrics, and delicate articles); a sink for soaking things and for doing hand wash; a place to hang drip-dry clothing where the water drains into the sink; a closet;

and a table for smoothing and folding items that need no ironing. The ironing board and iron can be stored in the closet along with soap powders, bleaches, and starch. If young children are around, this cabinet should be kept locked. The hamper should be ventilated, either to the exterior or to the room with a louvered door. Some people like a built-in ironing board; others find that they block traffic and are harder to get around as you iron.

Lighting, heating, and wiring are much the same as for the kitchen, although the heating requirement is less because of the warm, moist air from the washer and the heat from the dryer. Have a light over the sink or laundry tub, and counter lights under the wall cabinets.

Floors should be vinyl sheet, vinyl tile, vinyl asbestos tile, or asphalt tile. These flooring materials can be used directly on concrete floors and in the basement. Masonry floors are fine for the laundry, but tiring to work on for any length of time. Wood is very poor for the laundry floor since water is hard on it.

INSULATION

No matter what part of the country you live in, a house is more comfortable and easier to heat and cool at lower cost if it is well insulated, which will pay for itself in a short time by the amount you save on fuel consumption. Insulation is the least expensive material used in any construction work and is no place to try to save money.

It is difficult to overinsulate a house, but minimum values are recommended for floors, walls, and ceilings. You cannot judge the effectiveness of insulation from the thickness of the material.

Insulation is rated with an R value, based on its resistance to heat flow. The higher the R value, the more effective it is. This R value should be stamped on every package of insulation you buy. The minimum value for ceiling insulation is 19; walls, 11; floors over crawl-spaces, 13. Basement and concrete slab floors should have rigid-edge insulation between the foundation wall and the slab. The edge insulation should be at least one inch thick if it is foamed glass or plastic, and two inches thick if it is mineral wool. All insulation should be fireproof (not fire-resistant alone), waterproof, rotproof, and verminproof.

Rigid insulation is a form of board or self-supporting sheet; nonrigid insulation is in the form of a thick blanket; loose insulation is in pellets; and reflective insulation is of bright metal.

The blankets, or batts, come in long rolls from twelve to twenty-four inches wide and one to six inches thick. The batts are tacked or stapled between studs or joists. This insulation is made of mineral fibers, wood fibers, perlite, vermiculite, glass, or aluminum. A vapor barrier of metal, glass, or plastic may constitute one side. The vapor barrier should always face the warm side of the construction. It keeps moisture from condensing in the interior of the structure.

Rigid insulation is made of the same materials with various binders; it is also available with a vapor barrier. It is lightweight, and can be sawed and nailed or glued easily. The vapor barrier must form a complete seal between the inside and outside wall to be effective.

Loose insulation made of any of the same materials comes in a bag that can be dumped where you want it or blown through a machine into hard-to-reach corners of the interior structure. Perlite or vermiculite is recommended for this. You can insulate an old house in this way, but the insulation will be only as good as the contractor who does the job, because neither he, nor you, can see into the wall to be sure there is complete coverage. Cheap materials and poor installations are worse than none at all. They can be a fire hazard, support various forms of vermin, settle to the bottom and not even insulate, or become saturated with moisture and cause decay in your walls.

Reflective insulation is usually aluminum in some form of foil that is unfolded between the studs and joists. Many sealed air cells within several layers of foil act to keep exterior heat out and to reflect and contain interior heat. It is more effective in keeping out the hot rays of the sun than in keeping heat in.

An air space itself is insulation, but because of convection, the effectiveness of the air space within walls rapidly decreases if the space is less than three-fourths of an inch, and does not gain proportionately if the space is increased to six or eight inches; in fact, it hardly changes.

Older houses can be insulated from the inside or the outside. If the exterior structural walls are in sound shape but shingles or siding need to be replaced, you can apply a rigid insulation and then new exterior siding. This saves interior space and does away with a lot of patching and repairing, if windows, doors, porches, and other elements of the design are changed.

If you can afford to lose the space on the interior, you can insulate an existing house from the inside by applying furring strips, nailing insulation batts to them, and applying a new wall on top. You lose less space if you glue foamed glass to the walls and put the new wall over that.

When the existing interior wall is in poor condition or you want to save the several inches of space, remove the wall finish, insulate with batts, and either set up a new wall or put back the old one. When the existing wall is plaster, you have a mess; but if the plaster is in bad condition, it is worth the mess to be rid of the old cracked wall. Use sheet rock; it is inexpensive and goes on quickly, and there is no waiting for plaster to dry.

A new room addition should be enclosed and made weathertight, and all piping, duct work, electrical work, and carpentry should be installed and inspected before the insulation is applied.

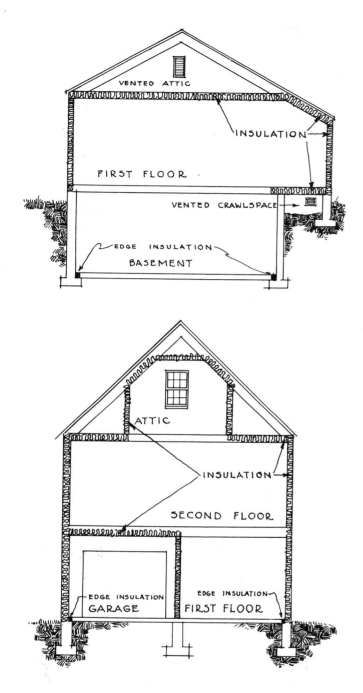

Unfinished attics are the easiest areas to insulate. Doing so can save you 25 per cent of the heat in winter and make your house more comfortable in summer. Loose insulation can be used and poured between the joists. Batts with a vapor barrier are better, however; nail them between the joists if you are not going to use the attic for storage or living space. If the attic floor is already in place, or if you plan to develop the attic some day, apply the batt insulation with vapor barrier between the rafters.

Insulation should be applied to any wall, floor, or ceiling between a heated and an unheated space. Rooms built over porches or garages should have insulation on floors, walls, and ceiling.

Air leakage occurs mostly around windows, not through them. An average-sized window leaks air around the edges, calling for weather-stripping, not clumsy and unattractive storm windows. Large areas of glass create down-drafts and draw off heat from your body to the cold surface. Often condensation forms on the glass and drips down to damage window sills. Much of this can be avoided by using an insulated lining on the draperies and drawing them after dark in the winter.

Insulating glass, which is several sheets with a sealed air space between, costs about a third or a half more than regular glass, but eliminates down-drafts, fogging, and chills. Storm windows raise your window cost as much as insulating glass and, if not carefully installed, fog up, get dirty, and drip condensation between the sash where you cannot get at it to mop up from time to time. If you weather-strip doors and windows and draw the draperies at night, the amount of heat you lose through the glass by radiation does not justify the cost of storm windows, taking them down and putting them up each season, and cleaning double sets of glass.

Houses that use a heating system fueled by electricity should be fully insulated because the cost of the heat is much more expensive, proportionately, than gas or oil in most areas.

HEATING

Central heating has been with us for a long, long time. The Romans used both convection and radiation systems before the birth of Christ. We in the United States have made central heating commonplace, inexpensive, and, too many times, uncomfortable and unhealthful. One of our biggest mistakes is in not taking advantage of the orientation of the house, its site, and such natural forces as the sun and prevailing winds for heating and cooling. Another error is in not making full use of advanced design and materials. We have added fans, motors, automatic controls, and electric devices, but our progress in creating a livable, healthy interior climate has been very slow. Our houses remain overheated, stuffy, dry, and drafty.

When we remodel, we should correct, as far as we can, the limitations placed on our physical comfort by inept heating, cooling, and design. The best interior climate is one that never enters our minds. We should never even be aware of it. The less noticeable the temperature, the more comfortable we are.

There are three methods of heating. Conduction is the principle that heats up a piece of metal which has one other end in the fire. Convection is similar to the heat that is carried on a warm breeze. Radiation is the heat that we feel from the sun radiating to us through millions of miles of space without warming the space or the layers of air that surround us. Heat is a positive factor; cold is negative. You cannot transfer cold or put cold into anything; you can only remove the heat.

Conduction in itself is not used to heat homes but is an element of heating systems that use convection and radiation. Our earliest heating system, if you want to call it that, was the fireplace, and few homes, Colonial or not, should be without one, even though we no longer need its heat source. After a while, our first space heaters, the pot-bellied stove and the Franklin stove, came along. Both are still produced. They function on the radiation principle and can be the perfect heat for a screen porch or sunroom addition in which you want to extend the usable season a couple of months. You can also use them in a sitting room, family room, or kitchen. They work very well on little fuel, which is either coal or wood.

Space heaters operate along the lines of the old stove, with some convection ideas sprinkled in. The electric ones can be quiet, efficient, and handsome enough in appearance. Others, however, manufactured to burn almost anything from kerosene to chicken fat, have been gussied up to resemble jukeboxes. At best they are offensive and ugly, and can produce noxious, deadly fumes. If your house is heated with one of these contraptions, you need a new heating system.

Probably all of us who remember the 1930's recall the pipeless furnace with the big square grille in the floor into which everything disappeared that could roll. The pipeless furnace was, and is, a combination space heater and warm-air furnace. The furnace is in the basement, the grille directly above; if there is a second floor, another grille there is supposed to lead heat to the bedrooms. This never did work well; it produced stupefying, dry, hot air in one room and left the others freezing cold.

This rudimentary convection method of forced warm-air heat was refined into a system of ducts and returns, with a fan to push the air around. A good system today is either forced warm-air or radiation, the latter using hot water, steam, or a radiant panel with either hot water or warm air.

The gravity-feed system was a development halfway between the pipeless furnace and the forced warm-air system. It has large ducts that feed warm air to each room. Furnace and ducts take up a lot of space and headroom in the basement. These big old furnaces may be satisfactory for a lodge or camp where there is no electricity and you are more or less roughing it, but they are not comfortable to live with all winter.

The developed system of forced warm air is the most popular in the United States, and for some logical reasons. Furnaces and ducts are small. The furnaces can be placed anywhere in a vertical or horizontal position. Ducts are small enough to fit in standard 2″x4″ stud walls. They can be metal or plastic, and are easily installed in most existing structures. The heat is quick, controlled by a thermostat, and responds in several minutes to changes in weather or heating requirements. If you are away for a time or want to take a winter vacation, there is nothing to drain or bother you. You simply turn the heat back to fifty degrees to keep the pipes from freezing. When you come back, reheating is only a matter of setting the thermostat to the desired temperature.

The warm air can be humidified easily and inexpensively in winter, dehumidified in spring and summer. Regular filters remove dust and dirt from the air; electrostatic filters go a step further and remove smaller particles of dust and pollens. Return air ducts circulate stale air back to the furnace where dust, smoke, and odors are removed; fresh air is mixed in, humidified, and pumped back to the rooms. The best furnace and fans work on an almost continuous cycle; the temperature does not vary more than one or two degrees, less fuel is consumed, and the motor does not go through a wearing on-and-off cycle. The registers are easily regulated for more or less heat in individual rooms. It is pleasant heat that provides slowly moving air with no stale, dead areas. In summer, the fan operates to clean the air and to circulate fresh air throughout the house.

Placement of registers on exterior walls and under windows is preferred. This is called perimeter heating. Warm air surrounds cool outside walls and counteracts cold down-drafts from windows. Do not place registers behind furniture or under windows where they will be covered by draperies.

Central air conditioning, using the same heating ducts, can be added to the small furnaces economically even if they are placed in a crawl-space, attic, or closet. It is better to insulate ducts that pass through unheated spaces. For air conditioning, ducts should be insulated to prevent condensation on interior walls and in spaces where there is no access or air circulation. Flexible insulated and plastic ducts can be snaked through existing four-inch stud walls as easily as BX cable. Simple plastic ducts are easily cut, much quieter than metal, and offer some insulation in themselves.

Noise from the fan and furnace motor can be minimized by setting the furnace on a rubber, cork, or plastic base and by insulating the space in which the furnace is placed. In many rooms, the carpet and underpadding are enough to muffle the sound of the furnace, although the new high-speed systems using flexible ducts and aspirating registers can be distractingly noisy due to the rush of air through the small (3″) ducts.

The location of registers and the noise of the fan are the main problems with warm-air heating. But you should not design your remodeling around the heating. Windows, furniture, and heat are all important to your house, and each should be planned in advance. Design your windows and furniture placement first; then locate the heating outlets, regardless of the kind of heat you have.

Most forced warm-air heating systems can handle an additional room or two; you do not necessarily have to get a new and larger furnace for every new addition. Even if your furnace is exactly right for your present house, sufficient heat can be squeezed out for new rooms by putting heavy insulation on new and existing ducts and by proper placement and sizing of windows, weather-stripping of doors and windows, use of insulating glass, and rebalancing of the entire heating system.

If your present heating system is already working at full capacity, you might install a small separate system for the new area. The furnace fits anywhere and the ducts are short. Though your present furnace might handle the increased load, it may be less expensive to get the small new system rather than run long ducts and returns.

In winter, the mass of warm, dry air can easily make rooms too dry. Forced warm-air heating allows you to humidify the air automatically, so that your house, your furniture, and you do not shrivel up like a prune. With a humidifier you find that floor boards do not separate and creak, windows do not suddenly become loose and rattle, furniture does not crack and come apart, static sparks are less frequent, your skin does not become parched, your nose and throat do not dry out and feel scratchy, and you feel altogether more comfortable with less heat.

Not that a humidifier is needed in every home. Your location and the construction of your house may allow enough of the moisture created within to circulate from the laundry, kitchen, bathrooms, basement, or crawl-space. Returns take this moisture and distribute it throughout the house.

Many humidifiers that are attached to furnaces are too small and function only a short time because they become clogged with impurities from the water. There are several kinds, but the best type is the atomizing humidifier, which injects water into the air flow in a fine spray. The size depends on the house, but you can estimate a capacity of roughly a gallon a day per room. Any humidifier needs attention and servicing to keep it in good working order. A humidistat controls the amount of moisture in the air. Too much humidity is just as bad as too little.

Excessive moisture is usually a spring and summer problem. Good ventilation is the best deterrent in any season. Basements, attics, crawl-spaces, and soffits should be adequately vented. Vapor barriers should be installed with the insulation in the walls to prevent moisture from penetrating the construction, but this is difficult to do in an existing house. There are, however, some interior paints which act as a vapor barrier and prevent further damage.

Hot-water heating systems do not offer as many advantages as forced warm air, but if you already have a hot-water system, you would be wise to extend it. The smallness of the pipes makes hot-water heat very adaptable for older houses and additions; pipes can be installed or replaced in small areas, and they allow almost full headroom in the basement. Because of the nature of these systems and their radiators, bulk insulation is not of the prime importance that it is with warm air, but reflective insulation can boost efficiency. The radiators act somewhat as the sun does, to warm you from a distance without regard to the temperature of the air between. Through the principle of conduction they also warm the air that passes over the heated tubes and set up a current of air that helps to warm you through convection.

Hot-water heating may be one-pipe, two-pipe, gravity, or forced-circulation systems. The reaction is slower than that of a forced warm-air system, but the heat, unlike steam, can be controlled by using water of different temperatures.

The one-pipe system is the simplest and easiest to design and install. Hot water flows from the boiler to the first radiator and then to the next. The radiator closest to the boiler is the hottest, and the one farthest away, the coolest. To overcome this, the closest radiator is usually the smallest, and the far one the largest. Since the hot water in a gravity system forces its way through the pipes by itself, the pipes must be larger than those in a forced system. You can increase the

heating capacity and efficiency of the gravity feed by installing a pump to force water through the radiators.

A two-pipe system has a return from each radiator to a main-line pipe which runs back to the boiler. All the radiators receive water at approximately the same temperature. This two-pipe system can also be improved by installing a pump to force the water to circulate faster and more evenly.

With forced circulation no basement is required, and the pipes can be smaller than those of a gravity system.

There is a vast difference between the radiators produced today and the old stand-up models. In many cases you can remodel your hot-water heating system, make it more efficient and less obtrusive, by using new baseboard radiators and a circulating pump. Perimeter installation is also the best for radiators. They warm exterior walls and counterbalance cold down-drafts from windows. Cast-iron radiators are better than copper or aluminum because they retain heat longer and provide more uniform heating. Aluminum and copper radiators usually have metal fins and are often noisy because of their rapid rate of expansion and contraction. Baseboard installations allow you to place some furniture against the walls, and if painted the same color as the walls, the radiators can be nearly invisible.

The old stand-up radiators can be improved with a reflecting sheet of metal behind them. Boxing them in cuts down on their efficiency but at least disguises them. Radiator covers should have an open grille over them and a space at the bottom where cool air at the floor is drawn up and warmed. If you paint the radiator a dark color with the cover and grille lighter, the radiator disappears; the grille can be quite open with the efficiency reduced only slightly. Metallic paint decreases a radiator's effectiveness. If yours are already coated with aluminum or bronze, repaint them with an oil-base paint.

Household hot-water and snow-melting equipment can be incorporated with hot-water heat, but air conditioning requires a separate system.

The obvious limitations of hot-water heating are its slower response and the dead, dry air it inevitably produces in winter. There is no air change, no humidification, and no effective way to rid the house of smoke and odors. If you are away in the winter and the electricity goes off, your heating system freezes up along with the plumbing unless filled with antifreeze.

Steam heat uses either one- or two-pipe systems. They have all the disadvantages of hot-water heat and none of the advantages except that the size of the radiators can be smaller. A one-pipe steam system offers no control. It is either on or off, hot or cold; because the steam condenses and runs back down to the boiler in the same pipe as the rising steam, it is uncommonly noisy. The two-pipe system, with the condensed steam traveling back to the boiler in a separate pipe, can be controlled a little better. It can also be converted to a hot-water heating system, which is a wise thing to do.

Steam is seldom installed in homes today, but if you have this system and it is working well, there is no reason to discard it. Usually it can be extended to supply another room or two, but because steam is so little used, parts and service may be difficult to find. Pumps and accessories can be added to improve an existing steam system. The cost, however, may be more than that of converting to hot-water heat.

Radiant heating, with pipes imbedded in concrete, progressed rapidly after World War II. It is similar to hot-water heat only in that it uses a boiler and hot water. The water is run through pipes set in concrete or other material, but heating does not depend on convection currents between the heated surface and the air. Radiant heat relies solely on the heated mass of floor, wall, or ceiling. The temperature of the air in the room can be quite cool. The occupants are warmed by the radiation of heat in much the same manner as the sun warms us through thousands of miles of unheated space and cold atmosphere. Tile and carpet do not impede the heating to any appreciable extent when the heat source is in the floor. On the other hand, the floor can become uncomfortably warm. Large glass walls do not unbalance the system, nor will they chill people near them if the heating is properly designed. Most radiant systems using copper pipe imbedded in concrete are expensive to install, but they operate economically. New installations lend themselves to the addition of rooms, and furniture placement is uninhibited.

This form of radiant heat is difficult to remodel, although its efficiency can be increased a bit with reflective insulation. But it is slow heat, slow to warm the house and slow to cool, so that in a changing climate you may be too cold one day and too hot the next. It offers no air change, no humidification, filtering, cleaning, or removal of smoke and odors from the air. Air conditioning must be a separate system.

Radiant heating, however, is not confined to pipes imbedded in concrete. Any large surface with any kind of heating coils can produce the same result many times more quickly and more efficiently. Large electric panels that can be fitted into the ceiling or wall are available. The wires are set in glass, and the entire surface radiates heat. This type is better in the ceiling where it is less noticeable and heats more uniformly.

Wall units that provide a combination of radiant and warm-air heating set in motion by a fan are shallow and can be placed between partition studs. Electric lights that produce heat have been used commercially for some time under marquees, at bus stops, and on railway platforms. Eventually we will be able to heat our homes quickly and economically with the same unit and wattage that we use for illumination. In the meantime, the heating lights can be used on the exterior to light and heat porches, garages, and entrances.

Radiant heating that warms rooms with the flick of a switch is also combined with plaster or wallboard in ceilings. Electric-resistant "wall-paper" can be obtained in sheets and rolls which is simply glued to the wall or ceiling to radiate heat. In time this will be extended to paint so that heating can be sprayed or brushed on, and there will be no more problems of cold surfaces or unheated corners.

The fuels we have today to fire our heating systems are limited. We are still pedaling along with wood, coal, coke, oil, gas, and electricity. But more advanced fuels, by-products of research programs, will become available, for example, in a packet that will last for years but be no larger than a cigarette.

The three principal fuels today are oil, gas, and electricity. The one you use depends on the area in which you live. Any furnace and any heating system can be fired with any of the three.

Wood, coal, and coke are, in that order, wasteful of heat. They take a lot of storage room and should be used only for fireplaces and stoves. Nothing will ever replace logs for a beautiful fire on the hearth. Coal is also very satisfying especially if you can get big lumps of anthracite. But if you have to shovel coal into a furnace, it is a messy, dirty chore.

Fuel oil must be stored in a tank, which makes it the most expensive to install. The 275-gallon tanks that are placed in the basement or crawlspace near the furnace in cheap housing need to be filled every month in cold weather. If you are going to have oil heat, get a big tank with a minimum capacity of 550 gallons, and bury it in the ground near the street and driveway. You save money because you can have it filled in the summer when oil rates are lower and there is no problem with the truck's getting stuck in the snow and possibly leaving you without heat for a day or two.

Fuel oil is a #2 grade of oil, a clear, light oil that ignites only when atomized in the furnace. A forced-draft furnace has a much higher rate of efficiency and lower fuel consumption than the old burners and does not require a chimney. Filters should be changed or cleaned two or three times every winter, and the furnace and spray nozzle should be cleaned every year for proper functioning.

Natural gas, if available at the location, costs less to install than oil. If both fuels are available, gas is probably cheaper. It is metered into your house in much the same way as electricity.

Some coal furnaces can be converted to gas or oil, but it is usually not a very efficient arrangement. The large size of the old coal burners and the low cost of the new furnaces combine to make conversion uneconomical.

Central heating systems run on electricity are not usually installed in remodeling, even in areas where the fuel cost is comparable to oil or gas. The operating cost is economical only if the house is very well insulated, in which case the other fuels would enjoy the same advantage. Electricity does lend itself to remodeling if you use unit heaters in any of their various forms to supplement the existing heat or to heat and air condition new space that cannot be carried on the present system.

The only way to decide which will be the cheapest fuel for you, oil, gas, or electricity, is to compare them carefully. The standard measure of heat is the British thermal unit (BTU). This has been established as the amount of heat required to raise the temperature of a pound of water one degree Fahrenheit. Without going into decimals, you can use a cost conversion factor for each fuel to translate it into the cost of producing one hundred million BTU's, the amount of heat most people use in the Middle Atlantic states during an average winter.

To find the comparative price for oil, multiply the cost per gallon by 952; for natural gas, the cost per 100 cubic feet times 1,270; for bottled gas, or LP gas (which stands for liquid petroleum) the price per decitherm times 13,300; and for electricity, the cost per kilowatt by 30,900. Remember that you can cook, heat, and run your air conditioner with gas, and you can get it a little cheaper because the more you use, the less you are charged per unit.

Electric heating is the cheapest to install because basically all you have to do is plug it in. You need no tank, chimney, or vent, and many times duct work is eliminated. Most unit heaters, whether the electrical radiant panel, the baseboard radiator, or forced warm-air wall or ceiling units, are made to be used on an occasional basis.

The electric heat pump, however, can supply year-round air conditioning for a single room or an entire house (in theory). Actually, they do not work as well as they are supposed to. The principle behind the heat pump is that something called absolute zero cannot exist. There is some amount of heat in everything on this earth, even in the air on a bitter winter day. If the air temperature is ten degrees below zero and goes down to thirty below, the heat pump, theoretically, takes these twenty degrees and whatever more it can get out of the air and pumps them into your house, raising the temperature by twenty degrees or whatever you need to be warm. It just goes on pumping, pumping, pumping. In summer, the cycle is reversed, and the degrees of heat are pumped out of the house air. Assuming that mechanically we can never reach absolute zero (comparable to a perfect vacuum), the pump works on the same basis as a refrigerator, using an expanding or evaporating liquid to absorb heat, while a vapor compressed back to a liquid releases heat.

The heat pump is more effective in warm climates where the major part of its job is cooling. They are more expensive than regular air conditioners and by the time you figure the cost of getting them installed, it may be less expensive and more comfortable just to air condition and use a few electric heaters where you want them.

Any heating and air-conditioning system is going to work better and more effectively if the remodeling and installation work you have done on it is undertaken by an experienced contractor and heating engineer. He gets you the best heat and air conditioning, but you or your architect have to watch to see that he leaves room for furniture and draperies, and eliminates as much noise from motors, pipes, and ducts as possible.

Window placement, a big factor in the success of heating, depends on the climate. In cold climates, large windows should face south; windows on the north should be small. The thermostat should be carefully placed. Do not put it on an outside or cold wall, on a wall where air from an opened door hits it, behind a door, near the television or fireplace, in a closet, bathroom, or kitchen, or on a wall backed up with an oven, range, or any mechanical equipment that generates heat.

The furnace needs oxygen to burn fuel efficiently; so do not enclose it in a small space without a window or vent from which it can draw fresh air. The first floor of your house is warmer and more comfortable when the basement or crawl-space is heated; it does not take much, but a register or radiator there makes a big difference in the comfort of your home.

AIR CONDITIONING

In crowded suburbs on the outskirts of large cities, in row houses, and in homes on heavily traveled streets, air conditioning seems to be the only thing that gets people through the summer in one piece, especially if you work in an air-conditioned office, travel in an air-conditioned train, bus, or car, shop in air-conditioned stores, and are entertained in air-conditioned theaters and restaurants.

If your remodeling design includes heavy insulation, reflective insulation, high ceilings, cross ventilation, wide overhangs, vented attic, soffits, interior fans, hoods and vents to conduct house-generated heat outdoors; if you put heat-reflecting colors on the exterior and have deciduous trees to screen the house walls and roof, you may be able to get by without air conditioning. And with these structural and mechanical factors your house is much easier to air condition (as well as heat).

Cold is a greater shock to our bodies than heat. We leave heated houses in the winter and venture into the cold at temperatures fifty and more degrees below that of the house. But we are insulated by layers of clothing which carry heated air within and which cool off gradually. One of the biggest mistakes we make with heating and air conditioning is to keep the house at about eighty degrees in winter and sixty degrees in summer; it just is not good for us. In hot weather air conditioning should be set so that it is only twelve or fifteen degrees cooler than the outside temperature . . . unless you are going to hibernate in front of the television with the blinds drawn all summer.

Air conditioning, properly controlled, is healthful and can be especially beneficial for older people. With it you can relax and sleep better, and your house stays cleaner, fresher, and quieter. Pollen, dust, and other irritants are filtered out, relieving allergies. To cool us more comfortably with less cost, excess humidity can be eliminated, reducing mugginess and the cold, clammy chill of old-fashioned air conditioning.

There are three basic types of central air conditioning: single package, split-system, and combination heating and cooling.

Single-package air conditioning has all the components, evaporator, compressor, condenser, and fans, in a single cabinet inside the house and is therefore very noisy. Vibration from this type sets the windows to rattling unless carefully installed with insulation and vibration pads. A rough comparison of the size of your refrigerator and the sound it makes cooling those few cubic feet with the size of your house provides a general idea of the noise you could anticipate.

The split-system places the condensing unit, the noisiest part, outside the house on an isolated concrete pad, eliminating some of the sound and vibration inside. Exterior components should not be near your bedroom windows or your neighbor's. Fencing and screening can help a "good neighbor policy."

The heating and cooling combination is the best

answer if you are installing a new forced warm-air furnace and heating system. Even if you do not want air conditioning now, provide for it so that you can add it inexpensively later on. Air conditioning is installed as part of the furnace and is usually attached to it, using the same fan and ducts as the heating system.

Individual room air conditioners are fine where you want to cool a new room or an existing area. A slightly larger unit, placed between two rooms, can cool them both. You can use the space at the top or bottom of a closet to house the air-conditioning unit with almost no ducting. Individual units should be placed through the wall, not in the windows. They are quieter, airtight, and watertight, and you preserve the full use of the window.

Before   After

With several individual room units you can run the fan of a forced warm-air furnace to circulate cooled air to other rooms through the registers. If you have more than three or four, however, the cost to buy, install, and operate individual units may be more than that of a central system.

If you have a hot-water heating system, it is possible to cool air by circulating cold water and replacing the radiators with fan-coil units. But this is expensive, and the result is just cold air, not air conditioning. Furthermore, it requires insulated piping to keep condensation from dropping inside the walls and is hardly practicable for remodeling. You are usually better advised to install a central system or use room units.

Sizing your air-conditioning requirements is a job for an air-conditioning engineer. Each house, each location, is different. The old rule of thumb which said that you need a ton of refrigeration for each six hundred square feet of floor area was only a general guide. Tons, horsepower, and amperes are not accurate measurements of output capacity. Air-conditioning systems should be rated in British thermal units per hour (BTUH). A one-ton unit is rated now at twelve thousand BTUH for every six hundred square feet, but let the expert guide you.

An air-conditioning operation that does not quite do the job is maddening; you do not know whether to open the windows and let in some fresh air, or sit in front of the thing and try to stay cool while your blood pressure and body temperature rise as you think about the money you wasted. Too large a system is almost as bad and results in uncomfortable temperature fluctuations.

Every central system or unit should be certified by the Air Conditioning and Refrigeration Institute, and bear its seal and initials, ARI. If it does not, do not buy it. This is the only way you can be sure you are getting what you paid for.

Central air conditioners are now so small that they can be fitted into attics, crawl-spaces, closets, or on top of the furnace. The size is not the problem, but the noise can be because cooling requires larger ducts than heating.

Ducts should be carefully sized and insulated to prevent condensation, reduce noise, and deliver cool air at the correct temperature. Plastic ducts are quiet, easily cut and shaped, and have a little insulation value in themselves, although without additional insulation they may sweat and drip.

Ducts in a combination air-conditioning and heating system should have dampers on them so that more air can be directed to upper floors in summer and to lower floors in winter. Directional grilles should be installed in the registers, allowing you to direct the air up for cooling and down for heating, or to the left or right.

Some systems use small (three-inch), flexible, insulated ducts for heating and cooling with special registers. These operate with high-speed forced-draft units but are prone to a number of problems, noisy operation being the obvious.

Air conditioning requires additional electric power in most homes. A hundred-ampere electrical system may be able to handle the added load. Usually a two-hundred-ampere system is needed. Consult your local utility for actual service capacity. Even if the air conditioner is a gas unit, the controls and other devices are electric.

WATER SYSTEMS

Whether we have city water metered into our homes or depend on a private source, a good supply of fresh, pure water is essential to our very existence.

A municipal water supply is usually taken from a lake, river, or reservoir. Though filtered and purified, it can have an unpleasant odor and taste, which may be removed with a water conditioner. This form of water system is subject to a number of controls, and because of increasing shortages in many areas, you may be restricted in the amount you can use during the hot summer months when you need it most. Desalinization, which converts sea water into fresh water, and electronic purification, which permits the reuse of industrial water must eventually come to our rescue, but until cheap processes of reclamation are found, municipal water supplies will fall shorter and shorter while needs mount ever higher.

Connecting to a city main for fresh water is, in some cases, limited to three-quarter-inch connections. If you have a small house with only one bath, one connection may be enough. With a large house and two or more baths, a dishwasher, and other equipment, you need more than one, perhaps three or four taps, if they are limited to three-quarters of an inch each. If the water pressure in your main is over sixty pounds, install a reducing valve to prevent splashing and excessive wear on the plumbing fixtures.

A private water system can be drawn from several sources but it usually means that you have to dig a well. In the United States we are fortunate in having excellent groundwater. You can use surface water, from lakes or streams, but the filtering and purification cost is more than that of a good, deep well, and you must maintain a constant check to avoid contamination. The inlet should be at least three feet below the surface and three feet above the bed. Strict control of drainage into the source must be maintained even in isolated areas.

Springs are another possible source. They can be surface water or groundwater. It is not advisable to use surface water, which is easily contaminated and difficult to control. You can detect surface water if the quantity of water varies with the season and climate. If the water stream is constant in volume and temperature all year round,

you may be able to use it for domestic water; it is groundwater escaping from the earth through a crack or fault in the rock ledge or bedding planes or through porous beds of sand and gravel. Any spring water should be chemically analyzed. Pollution at a distant source can travel miles and miles to contaminate otherwise pure water.

Artesian wells may also be a source of water for your home. Once water is reached in boring an artesian well, the flow of water remains constant because of underground pressure. But these wells also are subject to pollution from a distant source or from collecting surface water on the way out of the ground.

Rain water can be used for your home, but the system must be carefully designed and engineered. Local government authorities can give you annual average rainfall information. The water is soft, in that it has not collected minerals from the soil, but the old phrase "as pure as rain water" is outdated. Rain water picks up many impurities on the way down, even nuclear, in this age. In storage it must be filtered of all organic and vegetable matter, which can produce corroding gas and unpleasant tastes and odors. Such a system needs constant care and supervision.

A good well is your best source of pure, clean drinking water. There are four types: dug, driven, bored, and drilled. Their names are quite descriptive.

The dug well is one shoveled out by hand. It is shallow, dangerous, and obsolete, except for irrigation purposes. Seldom more than twenty-five feet deep, it is easily contaminated.

The driven well is hammered into the ground with a series of connected pipes. This is a quick way of obtaining water where the water table is close to the surface. But it is not a reliable source of good water, and the well cannot be driven through rock.

A bored well usually does not go deeper than fifty feet, although four-hundred-foot depths have been reached. A powered auger is used to bore through sand, silt, and clay. Bored wells are not a safe source of water in populated areas or in areas where diligent supervision of sanitary conditions cannot be maintained.

The above three types are classed as shallow wells and are not recommended.

The only reliable and constant source for a private water system is the drilled well. Where do you drill for water? You can try water-witching and hire a dowser with a divining rod (a forked peach or willow branch) to stalk around until by divine sign, intuition, or fatigue, he decides the well should be "here." You could also consult the United States Geological Survey, which has branch offices all over the country. They may be able to tell you through knowledge of the rock formations and charted information how likely and at what depth you may be able to find water. A local well driller will also be able to help you.

Only the best professional well driller should be hired. You can recognize him by his reputation, modern equipment, contracts, and past performance. You probably have to secure a permit to drill from local authorities. The operator may have to drill test holes and have the water from each analyzed. You may be able to tell how deep you have to go from the depth of neighboring wells. You cannot tap and remove the source of your neighbor's water. (Obviously it is unwise to place a well close to, or on the downside of a cesspool or drainage field.)

The amount of water, in gallons per minute, cannot be determined before you drill, but an experienced well driller can approximate the yield and distance. A well costs so-much-per-foot in depth. You should have a written contract, unit prices, and a complete report on the depth drilled, thickness and types of layers drilled through, results of pumping tests, size of well casing, size of filter screen, and the yield per hour, which should be tested over a period of continuous pumping for at least twenty-four hours.

A flow of six to eight gallons per minute is required for a medium-sized home. You can estimate the amount of water you need by figuring fifty gallons per day per person in your family. If your storage tank is in the basement, insulate it to prevent formation of condensation on the surface. A small pump and tank have to operate more frequently and therefore wear out sooner than a large pump. The pump can be installed in the pit over the well outside, which is quieter than putting it in the basement beside the tank.

Because of the minerals in all groundwater it is considered "hard" and a water softener is usually needed. The minerals clog pipes, stain plumbing fixtures, leave soap scum, and so on. You can have your water tested at any county center or health department. You may need a filter or a softener, or both, and they are worth the expense. They are quickly and easily installed.

Whatever your water source, do not contribute to general pollution of domestic water by using high-sudsing detergents in your household. Many of these cannot be filtered out readily, and one day you may get your neighbor's soapsuds in your tea and vice versa. No one today should knowingly use any of the packaged high-sudsing detergents still so readily available on all the grocery shelves. They pollute streams, lakes, rivers, and the land itself. If you cannot get the suds down the drain, common salt dissolves them. Use it, and then get a better low-suds detergent.

The difference in cost between the cheapest and the best water heater (and between one that is too small and one that is more than adequate) is little. Get an oversized one, and always be assured of lots of hot water. The large heating unit holds up twice as long as a small one that is constantly operating. The minimum size for any house is a capacity of thirty gallons. A forty-gallon tank is better. Get a quick-recovery unit that heats fast to replace water that is drawn off.

You can use electricity, gas, or oil to heat the water. If you have a gas furnace, it costs less to use gas; with an oil-fired furnace, an oil-fired heater is the least expensive; electricity is the most expensive and the most common. Get a glass-lined hot-water tank with a ten- or fifteen-year guarantee that replaces the entire heater and not just selected parts.

The hot water rises to the top of the tank, where it is pumped to spigots. Cold water should enter the bottom of the tank where it cannot mix with the previously heated water. There should be a safety valve on top to allow steam created by overheating to escape. A short pipe and drain at the bottom siphon off sediment.

If yours is a large house with bathrooms widely separated, you can cut water-heating costs and save a tremendous amount of water by installing a circulating hot-water system. The hot water circulates constantly through the pipes to the taps. With this instant supply you do not have to let faucets run, wasting water until it gets warm and wasting various degrees of heated water until it gets hot.

SEWAGE

Sewage is no more pleasant to read about than to write about, but it is one of the necessities that homeowners should know something about. Sewage disposal is definitely not a do-it-yourself project. Neither private nor public disposal should make use of a natural body of water or a stream; this has been done extensively in the past, and will, or should, be outlawed in the near future.

If you have a public sewer in the street, all you need do is to assure yourself that the line from your house is large enough and open . . . then skip to the next chapter. However, if you have a private sewage-disposal system and plan to add more plumbing, or if your plumbing is old and needs to be rebuilt, you had better read through this chapter.

There are two stages in the sanitary disposal of sewage. The solids must be contained in a receptacle where they can decompose inoffensively; second, the liquids, by far the major portion of all sewage, must drain into the soil where they can oxidize without odor and without endangering health.

Private sewage disposal usually employs a watertight septic tank built of brick, stone, or concrete and a drainage field to dispose of liquids. The solid sewage has to be emptied from the septic tank every three or four years, depending on the capacity.

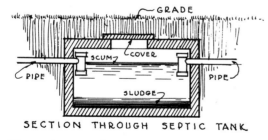

SECTION THROUGH SEPTIC TANK

If you have such a sewage system, you should understand something about septic tanks. In the watertight and largely airtight septic tank, there is an inlet pipe from the house sewer line below the water level in the tank. This disposes sewage in the tank, the solids settling to the bottom and the liquids being conducted to the drainage field.

Bacterial action takes place at the bottom of the tank, reducing the solids to liquids and heavier solids. Chemical agents that further induce this action can be flushed down the toilet several times a year. Detergents, cooking oils, and fat retard the bacterial action. High-sudsing detergents and cleaning agents can really gum up the works by killing the bacteria that work to decompose sewage solids into liquids which can be drained off. An automatic garbage disposer in your kitchen requires a separate septic tank.

When you add bathrooms and plumbing fixtures, you should construct a new septic tank, if the existing one is not large enough to handle the increased load. The minimum-sized tank is five hundred gallons, or sufficient to retain sewage for twenty-four hours at a rate of 125 gallons per person in the family.

Liquid sewage must be diverted from the septic tank to a drainage field or a cesspool.

The extent and size of the drainage field depend on the size of your family and the porosity of the soil. This is the job of a sanitation engineer, but you can make a quick check yourself by digging a hole one foot square and eighteen inches deep. Fill the hole with six inches of water. If the water level falls one inch in five minutes, you need twenty-five feet of drainage tile per person; if it takes ten minutes to fall an inch, you need fifty feet of drain tile per person.

Provided you have adequate space and porous soil, a drainage field made of open-joint four- or six-inch tile is laid in trenches eighteen inches deep with a slope of one inch in fifty. The tile is surrounded by gravel to allow the liquid to seep out slowly and disappear into the ground. A drainage field can get clogged with roots, or it can become inadequate if you add more plumbing fixtures and bathrooms.

If you do not have the required area, or your ground is not porous, you can use two leaching cesspools instead of a drainage field. Sometimes a charge of dynamite is set off in the cesspool excavation to loosen the earth and increase its absorption rate before the cesspool is placed. A cesspool is an underground chamber of stone or concrete with openings in the sides and an earth floor. The cover is removable and about six inches under the finished grade. The combined capacity of the cesspools should be about half that of the septic tank, or at least fifteen to twenty square feet per person. Usually they do not need to be cleaned out for years, unless they become root-filled.

PLUMBING

Plumbing generally refers to everything that has to do with pipes, because in remodeling you are concerned with both supply and drainage of water and waste.

In remodeling, enlarging, or adding a bath, laundry, or kitchen, you inevitably run into the subject of pipes. Is it cheaper and better to add a bathroom or more plumbing next to the existing plumbing, or is it best to place it where you want it, even though it may be a distance from an existing bathroom?

It is less expensive to add a bathroom backed up to another if you can connect to the existing vents and stack. These are the most expensive piping items. The pipes are large, and a new vent through the roof requires trimming and flashing. But if the new bathroom does not end up where you really want or need it, or if it is awkwardly arranged and inconvenient, what you saved on pipes, perhaps fifty dollars, certainly is not worth-while.

When you are remodeling the kitchen, replace the sink where the old one was if you can; this saves the cost of new pipes and the drain. But you should not inhibit the design of the kitchen (where you may spend several thousand dollars, not to mention some years of your life) merely to retain a length or two of old pipe. While the plumber is on the job connecting a new sink, the little extra it costs to have the sink where it is most convenient in relation to the rest of the kitchen is well spent. You are only going to do it once; so do it right.

In other words, if you can add the bathroom, kitchen sink, or new laundry next to, above, or below existing plumbing you may, but not always, save money. If you cannot, do not worry; it does not cost that much more.

Pipes for your water supply should be copper or brass. Copper is best, especially for the hot water, because when water is heated minerals tend to coat and clog other pipes faster. Copper bends, too, and so it is usually cheaper to use in remodeling; you avoid the many connections necessary with other pipe. Plastic pipe is still not really ready for commercial use in construction. Many codes do not permit it, and some plumbers refuse to work with it. However, because plastic pipe does not rust, rot, or burst from freezing, you can use it to excellent advantage for cold-water lines in the garden or garage . . . and you can, for the most part, work with it yourself.

Hot-water pipes should be insulated to deliver hotter water; cold lines should be insulated to prevent condensation from dripping into the structure. Consider circulating hot water for an instant supply from the faucet.

Each hot-water riser should have a vapor-relief valve to prevent steam from building up within the pipe. There should also be a valve at the water heater, allowing you to turn all the hot water off, and another valve at each fixture. Similarly, have a valve in the basement that controls the entire cold-water supply and another at each fixture so that individual fixtures can be turned off.

The size of the pipes to various fixtures is usually specified in the building code. As a general rule, the minimum for hot and cold pipes to the tub, shower, and kitchen sink is three-quarters of an inch (inside diameter); hot and cold pipes to the wash basin, one-half inch; piping to a toilet using a flush valve, one and a quarter inch; and with a flush tank, one-half inch inside diameter.

Getting the water into the house and to the fixtures is not half the problem of getting water and waste out again. It is all a matter of hydraulics and pneumatics. The best hygienic standards must be maintained, along with economical and efficient sewage removal, that does not permit waste and gas to back up into the house or fresh-water supply.

The house sewer extends from the public sewer, or septic tank, to the exterior edge of the house. It should be either glazed, vitrified clay six inches in diameter, sloped a quarter inch to the foot, or at least four inch cast iron. The vitrified clay pipe is a little cheaper, but the joints are not as tight, the pipe can crack if the drain settles, and tree roots can grow through the joints and clog the pipe. Cast-iron pipe lasts longer and has fewer and tighter joints, and you do not have to worry about its breaking.

Between the house sewer and the house drain you have the house trap, required by most codes, to prevent the sewage from backing up inside the house. This trap requires two clean-outs and also a fresh-air inlet on the house side of the trap.

A house drain runs horizontally, collecting sewage from the vertical soil and waste stacks. Never use clay pipe inside the house. The house drain should be of heavy-duty cast iron, with lead joints, sloped at least a quarter inch to the foot. If your remodeling or addition runs the drain below the house sewer, you need a sump pump to force the sewage out. Clean-outs should be placed at either end of the drain. You should also have a clean-out at the base of each soil and waste stack as it empties into the house drain.

Soil and waste stacks run vertically through the walls, rising as straight as possible through the roof; they are open at the top to allow balanced atmospheric pressure and air circulation. They should be of extra-heavy cast iron, brass, copper, or galvanized steel, if codes permit. The open extensions should rise a foot above the roof, and should be at least twelve feet away from windows or ventilators. The size of the waste stack depends on the number of fixtures it serves, but no stack connected to a toilet should be any less than three inches in diameter. Because of their size, the support required, the venting through the roof, and the flashing, stacks are relatively expensive. That is why designers and architects like to cluster plumbing fixtures around them. But this is often difficult to do in remodeling, and the finagling involved usually is not worth the cost of another stack.

Fixture branches are of the same material as the stacks, and are connected to the various fixtures through the traps. They go through the floor or wall with a slope of from one-eighth to one-half inch to the foot. Care needs to be taken in placing a fixture branch in an existing floor or ceiling to be sure you have enough slope to drain the pipes. Joists should never be cut away to run a branch to a waste stack. The plumbing and placement of the fixtures should be designed so that branches are parallel to the structural framing and not more than five feet in length. Vents should not be placed on the crowns of traps nor below the hydraulic grade, or they will become clogged and may allow gas to back up through the traps and fixtures.

Traps, those bent pieces of pipe you see below the sink and wash basin, are made out of the same materials as the piping, except in toilets, where they are cast integrally with the fixtures. Be sure you have them on all fixtures, even though you cannot see them as readily as the ones under old-fashioned sinks. They trap water in the lower part of the pipe and prevent bad odors from rising through the fixtures into the house. Of course they do not keep gas under pressure from coming through the pipes, and that is why vent stacks are necessary.

Vent stacks allow fresh air to circulate to each pipe, carry off gas and odors, and keep water from being siphoned out of fixture traps. Fresh-air inlets are also necessary to the proper functioning of the house trap. Local codes determine sizes and exact locations.

Venting the plumbing in an existing house can be a problem, but in connecting new fixtures to old plumbing lines you may be able to install a nonsiphoning trap approved by your local building code. These traps should not be used on new plumbing or in additions. They have to be cleaned and are at best only a half measure, but sometimes they can obviate the expensive venting when a wash basin or sink is being installed.

Floor drains in the basement, garage, or porch can discharge into a dry well, or, if you live in the city, into the sewer. If connected to the public sewer, they should have a full-size trap with a clean-out.

The most aggravating problem with plumbing is the noise it makes. This can be considerably alleviated. Bathrooms over or beside living rooms or dining rooms should have the floor or wall insulated. Soil and waste lines should not touch the construction. Bulk insulation, waterproof, fireproof, verminproof and rotproof, can be packed around the drainage lines. Wedge felt or rubber gaskets between the cast-iron soil pipes (or any other pipes) and the studs, joists, or other construction so that sound is not carried into other areas. Silent-flushing toilets also do away with some of the noise of rushing water.

When a faucet clatters and vibrates, the parts inside are loose and water pressure is knocking them around. Tightening the washer or replacing it stops this noise. A high-pitched whistle is due to a worn valve or one that does not close because of a worn washer.

Cold-water faucets turn clockwise to open, and hot-water faucets turn counterclockwise; the cold is on the right side, the hot on the left. Any fooling around with this arrangement, established through long custom, is bad business. Even the new faucets frequently drip. This does not make much noise, except in the middle of the night, and is usually due to a worn washer or faucet seat. A rag or washcloth connecting the drip to the bottom of the sink stops the noise, if not the leak, in such an emergency and gets you through the night. Frequent replacement of washers indicates need of a new faucet seat.

A great, crashing, slam-bang in the pipes when you turn the water off is called water hammer. When the flow is cut off, the water moves back and forth; the vibration set up can break pipe hangers, joints, seals, and the pipes themselves. This is usually a problem in large houses where the pipes carry water quite a distance. Bracing and supporting loose or sagging pipe can help. An incorrectly sized pipe may also be at fault, but a commercial shock absorber eliminates this noise.

Hot-water pipes pound and knock if the water temperature is so high that it makes steam in the pipes. Domestic hot water should never be hotter than 140 degrees.

Toilets are subject to the widest assortment of noises on the plumbing scale. While you may be able to fix this Rube Goldberg contraption yourself, chances are that you will finally need a plumber, perhaps several, and none of them will be able to fix it permanently. This does not mean that you should get a new fixture; all the works are just about the same.

The four-inch cast-iron soil-and-vent stack for the toilets requires a 2x6 stud wall to cover the hub of the pipe. When the stack is taken through the top plate of the wall to be vented to the exterior, the plate should be reinforced on each side of the hole with wood or angle irons. Wall-hung toilets need additional wall support.

Bath tubs need extra support in the form of double joists on the outer edges, and the joists in between must clear the drain. Blocks or metal hangers are used to support the inside rims.

Joists should be notched out for pipes only in the end third of the span. The notches should not be deeper than one-sixth of the depth of the joist, either on the top or bottom of the members. Do not allow the plumber to drill holes in the joists larger than two and a half inches in diameter, nor less than two inches from the top or bottom edge. Studs should not be notched to carry pipe; they should have holes bored in them instead.

WIRING AND LIGHTING

Electricity is a job for a qualified electrician, and we can promote safety and save lives by confining our involvement to designing our lighting, flipping the switch, and taking the cellophane off the lamp shades. Leave the wiring to the expert.

But we should know something about how electricity works if only to develop a healthy respect for those little wires. Without them our homes would come to a standstill.

Electricity runs through wires the way water runs through pipes. As homeowners we do not have to know what it is as long as we can measure it and know how it acts. The unit of measure used for the flow of water is the gallon; for the flow of electric current, it is the ampere. The pressure behind water is measured in gallons per minute; the pressure of electricity is voltage, and volts times amperes equal watts, the unit of electric power.

Electric service comes to us through wires on poles or cables underground. Originally it was carried on wires strung from wooden poles. But this method is wasteful of precious wood, unsightly, dangerous, and inconvenient in storms when wires go down under the weight of falling trees or ice. Today the more alert utility companies put wires underground where they belong.

If you have an old 30-ampere, 120-volt service in your home, you have a lighting capacity of only thirty-six 100-watt light bulbs, or 3,600 watts. That is hardly enough for anything these days, since even an electric toaster takes up to 1,150 watts. A 60-ampere, 240-volt service has a capacity of 14,400 watts, which is just enough to supply light, an electric stove, an electric water heater, and a few small appliances.

If you plan to do something to your wiring, have the entire service increased. The minimum that should be installed today is a 100-ampere, 240-volt system that gives a capacity of 24,000 watts. Should you plan on air conditioning or electric heat, or a number of added appliances, it costs only a bit more for a 150-ampere, 240-volt system that provides the 36,000 watts you need.

The 240-volt is called "three-wire service" because there are three wires; two carry 120 volts each to make up the 240-voltage capacity, and the third is a ground wire, which is a safety measure.

From the main electric board you should have a

branch distribution panel with fifteen to twenty available circuits. You may not use them all at present, but they will be there for future electric demands. These panels are known by an assortment of names; fuse box, electric panel, panel boards, distribution box, distribution center, control center, etc., but they all mean the same thing. All you need to know is where yours is and which circuit controls what. Each circuit should be identified on the panel as "stove," "water heater," "living room," or whatever it is, directly beside the fuse or circuit breaker. Never replace a fuse with one of a higher capacity than is specified; you could burn down the house. A circuit breaker is better than a fuse because it is safer and more accurate, and cannot get lost. When the wiring is overloaded, the circuit breaker simply pops out; then when the trouble is located, the load reduced, or the faulty appliance unplugged, you only need push the circuit breaker back in position to restore power.

You can estimate the number of circuits you need for general lighting; plan on a circuit for each five hundred square feet in your home. Use #12 wire for all general wiring, not the smaller size #14, which gets hot and wastes current. It is also easy to overload the #14 wire, blow fuses, or start a fire.

Each circuit should be limited to carrying one thousand watts, and not more than ten outlets for lighting fixtures. Incandescent light bulbs use from forty to three hundred watts each; fluorescent tubes from fifteen to forty. The wattage is stamped on each bulb; so it is easy to add them up and see if you are going to overload the circuit. Usually all the lights are not on at once. However, there is always the unusual time. You may be out one evening when something happens to frighten the baby sitter. She turns on everything all at once and blows a fuse to compound the situation. Plan ahead, and design your lighting to anticipate the unforeseen.

Small appliances and some large ones may be plugged into the general-purpose circuits. Each appliance has marked on it the number of watts it requires for operation. You should add these up, counting what you have now and what you plan to have later on. An electric clock uses only one watt, broiler 1,320 to 1,650, electric coffee maker 440 to 1,000, electric skillet 1,100, toaster up to

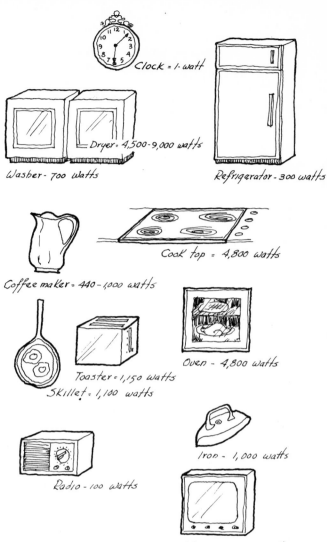

Clock = 1 watt

Washer - 700 watts

Dryer = 4,500-9,000 watts

Refrigerator - 300 watts

Coffee maker = 440-1,000 watts

Cook top = 4,800 watts

Skillet = 1,100 watts

Toaster = 1,150 watts

Oven - 4,800 watts

Radio - 100 watts

Iron - 1,000 watts

Television - 300 watts

1,150, mixer 100, waffle iron up to 1,100, blender 230 to 250, heated tray 500, electric fan 100, electric blanket 200, heating pad 60, iron 1,000, radio 100, record player 75, sewing machine 75, vacuum cleaner 125 to 700, television 300, waxer-polisher 350, shaver 12, toothbrush 2 watts.

Separate circuits of 240 volts should be provided for the electric stove, 8,000 to 16,000 watts; built-in cook-top, 4,800 watts; oven, 4,800; dryer, 4,500 to 9,000; electric water heater, 2,000 to 4,500; water pump, 700 to 1,500. Individual 120-volt circuits should be provided for the refrigerator (150 watts, but several times this on starting); the refrigerator-freezer, 300 watts; washing machine, 700; dishwasher-disposer, 1,500; freezer, 350; furnace control, 800; water pump, 700; sink-disposer, 500.

It is important, too, for each of the major appliances to be grounded. And all electrical work should conform to the local codes and the National Electric Code, as prepared by the National Board of Fire Underwriters. If it is not, you may not be able to get insurance or collect your insurance in case of fire.

BX cable is generally used to distribute current through floors and partitions to the rooms. This cable is insulated and incased in metal, but it is not waterproof and in masonry or concrete it should be laid in "raceways" or metal or plastic pipe.

Leave a circuit or two empty so that you can provide garden lighting in the future. It may not mean much to you now, but garden lighting will be more and more valued not only for security but for the appearance and enjoyment of your home.

At the door to every room there should be a switch controlling at least one light. For stairs or a room with two entrances, use three-way switches, which are controlled at two places. Use either silent switches or rheostat-controlled switches with no-shock grounds on them. The rheostat switches let you dim the lights for various effects in the room. There are also touch switches that go on and off with a touch of the elbow, knee, toe, or whatever. Switches are usually placed four feet from the floor, but this is a meaningless convention. You can have yours placed as high or low as you like. For special equipment, place the switches five or six feet high so that children cannot reach them. In children's rooms have the switches low enough to be within easy reach.

Silent switches, which you should insist upon, are now in general use. You can also have hidden switches and automatic ones. A switch under the threshold can turn on the lights when you step on it. Automatic switches in closets and behind doors give light as the door is opened.

Convenience outlets or plugs should be at least double. Continuous strips, with plugs every twelve or sixteen inches, are available for kitchens. There are floor plugs, waterproof plugs for the porch or outdoors, grounded plugs, and split plugs. The upper half of the split plug is connected to a switch by the door, and the lower half is live so that you can use it for a radio, blanket, or other device you want to control individually.

Convenience outlets are governed by most codes, which require you to have them every ten or twelve feet along a wall; sometimes the height is specified at sixteen or eighteen inches. If you do anything to your electric system anywhere in the house, the wiring must be reinspected and you may be required to install additional outlets, whether or not you either want or need them. You may be required to place convenience outlets under beds and behind bureaus and sofas. The twelve-foot distance was established because standard cord on lamps and some small appliances is six feet long. But there seems to be no logical reason for the height placement of outlets as required by codes. They should be high enough to avoid being hit with the vacuum cleaner or your foot, but this could be a few inches off the floor instead a height that necessitates running lamp wires down to the floor and back up the wall an arbitrary distance. You do not plug and unplug things often enough to make stooping a problem. Perhaps the higher placement was dictated by electricians who did not like to stoop over to install convenience outlets. Do not allow the outlets to be placed over the top of end tables or in cabinets or closets. You should have several extra ones in a room for the vacuum cleaner and other electrical devices. Design your furniture placement, and then arrange the convenience outlets. Switches should be on the open swing of the doors.

The plates on switches and outlets are metal or mirror, or they can be a fancy plastic or ornamental metal. The best are the least conspicuous. Outlets should be painted the same color as the wall. Any attempt to make switches or plugs more attractive only makes them more obvious.

The design of your lighting can establish the character of your rooms. Brightly lighted rooms make people talk more and create excitement, but they can also make people feel nervous. Low, dim lighting is relaxing and creates an intimate, friendly atmosphere. Warm lighting, yellows and pinks, is flattering to the face and figures, makes a cold room seem warmer, and mercifully overlooks smudgy walls, dust, and those so-called "architectural details." Cool blue or green lighting makes a room seem larger, but it also brings out any unfortunate details, separates everything into items, and can make people look ghastly.

Try not to light walls or ceilings in remodeling. Imperfections, patches, and lumps show up under concentrated light.

Valance Lighting

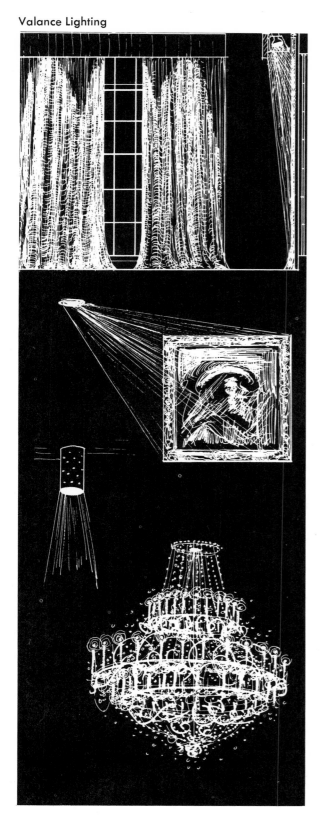

It is usually a mistake to have a lot of built-in lighting, except in the kitchen. Valance lighting over drapery or a spot to light a painting or favorite piece of furniture is enough for one room. Do not spotlight the fireplace. When the fire is going, it provides the best possible light, and when there is no fire, a light on the hearth only emphasizes the ashes and soot-blackened interior.

The selection of lighting fixtures and lamps themselves is not an easy proposition. There are .very few good-looking portable lamps. Out of the countless hundreds manufactured, you may see only two or three you would care to give house room to, which is unfortunate because lamps are among the most important furnishings in a room. A poorly designed lamp can give the best furniture a dime-store modern look. Most lamps are too low and squat. You should not be able to see the bulb from either a standing or sitting position; the shade should not dominate the base, and it should hover rather than squash. Though three-way sockets and bulbs let you control the amount of light, there is not much you can do about the design itself, except search for a good one.

The fixtures you buy for permanent installation are of two kinds, the ones you see and the ones you do not see, from a five-thousand-dollar crystal chandelier to a ten-dollar spotlight. However, do not overlook the pleasant atmosphere that can be created with candlelight.

Diffused lighting in the dining room makes it look too solemn and more like a boardroom. Small, bright pinpoints of light make glassware and crystal shine and sparkle; jewelry sparkles more, and so will your guests.

Do not get oversold on high-powered, high-wattage built-in lighting. You will not use it. The main thing to remember about built-in, or recessed lighting, is to replace the bulbs with the same wattage recommended by the manufacturer. Higher-wattage bulbs burn out faster and create heat problems that can start fires.

When buying a fixture, find out how the bulbs are changed. This is easy enough in the showroom, but when you have to change them at home you are on top of a ladder or chair, and it is much more difficult. Also see how the glass is cleaned on exterior and interior lamps. If the lamps are for the exterior, remember too that you will have to clean out the bugs, perhaps as often as once a week in summer.

THE PORCH

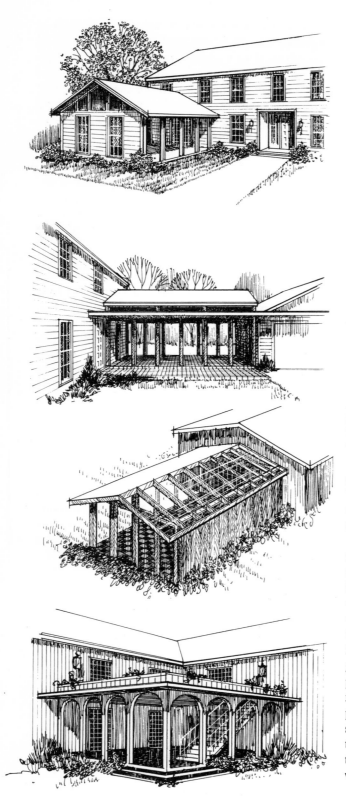

Any home can be made more attractive and enjoyable with a place outdoors where people can sit, lounge, and relax, sheltered and yet in the open air; that is to say, a porch. A porch is always roofed, with at least one wall of the house serving as backdrop. In North Temperate zones, it can be used as a second living room six months of the year, and its season of usefulness can be extended by heating. In the South, the porch can be enjoyed almost all year.

The usefulness of a porch depends on its location. I am not speaking about the "front" porch and the "back" porch, which are little more than covered platforms to get you into the house. Certainly you should be able to get to the garden from the porch, but it will be no place to relax if everybody and his dog charges through on the way to the bathroom or the refrigerator.

Design your porch as carefully as you plan your living room. It is actually a rather expensive room; so do not make the mistake of having it too small to be used by the whole family, unless you plan just a private porch off the master bedroom. Keep in mind that it is a genuine room, which should be designed, decorated, heated, and lighted to bring out its own special outdoor features.

The more walls of the house you can use to surround your porch, the less it is going to cost. You cut down on the breeze with each additional wall, but walls block off the wind in early spring and late fall.

A hot, sunny, public porch is worth almost nothing, but this does not mean that you should not put the porch on the front of the house, if that is where you want it. It may extend to the front with a blank wall on the street, opened perhaps with a tiny window or two. Elderly people sometimes feel shut off from the world and activity, but if they can be close to the street where things are going on, where they can watch cars and people passing and children playing, they feel better and not so alone. Placement of your porch should depend on your household, your house, and on the street in relation to the house. All three sides of the porch do not have to be open. Get the view, the breeze, the convenience, and the privacy you want by using full or three-quarter walls.

Make the overhangs extra wide so you do not have to worry about furniture or rugs getting drenched in a shower. A porch defeats its pleasant purpose if you have to run and take everything in when you see a cloud in the sky or cover things up when you go away for the day. Wide overhangs, four or more feet, keep out most of the rain and all of the hot midday sun.

Although screens keep out some of the breezes, they let you use your porch at night without being bothered by insects. Copper or fiber glass screening is the best. Steel screen rusts away in a year or so. Aluminum is beset with such problems as corrosion, sagging, ripping, and collecting dirt. Plastic gets burnt by cigarettes and builds up static.

Place the supports for screening at equidistances to avoid cutting of screen. Screen comes in standard widths, from twenty-four inches to six and eight feet. There may be a wait for some of the wider sizes; so check with your local lumberyard and hardware store to see what they have in stock or can readily get for you.

Do not put horizontal screen bracing, or a balustrade or railing, where it will be in direct line of vision when you are sitting down. Most screens need no horizontal piece at all. (*See p. 124 for screening sizes.*)

Copper screen can be electrified so that almost nothing gets through. See a demonstration of the screening in operation before you order this kind. Some installations make a distressing snap-crackle-pop every time an insect hits them.

There is also sun screening, like tiny Venetian blinds, which you can see through fairly well but which cuts off all but the early morning and evening sunset rays.

The roof of your porch can be flat or gabled, pitched or hipped to match the house. A flat roof is not necessarily the least expensive. In the North, it must be made stronger to hold snow loads. If you plan to walk on a flat roof from a second floor or use it as a deck, the finish material can be quite expensive. The pitched, gabled, and hipped roofs must be ventilated. It is wise to insulate the roof because insulation is cheap and you may want to enclose the porch into a room later on. A white roof reflects a lot of summer heat; an enclosed but ventilated air space keeps the porch cooler than an open-beam roof.

House #38

The construction of the porch should be as sturdy as that of the house because it has to hold up under all kinds of weather. The only difference between a porch and any other new room is that the porch does not have solid walls and usually has to have a better, more expensive floor than the enclosed room.

Concrete is about the least expensive masonry floor for your porch. It can look handsome when painted, but it sometimes gets slippery. Brick, slate, or stone give you a better floor. Wood floors are not recommended for the porch; they take a lot of care, need yearly painting, go right on splintering, and are slippery when wet. However, there is an exterior plywood with a roughed, slip-proof surface that holds up outdoors, and it might do nicely. You can also have wall-to-wall rubber or plastic carpet over a concrete slab; it is springy and soft, unaffected by weather, and neither reflects nor retains heat.

Heating can be installed in the porch floor in the form of radiant heat, using hot water, or in the ceiling, using electric panels or radiant heat. This form of heating is used primarily for northern or southwestern climates; in many homes in these areas a fireplace, prefabricated stove or Franklin stove on the porch is a welcome and charming accessory if correctly placed.

Lighting on the porch may include some ceiling lights and certainly must include several double, waterproof convenience outlets for lamps, coffee pot, toaster, and other cooking equipment, as well as for radio and/or television.

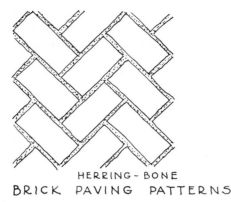
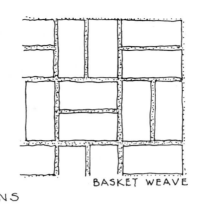

HERRING-BONE   BASKET WEAVE   RUNNING

BRICK PAVING PATTERNS

THE TERRACE

A terrace is a delightful addition to any home. Since it is not covered, it is not as useful as a porch, but basically it is easier and less expensive to build. On the other hand, since it is a room without walls and uses only the sky for a ceiling, it could cost you a great deal more than a porch, if you have to make it habitable with fences and hedges for privacy, tall trees for shade, and furniture that can live through any kind of weather.

The more natural shade and privacy an area of your property has, the better suited it is for a terrace. The more accessible a terrace is from the house, the more it is used and enjoyed. Terraces on the north side are cooler in the summer. A terrace on the east is a wonderful place for breakfast and is reasonably cool most of the day. A west terrace is pretty warm all summer, and you may get too much glare to be comfortable until after the sun goes down. A terrace facing south, unless heavily shaded by trees, may be hot all summer long, but it has the advantage of being usable in early spring, throughout the fall, and many times during the winter, if it is protected from the wind.

The floor is the largest structural element of the terrace. If you use a concrete slab, it should have footings and reinforcement, or else it will freeze out and crack in the winter. Brick, slate, or stone, if set on concrete, must have footings and reinforcement in the base slab. However, if laid without mortar you do not have to have anything under

brick, slate, or stone except a firm bed of sand. If the water drains straight through, there is no problem of freezing and thawing. To save yourself time and trouble in weeding, place strips of plastic in three- or four-foot widths to allow water drainage on the ground before you pour a two- or three-inch bed of sand. The plastic keeps weeds from growing up through the cracks, and any that do spring from seeds scattered by birds or the wind are easily removed from the sand. Slope terraces (even dry construction without concrete) away from house walls.

Gravel can be used as a terrace floor, an inch or two being laid directly on the plastic mat. But with gravel weeds are more difficult to keep down, high heels have trouble navigating, and small children tend to lob the tiny stones around. An edging of redwood, cedar, or creosoted telephone poles or railroad ties can hold the gravel and keep it from spreading onto your lawn or garden.

Although old railroad ties can make a good-looking terrace floor, they are not too compatible with children, because the ties splinter and the creosote can stain or make bare feet break out with a rash. Easy, quick terrace steps can be built with ties, held in place with spikes driven into the ground, and filled in with gravel or marble chips.

A plain concrete slab terrace should be painted to be attractive. Use shades of white and gray, or a light gray alternated with a slightly darker gray. Avoid dark, heat-absorbing colors, as well as stark, glaring white. A hosing down in the eve-

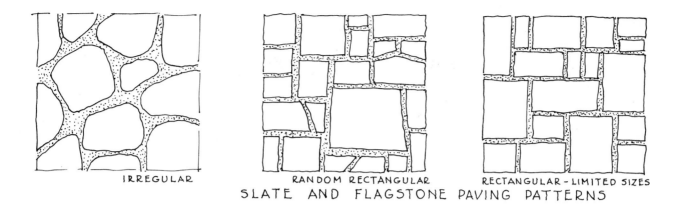

IRREGULAR   RANDOM RECTANGULAR   RECTANGULAR - LIMITED SIZES

SLATE AND FLAGSTONE PAVING PATTERNS

ning cools off your concrete terrace and cleans it in a jiffy.

A simple grass-surfaced terrace is the most difficult to build and maintain but it is one of the very nicest. It is cool, soft, and inviting but needs constant attention. Furniture should not be left in the same place for any time, or the grass bleaches and dies under it and little traffic paths get worn down in the grass.

If you live on the side of a hill, the only possible terrace may be a wooden one. Wood is comparatively light in weight and can be cantilevered on steel a great distance to compensate for sloping ground. Redwood splinters a lot, but it will not rot. If you can get an air space under part of the terrace, almost any wood can be used successfully, even though it must be surfaced and coated almost every year. Keep underbrush and anything else that can catch fire out from under the wood decking, and leave space between the boards for water to drip through.

Terraces around pools need special consideration. They should slope away from the pool and be able to withstand water and the chemicals used to keep the pool clean. Tile or painted concrete is indicated here. Wood presents no end of problems, slate is too hot, brick and stone are too rough, gravel is just too tempting for children to drop into the water, and grass attracts bugs.

Terraces can be heated to good advantage, especially around swimming pools. You can imbed radiant-heat pipes in a concrete floor and fill the pipes with antifreeze so that they do not freeze and break in the winter. Or you can use heating lamps suspended from trees, an arbor, or a tall fence. If the terrace is small, several lamps on a pole may be enough to heat it on cool nights.

Should you heat the terrace, you will, of course, need some wind protection. If you have a view you want to keep, build a wall with a low base and glass panels set in wood frames. Do not use glass windbreaks by the shore; the salt spray soon coats them and obstructs the view. Walls and fences should be eight feet or higher to break the wind. Some codes do not permit you to build a fence, wall, or screen more than four feet high on or near the property line. In this case you have to plant an evergreen hedge to block the wind.

Well-planned lighting can greatly increase your enjoyment of the terrace. Do not make the mistake so many people do in overlighting their terraces and grounds; that is, do not make it too bright or too obvious, giving the place a carnival atmosphere or the look of a drive-in restaurant.

Use lights that spread the illumination from a position lower than your eye when you are seated. On terrace steps use small lights at either side, lighting only the treads, not the entire night. If you have lanterns or carriage lamps on posts or hung from walls, keep the wattage low, barely brighter than a candle.

Lighting your terrace appropriately is just as pleasing in winter, when you may want to look at it, as it is in summer, when you want to be on it.

THE GARAGE

Today the automobile is a big part of our way of life. A great block of our economy is based on it, and the face (or defacing) of our nation and our homes has been transformed and often transfigured by our reliance on wheels.

Fifty years ago the automobile was kept in the barn. The barns went, and the auto moved closer to the house, first, into the shed out back, then into a more elaborate little house of its own, which got its name from the French word "garage," meaning a repair shop, and quite apt, since there was always something wrong with the machines. The garage came closer to the house until, finally, it wound up in it. Actually, as things now stand, that is where it belongs. Our cars have become extensions of our homes, heated, lighted, air conditioned, soundproofed, decorated, and color coordinated.

If you plan to remodel your garage or add a new one, do it so that you accomplish more than just a convenient storage place for the car. Never add one out front where the garage doors become the commanding element in the façade. It should be reasonably close to the street to shorten the driveway, particularly in the North to lessen the job of plowing out snow. But it should also be near the service entrance. Your back door should be handy to the garage, but you should not have to go through the garage to get to it.

You do not want to locate the garage where it interferes with a good view or a breeze, but you may be able to build it to cut off the sight of a neighbor's service yard or another dreary prospect. Try to use it to create a new view, perhaps to support a garden background or to enclose a garden. Design it to belong to the house and be equally attractive; do not let it look like an afterthought.

The roof line of your house and the new garage or addition must be considered together. With a structure as large as a garage, you can increase the apparent size of the house itself, make it more impressive, and even invest it with character that may have been lacking before.

Conversely, if not properly designed, a garage can do a lot to ruin the looks of a house. Remember that they did not have garages in the original Cape Cod houses, whose style we have inherited. Colonial houses often had many additions, but a garage was not one of them. Georgian and Federal houses, for all their dignity, look silly with a carelessly added garage. If your home is any one of the classic styles, extra skill must be exercised in the design of the garage and in its placement in relation to the house and garden.

While you are planning the project of remodeling your garage or building a new one, add some storage space, a workshop, a greenhouse, a porch, a loggia, or a room above the garage space itself. It costs very little more while you are building and increases the value of your home and the pleasure you get out of it.

The size of the garage proper is determined by the number of cars to be parked there, but do not necessarily plan it around the size of the car or cars you have now. Car sizes are like women's skirt lengths; you never know which way they are going to go. Design your garage so that you (or anyone else) can get the largest family sedan or station wagon into it comfortably. The average car is no more than eighteen feet long and about six feet, eight inches wide. This indicates a garage from twenty to twenty-four feet in length. When the car is inside you should have enough space to load or unload the trunk and close the garage doors without scraping your knees on the bumpers.

The inside width for a single-car garage should be eleven feet, six inches minimum. Even this does not allow much room to walk alongside without brushing against the car or the wall. An easier width is fourteen feet for one car. A double-car garage should be twenty-one feet, six inches wide, or else you will be chipping paint off one car with the door of the other. Opened doors project from three to three and one-half feet.

Some areas and codes require fireproof garages. This is more because of the junk people stack in the garage than because of the danger of cars' catching fire. Yet it is a good idea, especially if the garage is part of the house proper, since gasoline can ignite through a freak accident. When direct access from garage to house is through a connecting door, most codes also require that the door be fireproof and have a fire rating and that the floor be two steps below the level of the house floor. This floor specification is made so that if the gasoline does catch fire, water poured into the garage will not float the burning gas under the sill and ignite the house. It is a good requirement.

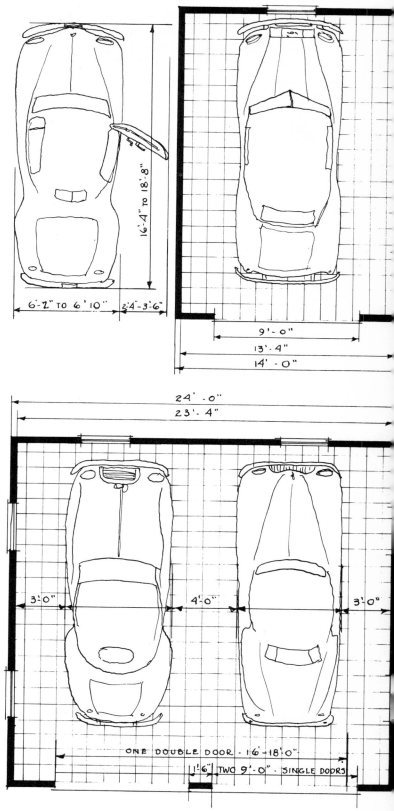

Garage construction is relatively simple. Footings must be carried below frost, just as in house construction. Walls can be of concrete block, finished on the outside to match the finish wall of the house, or regular 2x4 stud walls can be used for a frame garage. Usually code requirements can be satisfied by finishing the interior with a fire-resistant material such as wallboard, plaster, or transite.

Fully insulate the garage, by all means. The cost is small and the advantages many, not the least being the time and money saved if you ever want to convert the garage to an apartment or other livable room.

The garage floor is best made of concrete. You can paint concrete and clean it more easily than any other material. Provide a drain at one end and slope the floor to the garage doors so that water from washing floor or cars runs off quickly.

If you want to use the garage in summertime for a porch or play area for the children, you can put down various forms of tile or other floor coverings, but they should be able to withstand the drip of oil and occasional gasoline spills. Big screen doors could replace the regular door, making the garage convertible into a pleasant outdoor room.

Selection of a garage door raises a bit of a style problem, chiefly because so many of those available are distracting in design and poorly scaled. If your plan permits, place the door on the side where it is not seen from the front of the house or from the garden; even the best-designed garage structure has a blank, vacant look when the door stands open. A garage that, from necessity, is placed on the front of the house, should have individual doors for each car; one left open does not look as bad as a wide hollow space.

Today a mechanism can fold garage doors against the ceiling in one piece, or roll them up in sections. One-piece doors may be harder to operate, especially if snow piles against them, but you are freer to use a variety of materials and can get a better designed door. The door that rolls up in sections is counterbalanced, too, and works easily. Selection of design, however, is apt to be limited to those which are obviously planned around the usual four sections and are not suitably scaled for the detail of the house.

Automatic-action doors that operate from a switch in the car are disparaged by some but highly regarded by others who have them. They

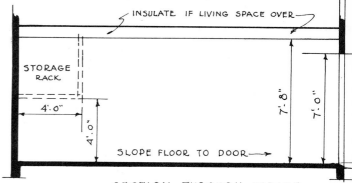

SECTION THROUGH GARAGE.

can often save you the cost of getting a suit or dress cleaned and pressed, and are considered indispensable by women who have to arrive home alone after dark.

Garage windows should be of the same design and type as those in the house, whether or not the garage is attached. There should be at least two windows for safety and ventilation. It is all too easy to be overcome accidentally by carbon monoxide; so have windows that open easily. Screen them for summer, and also provide one vent for each car. If the garage is on the front of the house, avoid large windows that have to be curtained to match the living-room or dining-room windows.

Wiring in the garage should include a ceiling light over the hood of each car and a light for the door. Place switches beside the garage door and at the exit door. A remote control operated from your car can also control these lights. Place convenience outlets on each side of the garage for a vacuum cleaner, polisher, and other equipment that facilitate keeping the cars and the garage clean.

A hose bib in the garage lets you wash the cars inside in the winter and is a great convenience in hosing down the floor. The latter may not be vital to the garage, but the cleaner the floor, the less you track indoors.

If your garage is in the basement, take special precautions to keep fumes from getting into bedrooms or other areas. Weather-stripping around interior doors and extra-tight construction are recommended. Fireproof or fire-resistant construction is usually mandatory here. Walls and ceiling should be fully insulated to prevent chilling the rooms when garage doors are open.

THE CARPORT

The carport is an adaptation of the old porte-cochere. A lot has been lost in translation, however, and today's carport usually has none of the advantages of the porte-cochere, which at least let you gain the house from your carriage without getting wet, plus the disadvantage of leaving your car in the open. In many cases, it really makes more sense to remodel your carport into a garage instead of developing it further as an exposed carport.

If you want to remodel your existing carport to improve its appearance, design storage space to get things out of sight. The storage can be self-supporting, and can also be built to provide additional protection for the car and to enhance the looks of the house. Exterior-grade plywood, board and batten, or second-hand shutters can be used, depending on the style of the house. The storage wall could also conceal a potting shed with its own sink. Since cold water is all you need in the shed, make the connection with plastic pipe, which will not freeze and break in the winter.

Exposed columns should be made two or three times bigger than they need be. A heavy-looking roof held up by toothpick columns gives an uncomfortable and insecure feeling.

If you wish to add a carport, by all means incorporate the good features of the porte-cochere. Place it where you can be protected getting from the car to the house in stormy weather. Build it over the drive, which not only saves you the cost of additional driveway paving, but can also give the façade of the house a new look.

At least two walls should be enclosed; the wall of the house is good protection, and you need only go to the expense of one new enclosing wall. Where space permits, plan to continue the drive through the carport to avoid having to back and turn.

Build the overhangs extra wide for shelter over the complete length of the car and room to load the trunk without getting wet. Where possible, low roof lines afford more protection; the roof can come down to within seven feet or so of the driveway level. Again, use columns of heavy wood, larger than the structural requirements, so that the port has a permanent and solid look. Low walls, planters, and trellises enclose and help hide the cars from the street and/or garden. Plants and vines soften and age the new structure.

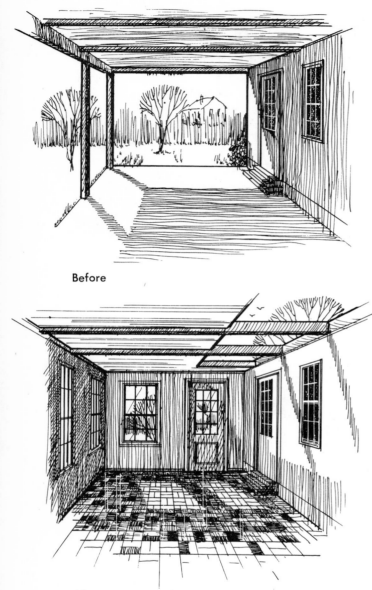

Before

After

It is wise to plan your carport large enough to accommodate two cars side by side, if it is in the form of a porte-cochere. One car may then remain parked without blocking the drive.

If you want to convert your existing carport into a garage, first consider whether the location is suitable. If it is not, plan to make a livable room of the carport and build your garage in a better place. Provided you have a good roof to work with—and that is about all a carport is, roof—making it into a garage is simple and inexpensive. All you need is a floor and walls. Since they need only be self-supporting, they go up quickly; in many instances, even a building permit is not required.

In remodeling the carport into a garage, the enclosed space should provide the same amount of automobile area as outlined in the preceding chapter. The roof structure should be studied to be sure that it can support the weight and movement of an overhead door. It may not, in which case you have to use swinging or folding doors. This is not as bad as it may sound because the old-fashioned swinging doors can be quite handsome.

The walls should be supported on footings built below the frost line. Sometimes the walls can be hung from the roof supports and columns, eliminating footings altogether. If a new garage wall blocks off an existing window in the house, the window should be replaced with fixed, obscure glass or closed up. You can get additional light into the room through a skylight in the garage or perhaps in the room itself.

An existing carport might supply a good beginning for another room of the house. Walls can be removed to open up rooms to the new space. Run sleepers over the carport paving to level it, if necessary, and apply new interior flooring on top. Insulation is not needed under the floor, but edge insulation should be used on the perimeter.

ATTICS AND ROOFS

The attic is the most desirable and usually the least expensive part of the house to remodel into living space. Developing it with a good design can mean much more to the value of your house than a finished basement.

First investigate the space to make sure you can get livable rooms out of it. Finished ceilings should not be less than seven feet, six inches high. Ceiling height is generally determined by the collar beams in the upper third of the roof. Knee walls lower than four feet restrict furniture placement; the measurements determine whether or not the attic is really usable.

Also have the structure checked to see that the floor is strong enough to take the additional load of furniture and people. If the floor joists are 2x4's or 2x6's, plan on reinforcing them with at least 2x8's every sixteen inches, or with larger joists, depending on their span. The existing collar beams should not be removed or tampered with since they brace the roof structure.

If the attic structure is made up of wood trusses, you have to be content with the existing free space they offer, because they cannot be moved or changed without adding enormously to the cost.

Check the roof and flashing carefully, too. A small leak that has gone almost unnoticed can be hard to find and correct after the attic is remodeled. If you plan to add a number of dormers and skylights, it may be better to reroof the entire house rather than try to patch and repair the present surface.

If your attic does not provide adequate headroom for more than a few feet down the center, a shed dormer can increase the usable floor space and allow you full headroom. Shed dormers are customarily placed across the back of the house because they are not thought to look well in the front, but correctly handled, they can be fine.

Little doghouse dormers are charming and rather romantic, both from the inside and outside. They are relatively expensive but give welcome light and air. Careful proportioning and detailing is required, or they may look too heavy and dominate the exterior. The wall should extend only a few inches on each side of the window before returning to the roof.

Flat-roofed dormers can be used on certain types of houses, and may provide a bit more interior space, but basically, these too are for light and air only.

Dormers can be taken to the knee wall or almost to the wall line of the floor below. Shed dormers may be taken to the wall below in order to furnish the maximum amount of floor space. Construction of shed dormers often utilizes the existing roof, which is cut away and raised into position; flashing is simplified, and the chances of leaks are less.

The usual design in a smaller home has the attic stairs in the center, with space for a bedroom at each side and a bath opposite the head of the steps. Enough light and air for the bedrooms can be brought in through the gables, and the bath can be placed in a shed dormer of its own for additional headroom and ventilation.

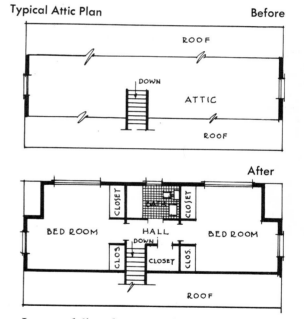

Typical Attic Plan — Before / After

In remodeling, however, the "usual" situations are apt to be exceptions. Stairs at one end may complicate things but not make them impossible. It may mean that the abandonment of separate bedrooms and substitution of a dormitory plan, with sleeping alcoves off a large central play or study room. It is only when we refuse to abandon preconceived ideas of what an attic should be that we get into trouble.

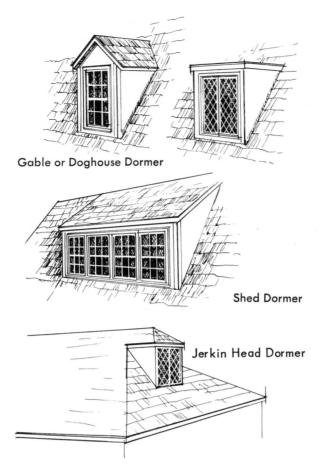

Gable or Doghouse Dormer

Shed Dormer

Jerkin Head Dormer

You need a bathroom on the same level if you are going to remodel the attic, even though the new space may only be used by occasional guests. In all probability you have a bath on the floor below. The least expensive location for a new one is directly above it or just to the right or left, just as long as the same plumbing stack can be used. If you cannot afford to install a bathroom now, at least provide the space and run the plumbing lines. Should there be enough headroom so that you do not have to build a dormer, you can get light and air by putting in skylights.

If the attic stairway is steep and narrow, you should build a new one. The same proportions and safety factors that apply to other stairs, as discussed in the chapter, "The Entrance Halls and Stairs," should govern your attic stairs. Rebuilding them is not too difficult or expensive. Each house is a separate problem, and the space is almost always limited, but wider, safer stairs can be designed.

If the attic is large, say fifty or sixty feet long, and the stairs are at one end, build a second stair either inside or on the exterior of the house as a convenience and as a safety measure. When the interior stairs are in the center of the attic but are steep and narrow, a new exterior stair should be built. This is a great convenience where the attic is on the second floor, and should be mandatory if it is on the third.

Light and air can be brought in by dormers, as mentioned before. Skylights are also good in attics, and new plastic domes are inexpensive and easy to install. End gables can be opened to more light. And you can also, cautiously, open the entire gable with glass. Even in a Cape-Cod-style house, this does not need to destroy the particular character of the house if properly designed.

When the house has a steep hipped roof and there are no gables, you can use dormers and put jerkin head dormers on the ends. However, because of the low pitch, a hip roof usually does not lend itself to an attic.

Consider raising your roof if it is too low for an attic now, and you would like to build additional bedroom space either by increasing the pitch of the roof or adding another story. This is more economical than you may think, because the foundations and floor are already there. Again, walls and floor should be checked for structural soundness, and walls must be strong enough down to the footings to support another story.

Heating, plumbing, and electricity are just a floor away from the attic, and only the heating may cause some difficulty, since forced warm-air ducts are comparatively large and sometimes awkward to extend to attic space. However, do not overlook the small furnaces that can fit into closets and provide completely separate and zoned heating for the attic floor. Electric heat in the form of small unit heaters may be sufficient.

Full insulation is absolutely necessary for comfort in both winter and summer. There is no such thing as too much insulation in the attic. For the ceiling, use at least six inches, or an R-value of 19. Use three or four inches or an R-value of 11 in the walls; the heavier, the better. Areas of the attic that are not open living space should be ventilated to the outside. This keeps moisture from condensing and increases the performance of the insulation.

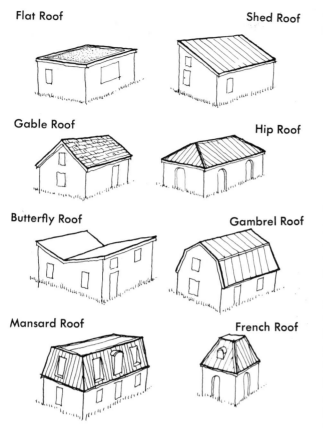

Flat Roof

Shed Roof

Gable Roof

Hip Roof

Butterfly Roof

Gambrel Roof

Mansard Roof

French Roof

Architecturally speaking, there are eight types of roofs: flat, shed, gable, hip, butterfly, gambrel, mansard, and French. Whatever your style or modification, the roofing material you use in remodeling depends on the slope or pitch of your roof and whether you intend to match an existing roof or add a new one.

The least expensive material is roll roofing. It is made of various mixtures of felt and tar, with a surface of granules, and is designed for roofs with a minimum pitch of three inches to the foot. This roofing has long been associated with farm outbuildings; it is not very durable and is quite inflammable. It can be made attractive in the hands of a competent designer, but the money you save on material is used up in the labor of nailing it down and sealing the joints. You still do not have a very good roof. The maximum guarantee a contractor gives on it is usually two years.

Asphalt shingles are ordinarily guaranteed for ten or fifteen years, and may be applied right over the existing roof finish if it is not waterlogged. The 235-pound shingle (the number of shingles required to cover 100 square feet, and weighing a total of 235 pounds) is the minimum weight accepted by the FHA. The roof pitch required for strip shingles is three inches to the foot minimum; four inches to the foot is better, and is required when the shingles are individual. On low-pitched roofs, a high wind may edge the shingles up, allowing rain to get into the roof, or the shingles can blow off altogether, unless special interlocking shingles or self-sealing tabs are used. Heavier three-hundred-pound shingles weather better. Asphalt shingles are not fireproof, but if the surface is in good condition, the mineral or mica granules can briefly retard a blaze that might be started by embers blown from a nearby fire.

Built-up asphalt roof finish is placed on surfaces of very low or flat pitch. A layer of hot liquid asphalt is alternated with a layer of felt or building paper. The surface is then topped with gravel, slag, or marble chips; but do not think it is meant to be walked on. On slopes running more than two inches in twelve, there is a danger of the asphalt melting in summer and running down the fascia. The topping also tends to wash off in heavy rains, clogging drains and leaving the roof surface further exposed to sun and wear. Guarantees are ordinarily given for ten to twenty years.

Built-up roofs are used in remodeling for either existing or new flat roofs. Small additions with flat roofs do not attract the professional roofers and are consequently hard to schedule unless you happen to catch the pros between larger jobs. However, remodeling with a flat roof has definite advantages in the ease and economy of construction, flashing, and insulation.

Wood shingles have been used in the United States for hundreds of years. They make as handsome a roof today as ever before. They cost more than asphalt, weigh less (about two hundred pounds per hundred square feet), and the minimum slope to which they can be applied is three inches in twelve. They last twenty years or more; durability is increased by dipping them in a preservative stain. Many codes prohibit wood shingles because they burn so readily. If you live way out in the country and some distance from a firehouse, it is better to settle for something fireproof for your own safety and for lower insurance rates.

Wood shakes have the same limitations, although being considerably thicker they do not catch fire quite as quickly as shingles. They are more expensive but give the house a sturdy, rustic appearance that can be attractive.

Asbestos shingles are fireproof and can be made to look very much like wood shingles or shakes, such as in the reconstruction of Williamsburg, Virginia. Minimum slope is five inches to the foot, and weight is anywhere from two hundred fifty to six hundred pounds per hundred square feet. They are guaranteed for fifteen years. Asbestos stays secure even in high winds, but it is brittle and breaks if walked on.

Slate shingles are fireproof, very good-looking, and very expensive. They can be used on roof slopes of four inches to the foot, minimum, and they last just about forever. They weigh from seven hundred fifty to twenty-seven hundred pounds per square (one hundred square feet). The structure of any addition must be reinforced to hold the weight; color should be exactly specified to match an existing slate roof.

Clay tile is in about the same class as slate, but each style has a different minimum-slope requirement. The minimum is about four and a half inches to the foot; some are slightly higher. Hard-burned tile should be specified; the soft-burned quality does not hold up too well. Weight is a consideration here also, and additions should be reinforced. Clay tile weighs from nine hundred pounds per square and up.

Aluminum shingles with baked-on finishes are relatively new and untested. Their main drawback is the poor imitation of wood and other shingles. Corrugated aluminum, on the other hand, can be an excellent roofing material for remodeling. It is light in weight, does not rust or burn, and is available in colors, even in stripes. The corrugated sheets are used on a minimum slope of three inches to the foot. Weight varies from thirty to sixty pounds per square. Some are so light that they must be supported by solid sheathing; heavier sheeting can span several feet without supports.

Other corrugated metal roofs weigh more than aluminum but have their own advantages. Galvanized iron and steel cost less. They require painting, but using a cheaper material cuts your initial cost. Also, since aluminum is so bright, you may want to paint it anyhow. The minimum slope for iron and steel is three inches to the foot. Weight is from seventy-five to two hundred pounds per square.

Corrugated copper is a fine roof, weathering to a soft green that is quite lush in character. Expensive, it will last for generations. Use it on a minimum slope of four inches to the foot. It weighs from one hundred to two hundred eighty-five pounds per square.

Corrugated metal can be used with corrugated plastic and is similar to crimped metal. One of the objections to metal is that it makes for a noisy roof, especially in rainy weather, but some people find this to be one of its virtues rather than a drawback.

Corrugated asbestos cement, sometimes called transite, is relatively expensive, much quieter than metal, and although brittle, is very durable. The minimum slope required is three inches to the foot.

Flat metal roofs are often used for houses of classic design as well as for small flat areas, such as those over bays. These are also very durable and tend to be expensive. Applied flat to the roof surface, they have either standing, flat, or batten seams, which must be expertly designed for the best appearance. Metals commonly used are aluminum, copper, lead, nickel-copper alloy, stainless steel, and terne plate, which is 80 per cent lead and 20 per cent tin. Batten seams can be used on very low slopes of one and one-half inches to the foot for aluminum, one and one-half to three inches for copper, and two inches to the foot for terne. Standing seams require more slope. Flat seams often limit the maximum slope. Terne is the heaviest roofing in this category, weighing about three hundred pounds per square. Aluminum and copper, of course, are the lightest.

Plastic finish can be sprayed or painted on plywood roofs of any slope from flat to ninety degrees. Naturally this finish is very thin and lightweight, but contractors now guarantee these roof finishes for ten or fifteen years. With proper application there is no reason to believe that they will not last considerably longer.

Copper makes the best flashing, but all metal in contact with other metal on the roof must be the same, or else electrolytic action will damage the two surfaces. On most roofs there will be valley flashing, chimney flashing, and ridge flashing.

BASEMENTS

At one time or other almost everybody with a basement has discussed the possibility of making it into something useful: playroom, study, additional bedrooms, or combination of all three. Basement ideas frequently die a-borning, which may be just as well. Unless you need the basement for living space more than for rough storage, do not undertake an expensive project to remodel it.

Your basement may have unusual possibilities, but psychologically the average basement does not make good living space. Most people think it would make charming quarters . . . for someone else. So-called playrooms, once built, are seldom used as originally intended except for playing inside on an occasional rainy day. Many adults were herded into the basement to play when they were children and do not particularly relish the idea now. And, no matter how attractively you decorate the interior, guests may get the feeling that they are being entertained in a subterranean kindergarten so that they will not disturb the better furniture, carpet, and rooms upstairs.

A study or den in the basement can have privacy and quiet, but dampness may make it a poor place for books. Basement bedrooms may make the children who occupy them feel neglected unless all the children are there. Older people, whether it is true or not, think that the dampness gets to their joints, that it is too cold, that there is not enough air, or that the stairs are too hard to climb; they feel cooped up and generally slighted.

The basement is not even a good place for a workshop. Noise from power tools carries throughout the house. Supplies and materials are messy and awkward to haul down, and with all the wood, sawdust, paint, lacquer, varnish, and turpentine, the basement shop can become a fire hazard.

Now if you still need to add rooms and this is the only space available, you can make the basement livable and attractive; but it is not particularly easy or inexpensive to do so. Whatever rooms you want, the requirements for any living area are the same: dry, safe, clean, warm, ventilated, and, if possible, a little sunshine.

Is your basement dry? This is a primary requisite. Dampness is caused by moist air and leaks or by penetration of water from outside.

Dampness due to interior conditions is generally easy enough to correct. It is generally a matter of warm, moist air condensing against cold masonry walls. Plenty of ventilation in the summer, heat in the winter, and furred walls over the masonry can take care of this dampness. Cold-water pipes can be insulated to prevent drip. Clothes should be dried outside or in a dryer ventilated to the exterior.

Dampness caused by outside water seeping in is much more difficult and costly to eliminate. If it is coming from a hydrostatic head of water (water from high water tables, springs, lakes, or rivers), you have to build a new basement floor and walls, reinforced like the hull of a ship, so that the water cannot force its way through or crack the masonry. If the condition is seasonal, a sump pump may be able to handle the water and drain it off before it has a chance to rise into the basement.

Outside water that does not drain away from the house properly is a troublemaker also. If your house did not have a tile drain around it and a layer of bituminous waterproofing placed on all the walls when it was built, you may have to have this done. It is expensive. All the foundation planting must be temporarily removed so that a trench can be dug around the entire perimeter. You could have the waterproofing done from the inside and lose some interior space, but it is difficult to get a guaranteed job.

Coating the walls on the interior with waterproofing paints and plastics may be enough to prevent the penetration of outside moisture. The work should be done by a contractor, and you should get a guarantee.

Water draining off the roof should be carried away to a storm sewer or to dry wells. Cracks in basement walls and floor can be sealed shut, and with proper ventilation and heat, you may not be bothered with dampness again.

While you are checking for dampness, have a pest control company look for signs of termites. These tiny insects build mud tunnels up the side of basement walls or crawl-spaces from the soil to the wood framing and structural members. If you suspect you have them (you can see the wings they shed when they spawn), call the termite man. Do not confuse termites with flying ants, which are not as destructive though just as annoying.

Masonry walls can be furred out to be finished with drywall or paneling; furring out makes them warmer, easier to keep clean, and prevents condensation in summer. If the walls are smooth and clean, you can glue styrofoam on directly, and apply the finish wall to that. If your basement is good and dry and has been all its life, you can simply paint the masonry walls or finish them with cement or a cement paint.

The basement stairs are of prime importance. Their location in the basement and the access to them from the first floor determine not only how much the new space is used, but whether it should be developed at all, and if so, into what types of rooms.

If you have to get to the basement stairs through a small, dark hallway at the back of the house, a playroom or bedrooms in the basement will not be used very much. It is best if you can get to the basement through a center hall on the first floor without having to go through any other rooms. If you must rebuild the stairs, make them wide with easy treads, incorporating the safety factors detailed in the chapter, "The Entrance Hall and Stairs." Do not enclose the stairway completely; try to make it as inviting as the stairs to a second floor, even if it must open into the kitchen or living room. The stairs should be well-lighted, carpeted, and have plenty of headroom.

Every basement should have two exits, for safety as well as for ease of moving furniture in and out. A door to the outside is usually simple and always necessary.

Light and air in even the darkest basement are available in several ways. You can increase the size of the windows. If you have light wells, increase them at the same time, not only in depth, but also in diameter. A continuous strip of windows can be used instead of the standard basement peepholes.

If the house is near the street, and windows would make the basement too public, extend the foundation wall and cover with a translucent plastic skylight. Even if you live in a town house and have to burrow under the sidewalk, you can get permission from the municipality to imbed glass blocks in the pavement, or cover the light well with a steel grille. Depending on the space and exposure, you can even build a little greenhouse off the basement.

If you are on a hillside, you can remove the earth from the down side of the basement and get full-length sliding doors and windows. A concrete slab will provide a terrace and prevent frost damage to the footings.

On a flat site or on the uphill side of the basement, you can get additional light and air or full-length doors and windows by building a retaining wall at a distance from the foundation wall and making the area into a sunken garden. If it happens that the garden must be in front of an entrance to the house, build a bridge to the door on the upper level; it even makes the garden and house more interesting.

Regardless of light, low ceilings may make basement rooms seem gloomy and oppressive. If the problem is serious, you can lower the floor. This is a rather costly operation, and care must be taken not to undermine existing footings. Unless they are held in place with jacks while new concrete is poured, serious exterior wall failures can occur and damage the structural walls and roof of the house.

Basement floors may also be lowered by removing the earth within a forty-five degree angle of the walls. This can be done and the wall next to the foundation left in the form of steps, to be used as shelves, but remember that every foot downward is another foot inside the basement wall, reducing the floor area.

Somehow basement floors have a tendency to feel cold, even if they are tiled with asphalt or vinyl. Concrete can be painted and waxed, but it is not a satisfactory floor for a basement bedroom. Put down wall-to-wall carpet for bedrooms. It looks and feels warmer, and in the long run saves hours of cleaning, painting, waxing, and mopping up the floor.

Interior partition walls can be built and finished like any other walls in the house. A fireproof partition may be required around the furnace.

Finishing the ceiling is usually difficult because of the pipes and ducts. Uneven heights can be taken up with built-in recessed lights and simple differences in levels. Drywall or wood paneling make the best and easiest finished ceiling; there is no problem of moisture, and you do not go through the drying-out period you have with plaster.

If you do not want to go to the expense of a finished ceiling, paint or stain the structure a dark

color, and suspend panels of thin plywood, fiberboard, or plastic on wires with lights behind them. Direct all the lighting down to the floor and away from the ceiling.

Heating, either with forced warm air or hot water, seldom presents any problems. Extra pipes and ducts are easily run from a nearby furnace. The warm mass of heated air on upper floors helps keep the basement warm. Its protected position, masonry walls, insulation, and furring keep out all but the strongest winds.

You need a bathroom if you are to get any real use out of your remodeled basement. If the floor level is below the sewer line or the septic tank, special drainage should be designed; otherwise a new septic tank or sewer connection may be required. New plumbing that eliminates under-the-floor drains is available; you do not have to break the floor slab to make the installations. Toilets designed to lift sewage to proper drainage levels now make these low basement bathrooms much less expensive than they used to be.

A utility kitchen in the basement is a good addition to any home, especially if there is a possibility of renting the space as an apartment sometime in the future. Meantime it makes the place much more livable for your family for serving luncheons and snacks, for the lemonade and root-beer trade, or for use during the dog days of summer, when and if the house is not air conditioned and the basement is the only cool spot around.

THE FIREPLACE

Fireplaces have been designed and built following the same principles and methods and on the same classic proportions for hundreds of years. The simple explanation is that if you deviate much from the basic form, they smoke you out of the house. If you are remodeling your fireplace, do not tamper with the interior if it works as is. If it does not, get an experienced mason to come in and correct the structural and design flaws.

A minor fault in the design of an existing fireplace may be remedied by changing the proportions of the opening or by adding a hood over it.

Sometimes a fireplace smokes, even though the front opening, smoke box, and flue are correctly proportioned, because there is a down-draft from a nearby hill, from dense planting, or from the roof. If there are no down-drafts and no obstructions in the chimney, your fireplace may smoke because the room is too tightly weather-stripped and there is no source of fresh air to help the smoke up the chimney. This can be corrected by opening a window slightly to supply a little moving air and more oxygen to the fire.

Fireplaces directly across the room from a door may smoke every time the door is opened because unequal pressure pulls the smoke back down out of the chimney. The door should be moved, or screened with a permanent partition. Cross drafts in front of the hearth can also cause smoking.

If you are remodeling and want to include a new fireplace, study its location carefully. Have it off the beaten path, off at one end of the room, and out of the line of main traffic. The psychology of the fire has come down with us from the cave, and we enjoy it more if it retains the intimate feeling and protective atmosphere of shelter. For this reason fireplaces "feel better" away from glass and across the room from large openings. Interior walls are usually best, but in remodeling an exterior wall is a less expensive location.

The flue should be 12 per cent of the area of the fireplace opening if the chimney is seventeen feet high or less. Higher chimneys draw better; if yours is eighteen to twenty-four feet, 10 per cent of the fireplace opening determines the size of the flue. The chimney should be at least three feet higher than the highest roof of the house . . . higher still, if a hill or planting shuts off the draft.

House #32

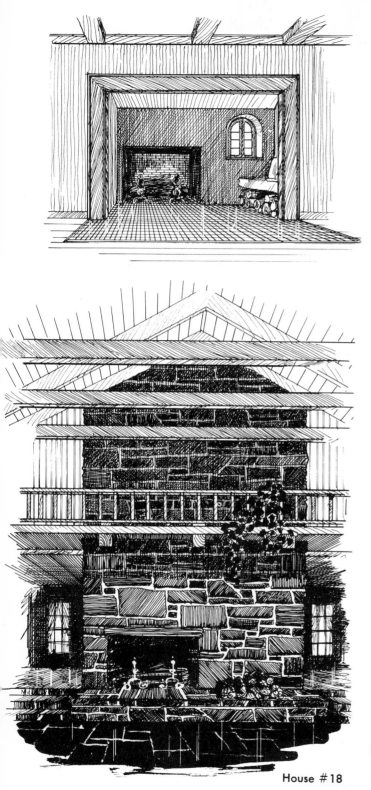

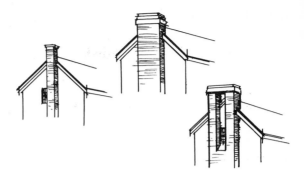

Chimneys on most houses are much too small and insignificant. If you are adding a flue, you can place it inside concrete block and veneer brick. But while you are at it, make the chimney massive, even if it means capping some empty space. You could also build a new chimney beside the old, connecting them only with decorative masonry. It will all appear as the same piece of masonry.

A fireplace in the basement demands a chimney to the top of the house, but a fireplace in the attic or on a one-story porch requires only a chimney over the rooftops. If you would like a fire for heat or just for cheer in an attic studio, on an enclosed porch, or anywhere else, consider a Franklin stove or one of the contemporary free-standing fireplaces. They are all inexpensive and work well, and none better than the old pot-belly style, or Franklin stove (about a hundred dollars mail order). They do make a lot of heat, and their stovepipes can get red hot and crack a window on cold days if too close. Keep all glass and drapery well away, and line the back wall of the stovepipe with asbestos or masonry.

Be very cautious about putting a fireplace in a small-sized bedroom. Although the fire itself may be kept small, sparks can pop out at night when you are asleep or during the day when you are not in the room. Beds and other furniture should be a minimum of six feet away from the structure and no furniture or any other object less than eight feet from directly in front of the opening without a screen.

Newfangled, avant-garde fireplaces, suspended, projected, cantilevered, or dropped, have an interesting novelty for a while. But the most satisfactory and perennially popular style is the old-fashioned, though not necessarily old-fashioned-looking, in-the-wall fireplace.

House #18

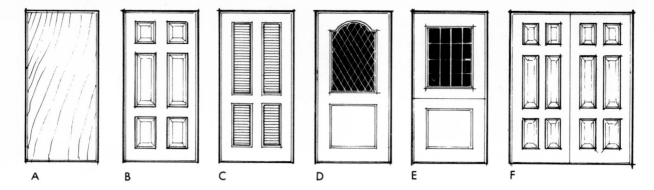

A   B   C   D   E   F

DOORS

Our doors should be more than just panels of wood with nondescript hardware, dull slabs that close one space off from another. Most of us pay more attention to the doors of our automobiles. We like them to sound substantial, to close on a luxurious and satisfying note without a bang, rattle, scrape, or shudder. The same should be true of the doors in our houses, and they should have personality as well. In remodeling we have an opportunity to study the matter and to try to make our doors beautiful as well as pleasant to use. Do not discard the old ones without considering what can be done to improve them. New doors are expensive to buy and hang.

All doors, interior and exterior, should be of similar design. This does not mean that they should be exactly alike. Your home is much more interesting if you have some variation within the design of the doors, but keep them in the same style and have similar, though not necessarily identical, hardware.

There are four main types of doors: hinged, sliding, folding, and swinging.

With the exception of the closets, most of the doors in your home are the hinged type, hung at the side with simple hardware. They are easily sound- and weatherproofed. Their only disadvantage is the space they require to swing open.

Until recently, panel doors have been the most commonly used hinge types. The familiar six-panel Colonial is a good example. Cost depends on whether it is an interior or exterior door, the kind of wood used, and the number of panels, which may be from one to fifty-four; usually the more panels there are, the more expensive the door. Most interior doors are one and three-eighths inches thick; exterior doors are one and three-fourths inches, or more. (For costs of doors see page 236.)

Standard sizes available in single doors vary from one and a half to three feet in width, and from six to seven feet in height, in increments of two inches.

Double doors come in the same sizes and are experiencing a revival in popularity. They are particularly gracious at the entrance. Styles vary from informal to formal. They cost more to weather-strip than single doors, and of course the hardware is double.

Flush doors are the least expensive, but they have a blank, vacant look unless the wood and hardware hold some interest; paint alone seldom helps them. However, they are invaluable when you want to make as little of an opening as you can. Thus if a secondary door to the garage or storage room on the exterior, or to the kitchen or closet on the interior, is close to a more important door, such as the entrance or the door to the dining room, a flush door painted the same color as the wall lets the eye slide right over it. Used indiscriminately throughout the house, though, flush doors can be characterless and flat.

French doors are glazed instead of paneled. They have fallen into disuse in the past twenty years because of the new and cheaper sliding glass doors, and this is a shame. Although they can be hard to lock and expensive to weather-strip, French doors more than make up for this with their fine scale, inherent charm, and grand sense of freedom.

Louvered doors combine ventilation with a most agreeable appearance and are finding more and more application in today's homes. They can be used to good advantage as bedroom doors where cross circulation of air is needed. If you want a screen door on the exterior and privacy too, a louvered screen door is a very handsome answer.

Any screen door you use should reflect the design of the solid door behind it. The hardware should also be similar.

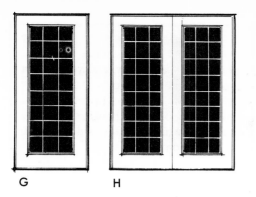

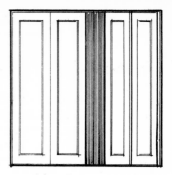

G   H   Sliding-Glass Doors   Bi-Folding Doors

Dutch doors are divided horizontally, with either a paneled or glazed top and a paneled bottom. They were originally designed to admit light and air through the opened upper half, while the lower half was kept closed against the barnyard animals. Though picturesque, they soon lose their romance because they cannot be screened.

Sliding doors slide over each other, over the wall, or into a slot in the wall. Since the slot has to be built in, the doors that slide over each other are better adapted to remodeling. Tracks at the top or bottom, or both, hold the doors in place and must be kept free of dirt and impediments. If not in almost perfect alignment, the doors jump the track. Sliding doors make more noise than hinged doors, but they take up less room. Usually their weight must be taken into consideration. The wall over the door may have to be reinforced if the sliding door is hung without floor tracks.

Sliding doors can be very useful or quite annoying, depending on where they are used. It is not a good idea to have them on bathrooms, even though they save space. They can be jammed easily, and at night or when someone does not feel well, this could create a panicky situation. They are far from convenient on closets because they reduce the size of the opening, require constant shifting, and expose only one section at a time. Where, for one reason or another, you have to use them for a closet, be sure the opening is at least five feet wide. An opening of less than five feet will not allow you space to maneuver things in and out.

Sliding glass doors to a terrace or porch, or even from one room to another, can be very handsome and convenient. Any number of sizes and combinations can be had, with or without sliding screen doors. They can be weather-stripped and insulated with ease.

If you plan to install a large sliding glass door, provide additional support with several wood members held together to form a beam or a small steel beam enclosed in wood.

Insulating glass adds to your initial cost, but it reduces the amount of heat loss in the winter and keeps out the heat in summer. If you get tinted glass, use gray tones, not blue or green, which change interior colors.

The most common mistake in installing sliding glass doors is in using large sheets of undivided glass in homes better suited to traditional treatment with paned glass. Mullions that snap in and out help reduce the scale of such an expanse of glass, yet keep it easy to clean.

Bifolding doors are the best doors made for closets. They work easily, quietly, and expose the entire contents of the closet. Numerous designs are available in stock sizes. Aside from their use as closet doors, they are convenient between rooms where you do not need complete privacy and sound control. They are not manufactured in exterior grades because they cannot be weather-stripped or locked easily.

Louvered bifolding doors permit air circulation in closets and from room to room. No more than two should be used in series because the hinges bind and the doors sag.

Multipanel folding doors can be locked, and soundproofed to an extent, and may be used to close off large areas, but they are usually associated with commercial buildings and are not recommended for homes.

Used almost exclusively between the kitchen and the dining room, swinging doors should be three feet wide so that you can easily carry a loaded tray through. Have a stop mechanism on the hinge to hold the door completely open on either swing. Because the clearance is necessarily larger than for other doors, there will be a crack of light all around the frame when the kitchen is brightly lighted and the dining room is lit by candles. This is inevitable and should be expected.

WINDOWS

Windows, sometimes referred to by the more architectural name, fenestration, are one of the most significant elements in the character of a home. Windows contribute more than any other single element to establish and verify the style and architecture of the house. Double-hung Colonial windows would be as out of place on a contemporary house as window boxes on a space capsule.

On the exterior, windows help determine the specific style and character you have chosen for your home; from the interior they establish furniture placement. Unlike furniture, however, windows are not so easily moved, but they should be designed with both the interior and exterior conceptions of architecture and furniture in mind.

Primarily, windows should be placed to bring light and air into the house, but keep in mind that they also keep out weather, frame views, and control privacy. Windows also help determine scale in a house, and can make it seem larger or smaller. They should be easy to clean, screen, and curtain, although not all windows have to be curtained and not all have to open and close. The glass itself can be part of the design of the window and can be textured, tinted, or treated to admit as much or as little sun and view as you want.

In Colonial times window glass was tediously made by hand in small rectangles and was very expensive. Even after the manufacturing process became less complicated and cheaper, glass was still considered a luxury and taxed. Each window was taxed per pane every year; so people kept the windows as small as possible to reduce the tax and keep the initial cost of the windows down. In fact, when settlers moved on to new lands and abandoned their old houses, they took all their windows (or at least the panes) with them.

Most of the traditional styles of architecture in the United States have been brought to us from Europe, and these designs were originally scaled and refined through the years to use small panes of glass, the only ones available when the designs were conceived.

Even with all the types we now have to select from, there is still no one perfect window to solve all your lighting, ventilation, and esthetic aims.

But today's possibilities are wider, and you do not have to replace old, rattly windows with exactly the same style in a new, weather-stripped version. The scale and design of your house should be studied to determine which window suits it best.

Changing the location of windows is more expensive than replacing them in the rough openings, but it is often necessary. Too many builders have lined up the windows on the front, perhaps using two or three different styles, and then centered others on the sides and back of the house in the middle of each room. If you are getting new windows, try to correct as many of these design errors as possible beforehand.

There are fixed glass, double-hung, single-hung, casement, sliding, awning, hopper, jalousie, and pivoted windows. You can use them singly, in groups, and in combinations.

Fixed glass, used in combination with operable sash where more light and view are wanted, is inexpensive and needs no screening or weather-stripping. Often it costs less to use fixed glass as a finish wall material because the interior and exterior are completed in one step. If obscure glass is used, you do not have to clean or curtain it. Fixed glass is also excellent for small irregular places in the façade that allow you to bring more light to the interior. Overuse of fixed glass, however, may let the summer sun pour in and heat rooms beyond a tolerable level. Shading and curtaining and cleaning must be well worked out.

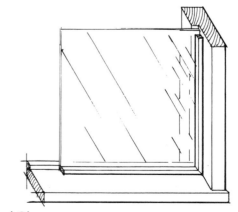

Fixed Glass

Double-hung windows have been the most popular for several centuries. They provide the best-controlled ventilation of any window, even though only 50 per cent of the space can be open at one time. Warm, stale air goes out at the top; fresh air comes in below. Those used in new construction today are counterbalanced with springs and work smoothly and safely. All can be washed fairly easily from the inside; some come completely out of the frame for cleaning, others pivot on the frame. Some manufacturers combine storm sash, screen, and window in a single sash that is pre-weather-stripped.

Meeting rails can sometimes be heavy and distracting; mullions may be deep and clumsy. Mullions must be kept puttied and painted. New snap-out mullions speed up painting and cleaning time, but they can have an ersatz look. Double-hung windows should only be used singly, never in cross-eyed tandem.

Single-hung windows have a fixed upper and an operable lower section. About all that can be said for them is that they are cheap. They do not provide good ventilation and are hard to wash.

Casement windows, the oldest-known type, have some design advantages. They open 100 per cent of the area to ventilation, there is no crossbar to obstruct the view, and, unlike double-hung windows, casements look well when used in a row for greater exposure. But with the window opening to its full height, ventilation is more difficult to control. Casements that open in are easy to clean and screen, and storm windows are not a problem. They take up a lot of space inside the room, however, interfere with curtains, and are liable to leak. Those that open out can be hard to clean and screen. They keep slowly moving currents of air away from the open window and may be blown about in a strong wind. Some types open with a space between sash and frame that lets you reach through to wash the outside. The best have screens that roll up and store in the window head. Usually operated with levers or worm gears from the bottom, you can also get them with a chain drive which extends from the center as the windows open and which braces them against the wind, but the mechanism obstructs the view and can rust and get out of kilter.

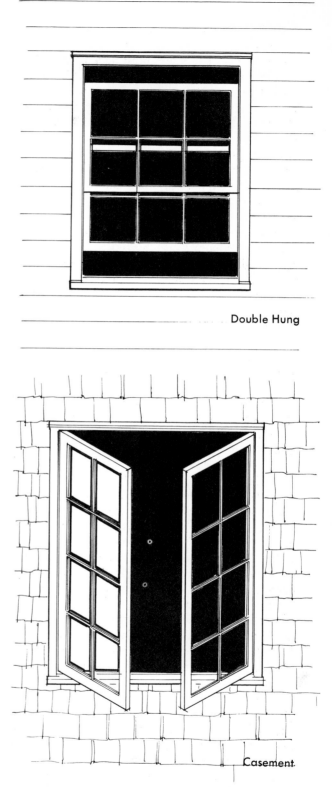

Double Hung

Casement

Sliding windows operate on tracks built into the frame. Storm sash and screens have separate built-in tracks. The tracks must be kept clean, and even then are prone to stick and bind. Ventilation is hard to control because the window opens to its entire height with never more than 50 per cent of the opening available for air. Some designs slip easily out of the frames for cleaning. Swelling and shrinking of wood makes sliding windows of this framing subject to sticking and rattling. Because the glass is supported, small mullions of either wood or metal can be used. This gives a distinctive appearance on the façade and on the interior when strips of many windows are used together.

Awning windows are hinged at the top and project out from the bottom. Operated by a worm gear or lever, their angle and projection keep the rain out. They open completely and offer good control of ventilation. Screening must be on the inside, and no storm sash can be used. Some awning windows can be washed from the inside; by the very nature of their design, they need cleaning more often than other types. Designs are usually heavy, however, and since the frames must support a good deal of glass, they may suggest an industrial appearance. You can avoid this look and achieve good design and some ventilation by combining awning windows with fixed glass.

Hopper windows drop in from the top and are hinged at the bottom. They can have storm sash and screen, and are easily cleaned from the inside. Hopper windows are mainly used in basements. They may be in series or used at the top or base of a fixed glass window. Combining them with fixed glass lightens the scale. Air control is fair where you have enough operable sash. When open, though, hoppers interfere considerably with window shades and curtains.

Jalousie windows are narrow strips of glass opened and closed with a lever or worm gear. Closed, they are reasonably airtight. Ventilation control is good, from a tiny crack to almost 100 per cent of the opening. Screen can be applied on the inside, but storm windows or insulating glass do not work. The angle of the glass keeps out rain, which makes jalousie windows valuable in certain climates. Open or closed, however, the narrow slats create disturbing lines across any view. In addition, the closed windows do nothing to establish character or to give a feeling of

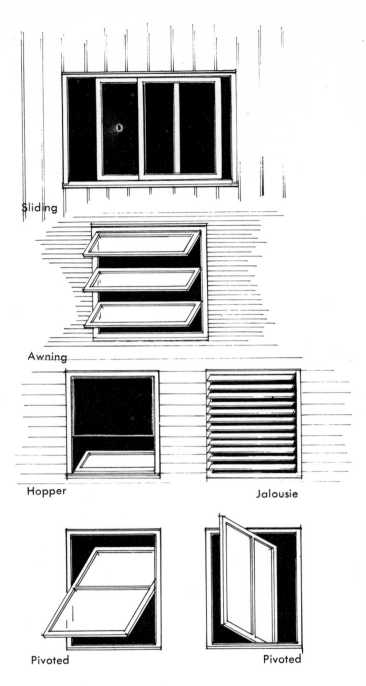

Sliding

Awning

Hopper

Jalousie

Pivoted

Pivoted

enclosure or protection. They are expensive, and their use in remodeling should be carefully studied since they adapt to few homes. Too often we see them applied to the sun porches of older houses in the hopeful attempt to get something better in the way of 100 per cent opening and summer breezes; the disquieting effect is one of a pleasant old home addled with modern contraptions.

Pivoted windows have very little use in remodeling because they cannot be screened. It is possible to use them, however, if screening is supplied by a porch or loggia. They are easy to clean and can provide adequate, if hard to control, ventilation.

Aside from these windows, there are also special styles: bay, bow, projected, clerestory, and oriel.

A bay window is three windows in one, extending beyond the face of the house wall. Usually the two side windows set at an angle are operable, and the center window is fixed. Bays offer an excellent means of gaining extra light and space within a room if they are carried down to the foundation and the floor extends into them. Less expensive is the bay window that cantilevers over the foundation. The least expensive type projects only the window area, with solid wall below, which gives you more light but space sufficient only for, say, plants.

Bow windows are comparable to the bay, except that they take the form of an unbroken curve and are considerably more expensive. Operable sash on them has never been successful. If you want one, by all means avoid the operable sash seen so often; it interrupts the window and the view and is quite costly. Both the bay and the bow were originally used on shopfronts so that merchants could display their wares. They were fixed windows, with no ventilation at all. We all know their charm, if only from an old Dickens movie.

Projected windows are actually square bays taken out of the house wall at right angles. The two sides are usually very narrow, and can be solid or filled with glass. Glazing the sides is a good way of getting east and west sunlight into a room with a northern exposure. Because of the straight lines, projected windows are less expensive than the bay or bow. Roofing is usually copper or, if the slope is sufficient, the same material as the house roof.

Clerestory windows, formed between two intersecting planes of roof to shed light into a room or hallway, can also be useful in remodeling, particularly where an addition may close off an existing opening. Properly designed, they are an attractive and compatible means of reintroducing light to the interior.

The oriel window has limited application but is decorative and romantic for a house whose

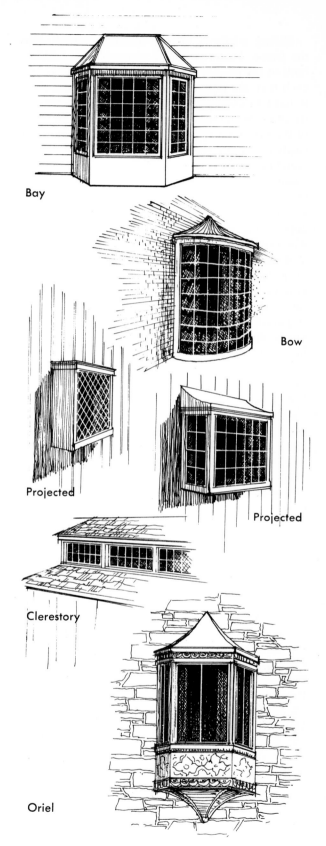

Bay

Bow

Projected

Projected

Clerestory

Oriel

design can take it. Usually in the shape of a bay, it projects from the wall and is supported by a decorated brace of masonry or wood.

Whatever type of window, or style you use in your remodeling, keep in mind the importance of scaling the windows and panes to the façade of your house. It is unwise to mix shapes and scale unless the design is being planned by a highly qualified person. Never mix two pane sizes on one window or series of windows.

Everyone likes diamond-shaped panes, but they should be used sparingly. Do not just turn a rectangular pane on point and combine it with squared ones; the angle must be sharper. Imitation diamond panes glued onto the window are obvious and ugly. Diamond-paned glazing draws attention to itself, and therefore should not be used on bathroom or service windows.

Remodeling existing windows is a hard job; each element is so dependent upon another that by the time you get everything fixed up, it may have been cheaper to buy new windows. However, some things can be corrected fairly easily. If you are stuck with horizontal mullions used by so many builders to cut windows into unpleasant rectangles, add vertical mullions inside and out; simply glue them to the face of the glass. Other large double-hung windows can have snap-in mullions fitted to them. Mullions actually do more than create scale. Painted a light color, they can help obscure the room behind.

Patterned glass can also be placed in existing sash with good results. Old windows can often be fixed up for another year or two with repainting, and the screens can be painted to match or contrast. Screens painted in light colors are more obscure from the outside than those painted dark.

If you are getting new window sash, you have a choice of wood or metal. The metal is usually aluminum, though steel is not unusual.

Wood sash has the advantage of being inexpensive, quiet, and easy to fit and shape to existing window openings. But you have the upkeep involving painting or varnishing the mullions and keeping them puttied.

Aluminum sash does not need painting in some localities, but chemicals in the air usually start to pit and corrode it in a short time. The color of the metal, either new and shiny or a dull and corroded gray, may be so noticeable as to detract from the appearance of your house. The price of this sash varies from the very cheap, which should not be permitted in any house, to the moderately expensive. On the other hand, aluminum windows with a permanent finish either baked on or adhered through a chemical process are very good windows and require no upkeep at all. They are fairly expensive, but if combined as storm sash or insulating glass and screen, with easy cleaning, they are well worth having.

Steel windows must be painted, are heavy, and have proved to rust. In special cases they may be suitable for remodeling, but their main application is in industrial and commercial work, where fireproofing and special requirements must be met.

The principal advantages of metal windows are the slim mullions and the greater expanse of glass they can carry without becoming clumsy.

Window screening is available in plastic, fiber glass, copper, and aluminum. While the most convenient is the kind that rolls up and stores in the head of the framing, it may not be applicable within the scope of your remodeling; therefore other screening methods should be considered.

Plastic screen has a tendency to sag in the heat and melts if touched by a burning cigarette. Some of it is also difficult to see through; however, it needs no painting.

Fiber glass is strong and light and, like plastic, does not need paint. I believe it is the best of the present screening materials.

Copper screen looks well when first put up but bends and gets out of shape. As it weathers it gets more difficult to see through and discolors the wall and window sill.

Aluminum screening is not satisfactory, especially in a metropolitan area or near the shore. At first, like the sash previously mentioned, it is smooth and shiny; then it roughs up in the weather, catches all the dust, streaks the wall beneath, corrodes, and breaks. It can and should be painted, but paint further reduces your ability to see through it.

Screening comes in a number of sizes, specified by the number of spaces per inch. For example, 16-18 screen has sixteen spaces per inch horizontally and eighteen vertically. The higher the numbers, the smaller the openings. In some areas, such as along the shore, 20-20 screening is specified to keep out the gnats and nits, but they always find their way in, and what you need here is special candles and bug lotions.

CASE HISTORIES

SECTION FOUR

Facelifting

When houses are remodeled and improved, it is only natural that a part of this additional investment will be reflected on the exterior. Many times, however, the interior is quite suitable and it is only the outside of the house that shows the effects of time, weather, and changing tastes. It requires more than general maintenance to rescue a house from dowdiness and lift it out of the ordinary.

The first chapter concentrates on the changes that can be made in the exterior appearance, or façade of a house, with little if any changes in the basic plan. Small alterations of the interior may be inevitable as windows are changed and projections added or eliminated, but primarily we are interested only in the way the house "looks."

Some houses have character that needs to be uncovered, others require only a nudge in one direction to assume a fresh personality. It may be simply a matter of removing distracting details and adding certain new elements to emphasize the existing character. At other times the house may need to be supplied with more deliberate individuality, and this is not a question of simple cosmetics.

Usually more is removed from the façade than is added. Always avoid the "cute" look; you will tire of whimsy as quickly as women change fashionable clothes. If there is any real doubt in your mind as to adding or removing something from the exterior, do not make a change. You will usually be right in leaving it as is.

While remodeling the exterior to improve its appearance, you should also increase the value and convenience of the house. Steps and doors can be sheltered to keep off the rain and snow; porches and windows can be screened for privacy from the street, second-floor windows may be made easier to clean with a small balcony, or the walls can be shaded and cooled in the summer with a porch. Additional interior wall space might be gained with the selection of one window style over another; winter drafts may be eliminated by the addition of an entrance-way. And it is not surprising that these facelifting operations are usually the least expensive of all remodeling work because there is no major mechanical work involved such as plumbing or heating, and structural changes are minimal.

COSTS FOR THE REMODELING CHANGES ON ALL THE HOUSES ILLUSTRATED ARE GIVEN IN THE CHAPTER, "THE COST OF REMODELING."

OWNER   Byron W. Crider
LOCATION   Fullerton, California

House #1   Before

Small houses such as this one need simplification so they do not look as though they were assembled from another structure's leftover materials. The front wall is evened out by adding twelve inches to the dining room. Narrow strips of floor-to-ceiling French doors spaced across the dining and living room increase the apparent size from both inside and out. Shutters are split so the bottom half can be closed separately—a combination that is flexible for maximum air, sunlight, and privacy. A skinny chimney looks ineffective and temporary. This one is designed three times as big as it need be so the house has a settled and permanent look. A portico shelters the way from the drive to the door in rainy weather and protects the French doors so they do not have to be closed for every summer shower. The clapboards on the right have been carried to a logical conclusion instead of stopping halfway down the wall. The bit of brick under the living-room window is eliminated. Brick is used for the drive and the portico floor leading to the front door, and the small site is not broken up with various paving materials. Landscaping should be kept simple and on the lot line so there is a feeling of space between the house and the hedge that frames the site.

OWNER Carl Lugbauer
LOCATION Gardner, Massachusetts

Before   House #2

There was nothing wrong with the big, old-fashioned front porch that surrounded this house, but the owners found little use for it and were attracted to a more formal design. The old materials and railing are re-used to construct a more or less classical façade. The new windows on the first and second floor are now much less vague than the blank and mismatched original openings. The new porches on the second and third floor make window washing easier and less dangerous. The columns unify the front and emphasize the entrance which has been redesigned with a traditional door and sidelights, although the door is not the conventional six-paneled Colonial style. If the exterior walls are in good condition and can be patched and repaired after remodeling, there is no reason to change them. However, if the surface is in poor repair, or if insulation is applied to the exterior, another wall surface may be less expensive in terms of maintenance. Materials should have a logical placement and should never stop abruptly on an exposed corner. If for the sake of economy or design, brick is used on part of the façade, terminate it at the second floor and sheathe the upper wall in wood, which is lighter in weight and in character.

OWNER   Edward J. Bara
LOCATION Syracuse, New York

House #3   Before

On narrow city lots where site restrictions limit the direction and the area in which you can remodel, you also have similar problems of urban living—lack of sunlight, fresh air, privacy. The solutions, however, can always be individual. Here on a lot that slopes two ways the house needs to be steadied and related to the site. The brick retaining wall at the sidewalk levels the site and becomes the base of the remodeling. The hedge, which should be as high as the law allows, screens out headlights, noise, heat, and a view of the windows across the street. The view from the sunporch is turned away from the street to an enclosed garden which is also viewed from new living-room windows. The garden is closed off from the entrance with a brick wall similar to the one used on the new street wall of the sunporch. Open beams hold up wisteria and trumpet vines in the summer and block out the hot sun. The roof line of the porch is carried over the entrance where shelter is obviously needed for the front door. Equal column spacing is not always required, and here the wider space in front of the door emphasizes the entrance. The object is to lower the line of the house and tie it to the site while providing privacy for the existing rooms built overlooking the street.

This little square house with its front porch was practically built on the sidewalk. The porch was too public to be used and darkened the living room. Reusing the same materials the porch is reconstructed in the back where it could be put to better use. By removing the porch and then building a low retaining wall at the level of the first floor, the house loses some of its height and now seems to move back from the street. The doorway is indented into the front hall to provide some cover for the entrance and is lighted by concealed fixtures in the entry ceiling. The square bay window is not out of place on this quiet tree-lined street, and mullions with rather small panes obscure the interior. New casement windows on the second floor and in the attic dormer maintain the same small scale and provide interest for an otherwise plain façade. Landscaping must be kept low and refined in scale with the house. Any ornamentation such as light fixtures or railings would be distracting and out of character with the restrained simplicity of the façade.

OWNER John Harris
LOCATION Monticello, New York

Before   House #4

OWNER Dr. Z. Szaloki
LOCATION Whitinsville, Massachusetts

House #5   Before

Behind the awkward and glassed-in front porch there was quite a pleasant and well-detailed house of colonial design. The owner was most interested in a suitable entrance and in improving the exterior. The straightforward solution is almost automatic. An entrance terrace along the side of the house using the old porch foundations connects the back door with the street. The dining-room bay and windows are replaced with a double-hung Colonial sash. The second-floor dormer is trimmed to simplify the roof line. The entrance is very quiet and lighted with soft down-lights concealed in the fascia. A few details are altered slightly to eliminate some of the shadows and give the corner trim a firm appearance. Various colonial entrances are available ready-made at lumber yards at reasonable prices, but in this instance when combined with the existing details they would have proved incompatible. Simple shutters are placed on each side of the standard six-panel Colonial door. The shutters are operable, of course, and may be used during the winter as a handsome escape from the regular storm door.

This suburban home is typical of many houses throughout the country, and presents many possibilities for remodeling. In this case the front wall is projected out several feet to contain the entrance and to place the steps up to the first floor inside where they would remain free of ice and snow. The portico around two sides of the house is covered with a low pitch roof so it does not interfere with the second-floor bedroom windows in the gable ends. The broad low roof gives the house a distinctive sheltered atmosphere that is almost a cross between Japanese and French farmhouse dwellings. Single French doors are used because of their small size (two feet four inches wide) instead of more complicated and expensive windows. The exterior of the first floor is sheathed in scored plywood. The most important thing to avoid with this or any other portico or loggia is small spindly columns. Structurally, columns or posts one third of the size used would have easily supported the roof, but they would have appeared out of proportion to the rest of the extended roof and design.

OWNER   Harry Friedman
LOCATION   Woodburne, New York

Before   House #6

Although this house was well-planned on the interior, the façade was a confusion of intersecting roof lines, different materials, and windows. The conflicting roofs are simplified by extending the roof of the main block of the house, eliminating the hip, and forming a gable supported by four husky two-story columns resting on the existing terrace. With the little doghouse gable over the front door removed, a small balcony is built the width of the front, shielding the new French doors of the bedroom. The existing doors of the living room do not appear as isolated or public then and receive double weather protection by the balcony and the roof so the interior may be opened to the outdoors. The front door remains prominent, but it is softened and becomes a part of the entrance terrace reached by a double-curved staircase.

House #7   Before

OWNER   William V. Jackson
LOCATION   Grosse Pointe Farms, Michigan

Remodeling with Paint

Paint, more than any other single material, is the most useful tool in remodeling. With color it is possible to change the apparent size and shape of a house, paint out ungainly features, and make good lines and details stronger and more dominant. Even the ugliest house can look almost 100 per cent better through the proper use of color.

Although some houses would not look well painted in any other color, far too many houses are painted white. White, used indiscriminately over the exterior, can be dull, show up all the defects, and highlight poor design elements, giving equal importance to both good and bad aspects of the house. White houses in the North can look bleak, almost disappearing against the winter landscape, or seem gray and soiled against the white of new-fallen snow. In the South, white houses produce a sharp glare in the sunshine. White reflects heat and keeps homes cooler in the summer, but other, softer colors keep it just as cool and prevent harsh shadows and glare.

White makes a house look larger, but so can many far more interesting colors. There is no color chart or general guide you can spin to select colors for walls, roof, and trim. It is best to avoid trimming a white house with bright red or blue, which is too reminiscent of the ten-cent store or a gasoline station, but do not be afraid of using color over the entire façade.

Primary colors, red, blue, and yellow, are ordinary and soon lose their interest. Secondary colors, a mixture of any two primary colors, are green, orange, and purple. They can hold your attention, but should also be used sparingly. Pastel shades of light blue, pink, and pale green usually give the house a candy-box look and do not wear well unless the house is located in the tropics or where the sun is so strong that the walls seem almost white in contrast to the strong blue of the sky.

In most areas the grayed tones and subtle mixtures of olive-greens, golds, and browns are more satisfactory over a period of time. They tend to make a house warm and restful and tie it in with the landscape.

Monochromatic color schemes, several shades of the same color, enhance a small house and also make it seem larger. A lighter shade on the side walls with a darker window trim can enlarge the apparent size of the windows. A lighter shade on the windows makes them more prominent but apparently smaller. Sharply contrasting colors on walls and trim emphasize the windows and trim but often make the house seem jarring and the windows spotty.

When windows are not classically arranged one above the other, the house seems better balanced if the windows are painted the same color as the exterior walls. This also saves time and money because the painter does not need to be so careful in making precise lines where the colors meet. All windows and trim do not require the same treatment. You may wish to emphasize the symmetrical windows by painting them a different shade from the walls and minimize the irregular windows by painting them the same color as the walls. If you want some color contrast, concentrate the color on the entrance or on a particularly attractive window, drawing the eye away from the garage door and basement windows.

Awkward dormers and odd projections on the roof can be painted the same

(*Continued on page 137*)

House #8   Before

OWNER   John Faber
LOCATION   Mountain Lakes, New Jersey

A fresh pale yellow is used on the stucco exterior, held in by the white frame of new corner boards and fascia. The dormers are painted to match the roof and minimize their importance. A windowbox under the kitchen window lowers the apparent sill and brings it to the level of the living-room windows. To emphasize the entrance and at the same time minimize its unbalanced aspect, the center section is covered with wood paneling painted white. In all examples, landscaping and foundation planting are kept to a minimum although in many cases existing or new landscaping would complement the solutions.

OWNER   Evan S. Nelson
LOCATION   Iron Mountain, Michigan

Scheme A   Red was the first color used in America to paint houses and barns. It was made from red lead and it was cheap. Later, more expensive white lead paint was used on homes, but to the present day, red remains a favorite for barns and can be used effectively on suburban homes especially when the roof is gray or black. With the porch removed, a new entrance platform leads to the standard six-panel Colonial door from the drive. Because the door is unevenly placed in relation to the windows, a single lamp is placed to the left instead of the usual arrangement of one lamp at each side of the door.

Scheme B   A navy blue house—why not? Navy blue will cover many defects and patches in old siding and is an excellent background for plants. Although touches of white are necessary with blue, they should not be on it because of the stark contrast and the tendency of most white paints to chalk. Use a little darker blue than desired because almost all blue paint will fade. Any disparity in window and door spacing will become more obvious and here the entrance area has been paneled to include a new window. Exterior lighting for the double-curved entrance platform is placed in the ample roof overhang.

House #9   Before

Scheme C   Many houses of this type have been built with a particularly unattractive shade of green shingle and special consideration must be given to choose a color that can be used with them. In Scheme B, the windows, door, and trim are painted the same color as the surface on which they are placed; this makes the house look longer and lower than the house in Scheme A.

Scheme D   White, of course, emphasizes the irregular placement of openings but sometimes it is the only acceptable color. This is a more formal and ambitious solution with a brick terrace replacing the porch. The front door is relocated and glazed doors from the living room replace the triple window.

House #8 After Remodeling

House #9 Scheme A

House #9 Scheme C

House #9 Scheme B

House #9 After Remodeling

House #9 Scheme D

House #10   Scheme A   After

House #10   Scheme B   After

OWNER Edward Howe

LOCATION Stillwater, New York

House #10   Before

Scheme A The most obvious need is to remove the ramshackle porches and soften the edges of the house with foundation planting. The projected gable and second floor over the entrance, although disturbing, does protect the front door and can be minimized by painting the window trim and mullions the same color as the house wall. However, a structural element as prominent as this should either receive special treatment or be removed. The double window is replaced with casement sash to retain the interest and detail but not the coarseness of the old window. The windows are not new, but snap-in mullions put them in scale and reduce their raw, unfinished look. White on the front door brings out the old paneling and fine millwork.

Scheme B A few inexpensive changes in the elevation and corrective painting will completely alter the complexion and simplify the problems in the façade. Porches and the second-floor projection are removed and the side door is moved into the space previously occupied by a window. The entrance is recessed into the large front hallway. Considerably more freedom with less chance for mistake is available in the choice of colors. White would still be a bad choice for this house because of the anonymous quality of the design which would not be improved by adding shutters as most people are tempted to do. Use of good strong color, and no ornamentation, will give the house character.

(*Continued from page 133*)

color as the roof, even if it is dark gray or black, so that they do not stand out and detract from the sweep of the roof line.

Masonry and natural shingles can be painted, but it is usually a mistake, because once they are painted they continue to need paint. If you want to change the color, both masonry and shingles can be stained or bleached and then left to weather and mellow.

Good repainting of any house depends on the quality of paint used and on the preparation of the surface. Exterior paint, usually called house paint, and interior paint can have any number of common flaws, such as alligatoring, bleeding, blistering, chalking, checking, cracking, crawling, and mildew, which should be scraped, sanded, and cleaned away before the fresh paint is applied.

Good paint is expensive, and cheap paint is no good. Always buy a reputable brand, and never mix two kinds or brands together to stretch the paint or get the color you want. Every paint is a mixture of at least two components, the pigment and the vehicle or base. Besides giving the paint its color, the pigment seals the surface against wear and moisture penetration. Paint usually gets its name from the base, and there are three main types for the exterior of a house: oil, alkyd, and latex.

Oil-base paints have been standard for exterior work until fairly recently. This group includes the white-lead paints, the titanium-lead-zinc, and titanium-zinc. Pure white-lead paint holds color better than the others and does not chalk perceptibly. It costs more, and dirt tends to gray it sooner. In industrial areas where hydrogen sulfide is carried in the air, white-lead paint darkens severely, almost turning black. Titanium-zinc paints are sometimes called "fume-resistant" because they do not turn black in industrial atmospheres. They do chalk, but if this is not excessive it keeps the paint fresh-looking and obviates the buildup of layers and layers of paint on the wall. However, do not use a paint that chalks above masonry or where it can stain and discolor lower walls or roofs. For good color retention in an oil-base paint, use a chalk-resistant titanium-dioxide paint.

Oil-base paint can be used on wood or masonry and dries in forty-eight to seventy-two hours. It is brushed, sprayed, or rolled on the wall. One gallon covers five to six hundred square feet on wood,

(*Continued on page 142*)

OWNER   John J. Brittan
LOCATION   Alliance, Nebraska

House #11   Before

OWNER   Charles Giuri
LOCATION   East Paterson, New Jersey

Scheme A A permanent extension of the roof over the front door will keep the rain off and protect it from the weather. Moveable shutters over the windows are far more attractive and much less expensive than tin awnings to control the light and air in the house. Dark, reddish brown shingles so often associated with these houses can be bleached and restained a better color.

Scheme B Many times, instead of being reddish brown, a little house like this may be stained an ugly shade of green. The color of the stain can be changed completely, painted, or in this case only altered. The dormer is made darker; windows and trim are painted the same color so they fade into the roof. The bottom half of the house is somewhat brightened and becomes more important. The roof extension is supported by two columns to draw attention to the front door.

Scheme A The stairs at the front door are eliminated and a low brick wall and steps constructed at the property line lowers the house and gives it a setting of its own. The entrance is at the front door of the porch so it becomes a part of the house and not just some sort of "no-man's-land" between the front door and the street. The flimsy porch door is then exchanged for a proper entrance door. Classical columns such as these are white with no competition from windows and trim painted in contrasting colors. Because the roof is black, trying to minimize the dormer by painting it dark gray or black would only make the house too somber. On this façade, the columns and the horizontal fascia of the porch should be emphasized. Other details can be removed or painted out.

Scheme B When red brick is used, it is better to avoid warm shades of yellow. Essentially the same design elements are present as in Scheme A, but the colors—elephant gray, white trim, and an egg-plant-colored door—are more sophisticated and considerably less cheerful.

House #12   Before

Scheme C Painting the corner boards, shutters, and trim a dull gray adds strength to the façade and makes it look less spotty and contrived.

Scheme D If you prefer not to have shutters over the windows, extend the roof to keep out sun and rain. A new roof surface is applied because of the patch work involved. A white roof usually looks better with a house that has dark walls. The shutters are a variation that could be used on any of the other schemes to replace the flimsy awnings.

House #11   Scheme A

House #11   After Remodeling

House #11   Scheme B

House #12   Scheme A

House #12   Scheme C

House #12   Scheme B

House #12   After Remodeling

House #12   Scheme D

House #13 Scheme A

House #13 Scheme B

House #13 Scheme C

Scheme A   The center posts of the porch are shifted a bit to make room for another and to create equal spacing between them. For esthetic reasons, all the posts are made heavier than actually necessary to support the roof. The walls of the porch are painted white to focus attention on the entrance. The eyebrow windows over the porch roof are painted with the wall to avoid attention and to attenuate the narrow surface. The symmetrically placed windows in the gabled wing, however, should be emphasized and are drawn in white to tie them in with the rest of the façade.

OWNER   John R. Lane
LOCATION   Wauseon, Ohio

House #13   Before

Scheme B   If the roof were black (or white) a more dignified approach to the farmhouse might be made using natural finished posts and doorway against a background of Madison-Avenue gray. Because of the uneven placement of the windows in relation to the posts, the windows are painted the same color as the walls. Just a touch of the natural wood is carried to the windows over the porch roof, so the doorway, in a provincial French design, is not unrelated to the rest of the house.

Scheme C   Barn red again has the warm farm-like quality that is distinctively American and it looks especially well when the surrounding fields are covered with snow. Here too, the posts of the porch are emphasized and the porch windows painted with the walls. To lower the height and lengthen the line of the house, the section over the porch is painted white. The front door is dull orange, but it still relates to the eyebrow windows through the use of diamond-shaped panes. Black could have been used for the door, but somehow black seems more appropriate for the entrance to a house in town than to a country farmhouse.

(*Continued from page 137*)

and one hundred fifty to two hundred square feet on masonry. Oil paint is thinned with turpentine, and brushes are cleaned with turpentine or another solvent. Repainting is usually required every four or five years.

Alkyd paints are made from synthetic resins that produce a tough, quick-drying coat, much harder than the standard oil-base paints. Considered an improvement on oil-base paints, alkyd paint is excellent for color and can be used on wood or masonry. Sprayed, brushed, or rolled on the surface, it dries in twenty-four hours. One gallon covers two hundred seventy-five to three hundred square feet on either wood or masonry. The paint is thinned with mineral spirits or naphtha, and the brushes are cleaned with the same liquids. Repainting is required in from six to eight years.

Latex, or vinyl-plastic, paint is more expensive than either oil or alkyd paint, but it is quicker and easier to apply and lasts longer. Latex paints are thinned with water, and even an unhandy amateur can apply a professional-looking coat with them. Marketed under various and rather complicated trade names, you should buy only from a reputable manufacturer and then follow explicitly his directions for surface preparation and application. Brushed, sprayed, or rolled on, these paints stick to almost any surface. Metals and new wood may need to be primed, old painted walls may have to be washed, and blistered or scaling paint may have to be scraped off as with any new coat of paint.

The latex paints do not blister or chalk and can be applied in damp weather. They hold color well and are not bothered by industrial fumes. Some manufacturers have added "mildewcides," which is helpful if you live in an area where mildew is a problem. Latex paint can be cleaned off hands and brushes with soap and water. It covers three to four hundred square feet per gallon, dries in an hour, and does not need repainting for eight to ten years.

Interior paints are not exposed to the constant wear of the sun and weather, but they do have to withstand washing with soap and water. Here, too, cheap paint is no bargain, and the latex or vinyl paints are by far the easiest to use because spills, hands, and brushes can be cleaned with water. You do not have to have dangerous inflammable liquids in the house, furniture and pictures can go back into place in an hour, and you do not need to leave the windows open to get rid of paint odor and fumes.

Color on the interior is a more particular subject because it involves decorating. A color that works well on the exterior may be out of the question inside a room because you live in closer proximity with interior colors. You may not tire of barn red on the outside of the house, but you may find it very tiring to live with inside.

Aside from personal taste, the condition of the wall surface can influence the color you choose to paint the walls. Stark-white paint does not cover discolored and patched walls well, and it may take several coats to bring the walls and ceiling to a uniform level of whiteness. The covering power of white paint can be increased by adding a tint of another color, usually raw umber; instead of taking two or three coats, one coat of paint then covers evenly. With white or light colors, however, rough spots and patches show more than if a darker color is used. A warm dark gray shows the least amount of patching an unevenness in an old wall.

Flat paint in any color shows wall and ceiling defects less than shiny or semigloss paint. Shiny paint, such as enamel, catches and reflects light from every uneven surface and patch in addition to producing a harsh glare. Shiny paints are no longer considered necessary in kitchens and bathrooms. The flat latex paints now available can be cleaned and washed quite satisfactorily, but they are so simple and convenient to apply that it is almost easier to paint than to clean.

Ceilings are the hardest part of the interior to paint, and the most popular colors are white or a neutral shade because you may want to change the wall color several times before the ceiling needs to be painted. A white ceiling also distributes light from table and standing lamps more evenly throughout the room. The apparent size of a room can be increased by painting the inside wall a darker color than the other three walls. If more than one color is used in the room, the lightest should be on the outside walls. Dark colors around windows accentuate the daylight and make the room seem smaller. This intensified daylight can also produce a distracting glare that would not be noticeable if a light color or white were used on the outside wall and around the window.

Remodeling Interior Space

Before we begin adding new rooms and wings to a house, we should use all the available existing space within it. The ideas expressed in the Facelifting and in the Remodeling with Paint chapters will also apply to the houses shown here, just as the principles of using all the space in a house will apply to any remodeling project. Good use of the site is equally important in creating a feeling of space and privacy around your home. The smaller the house and lot, the more important it is to use the space well.

The concepts of the three main areas of the house—public, private, and utility —must be kept in mind, and if they are not established, then an attempt must be made to define them. It does not have to be an arbitrary ruling; sometimes only an approximation is possible with an existing house, and areas may inevitably overlap.

It is also well to remember that there is nothing inflexible about the arrangement of the rooms. The only rigid parts of the house are the walls and the few bearing partitions that hold up the roof. The rigidity in planning is much more apt to be in our conception of the rooms, their use, and the dependence on the plumbing that runs through the house. Some time and money might be saved by rebuilding the old kitchen where it stands now, but the entire plan of the house should not be conceived around the existing arrangement of the pipes. If the main entrance is presently on the front of the house, but the plan works better with the door on the side, there is no reason not to move it.

You have the distinct advantage of knowing what is wrong with the house after having lived in it and being able to plan where you would like things to be. If you have a front entrance, and everyone still uses the back door because it is more convenient to the driveway, then the front entrance should either be made more convenient or the back door should become the entrance to the house. If you live in the kitchen and the living room is unused, make the kitchen larger and attractive enough to be used all the time as the living room and put the living room space to better use.

OWNER   Judd Woldin
LOCATION   South Orange, New Jersey

Built in the 1890's, this grand old shingle house
is the home of a pianist-composer, his wife, and
four small children. It is a big, happy house in
spite of its foreboding appearance. The ponderous
gable that hovers over the entrance only focuses
attention on the ersatz window and emphasizes the
ungainly height of the roof, which is basically
seventeenth-century English. (Dutch and Flemish
gambrel roofs are not quite as steep.) Windows
of different sizes and shapes helped to produce a
restless cold façade and give the house an empty
look. Removing the gable and continuing the
dormers across the roof make the façade less
top-heavy and move the center of interest down
to the entrance. The front door is painted so the
entrance stands as a unit, but the nice old woodwork and careful details are left just as they were.
The new sash with diamond-shaped panes recre-
ates some of the English character, fills up the
blackness, and removes the vacant appearance of
the windows. Rectangular mullions, if small in
scale, would have done just as well.

House #14   Before

The site slopes sharply to the back and down to the existing garage. If you had a horse and buggy you would probably want them stabled away from the house, but it is much more convenient to have automobiles closer. The garage is reconstructed against a wall of the house for economy using the existing materials. The attached garage lengthens the façade and helps to lower the height of the house. In this way a more economical use of the lot frees the backyard for a garden and outdoor living areas. In making the driveway shorter, an advantage in itself, the traffic is kept safely away from where the children may be playing. The entrance terrace, up a few steps from the drive, leads easily to the front door. Landscaping should be kept simple, extending beyond the foundations so that it frames, but does not overpower, the house and make it look too dark.

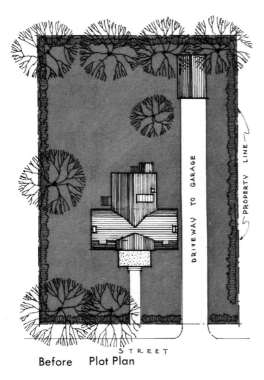

Before   Plot Plan

After   Plot Plan

House #14 *Continued*

One of the Woldins' first requirements was to move the piano and recording equipment out of the living room and away from the noisy activities of the children. An attic room is ideal for the new studio. A bath is economically provided by using the same location over the plumbing on the second floor. Before anything as heavy as a piano is planned for an attic or an upper floor, the stairs should be checked for adequate clearance and an architect or engineer should determine if the stairs and floor will support the additional weight.

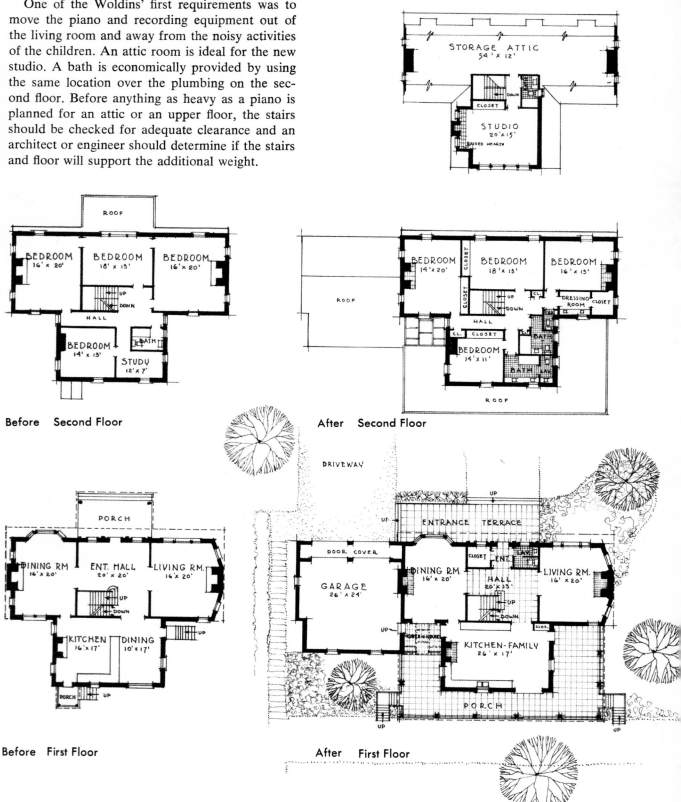

After   Attic Plan

Before   Second Floor

After   Second Floor

Before   First Floor

After   First Floor

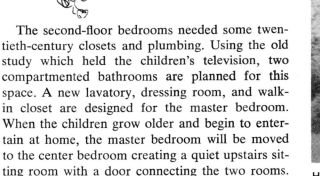

The second-floor bedrooms needed some twentieth-century closets and plumbing. Using the old study which held the children's television, two compartmented bathrooms are planned for this space. A new lavatory, dressing room, and walk-in closet are designed for the master bedroom. When the children grow older and begin to entertain at home, the master bedroom will be moved to the center bedroom creating a quiet upstairs sitting room with a door connecting the two rooms.

The entrance hall has been redesigned to provide a powder room and a walk-in closet for coats and sports equipment, but the hall still remains big by today's standards. The central axis of the gracious twin fireplaces in the living and dining rooms is retained. The greenhouse creates a garden view from the dining room all year and is large enough for a quiet breakfast for two after the children are off to school. It is also a convenient connection between the kitchen and the garage. The old kitchen fireplace is uncovered,

House #14 Before   Back

and counters and appliances are rearranged to form a large open space. The ovens and a bar are placed on the inside wall out of the way and close to the dining and living room doors. Because the back of the house is a full story above the ground, a porch on three sides of the kitchen-family room opens the first floor to the outdoors overlooking the gardens and children's play areas behind the house. The low flat line of the porch roof improves the back and ties the house to its surroundings.

OWNER   Stephan Kucko
LOCATION   Brookfield, Illinois

House #15   Before

Solid and compact little houses like this were built by the thousands during the twenties and thirties and called "bungalows" after the one-storied dwellings constructed in India. They had as much relation to their predecessors as the so-called "ranch houses" of today. You could get the design (always named something like "The Beverly" or "The Elmcrest") from any number of plan books, but unlike our instant housing these were built to last forever and they almost have.

Before remodeling, the house was a clutter of small, poorly placed rooms. Due to the narrow lot the house could expand only up or down, so it was decided to develop the existing basement and do away with any livable rooms in the low, hot attic. In order to get the circulation into workable form, the entrance was moved around to the sideyard that was too small for anything else. The rooms then fall off more comfortably to the left and right of the entrance halls on each floor. Having a bedroom off a dining room or a kitchen is not ideal, but in this case it worked out well and created fewer problems and less expense in partition changes. A combination dining room and kitchen twenty feet long and twelve feet wide is better than two cramped ten by twelve foot spaces.

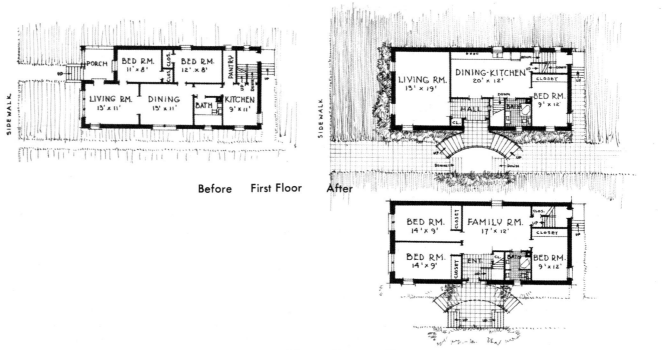

Before   First Floor   After

After   Basement Plan

After Remodeling

Since the children's rooms are downstairs, the back hall is retained, not only for the extra convenience, but also as a safety factor in case of fire. Children (or anybody else for that matter) should never be permitted to sleep in a basement without two exits in case of fire. A new furnace is placed in the attic and allows full use of the high, well-lit basement.

The windows are lengthened to the floor for additional light and air without really disturbing the arched windowheads and expensive brickwork. The removed bricks are to be reused to fill the openings left on the front, and this will also solve the problem of matching the old bricks. Simple flush balconies that neither add nor detract from the façade are placed in front of the French doors. The roof is trimmed up considerably by the removal of the bulky dormer. The gently curved reinforced concrete exterior entrance staircase may be extravagant, but it shelters the children's entrance and the little courtyard sunk below the level of the basement floor. The house assumes a French atmosphere, which is further heightened by touches in the woodwork and hardware.

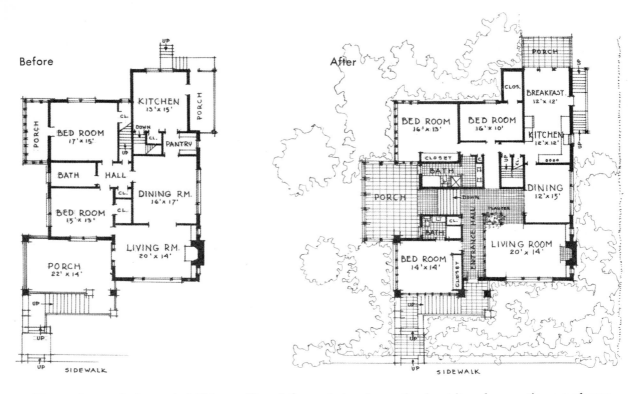

Before

After

The ageless and almost indelible quality of the Florida cottage is difficult and expensive to change. In the Cramer house, though, there is a streak of the Oriental often found in homes built around 1915, when the Japanese nation grew more important in world affairs and their culture more widely popularized. The influence is seen in the wide overhangs, the overlapping eaves, the suspended porch roof, and the gable vents. Without being dogmatic about it and recreating a teahouse, we can generate more of this charming character by using a ribbon of sliding windows in the new room. The plan requires a new bedroom and bath with some rearrangement both functionally and esthetically. By using the front porch and by filling in the odd corners at the back of the house, a better plan evolves. The hallways are used to circulate cool breezes through the house in both direc-

Before   After

OWNER   Katherine Cramer
LOCATION   Jacksonville, Florida

tions and yet block unwelcome views of bedroom and bathroom doors. The new porch is down a half-flight of stairs from the main floor and has a sloping ceiling that funnels the breeze up through the attic and out the other side of the house, thus creating its own movement of air even on the muggiest of days. The outside basement entrance is under the porch, cantilevered off the breakfast room into the dense green foliage in the back.

Before   House #16   Before

After

OWNER   E. A. Shelby
LOCATION   Dayton, Ohio

House #17   Before

Early, poorly planned prefabricated houses are sometimes thought to be "impossible" to remodel without extensive rebuilding, but this is not true. Because of the structural complexities involved in the prefab, a certain amount of extra care should be exercised in removing walls and partitions and changing the location of windows and doors. As happens so often in any house, the automobile was given the first consideration in the original house plan, and the garage was the most prominent section of the house. People had to fend for themselves in finding and getting to the front door hidden on the far side of the picture window—a good fifty feet from the driveway. A new loggia obscures the garage and changes the front of the house to the side away from the garage doors. The front door is moved so you can see it from the drive and framed by the loggia which leads you naturally to

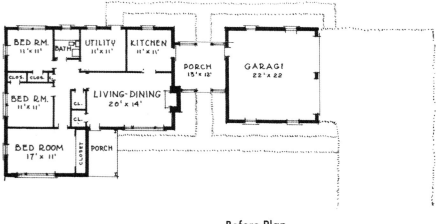

Before Plan

the main entrance. The interior changes are minimal but effective. The open porch is enclosed to provide a powder room and bath for the master bedroom and a hall so the entrance is not directly into the living room. It would be better if the living-room windows were not right beside the front door where arriving guests may have a full view of the interior if curtains are not drawn, but in this instance the situation was unavoidable. The kitchen is moved to make way for a dining room and a combination kitchen-family room is built into the enlarged porch connecting the garage to the house. New casement windows replace the ill-conceived picture windows. Some new garage doors have a less industrial appearance and are protected from the weather by the loggia.

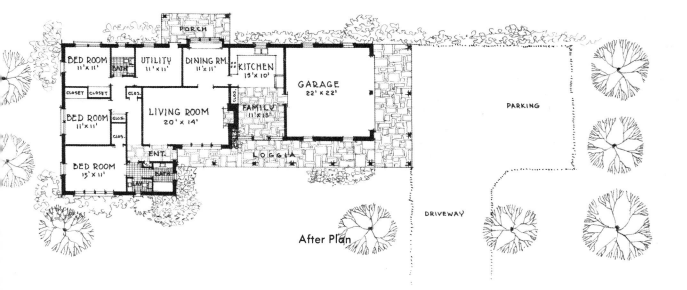

After Plan

When a large estate outside Philadelphia was subdivided, this carriage house and stable attracted everyone who saw it, but few knew what could be done to make it into a home. Dividing the interior space into rooms is not a serious problem. The most difficult part of this sort of remodeling is in keeping the robust charm that attracted you in the first place and still be able to add enough polish to make it habitable. Details must be refined to the basic elements and kept as simple as possible. One must resist the impulse to relax and just add shutters to everything. The old door, for instance, almost disappears, which is fine for a barn, but as a residence the entrance should make a statement—however quiet. With the door recessed to give it cover, and lumber uniting the two windows and door, the architecture is neither French nor Italian nor American Colonial; it is simply provincial. In other words, it's a farmhouse in any language. Masses of formal planting around the house would be pretentious and out of character. The fenced garden limits the gardening needed and keeps the headlights of oncoming cars out of the living room. On the interior, the living room is several steps above the dining room, separated by a massive stone fireplace. On the dining side the double steps flank a raised hearth, and a balcony off the master bedroom on the second floor overlooks the open-beamed ceiling.

OWNER   James E. Carberry
LOCATION   Easton, Pennsylvania

House #18   Before

Entrance After Remodeling

Before

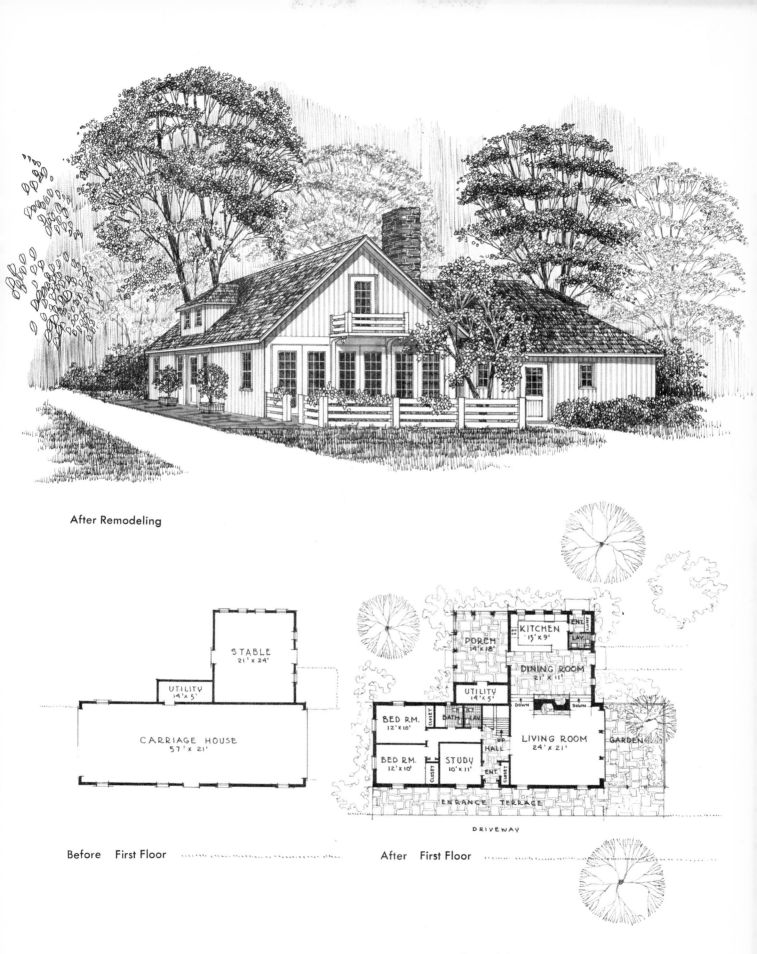

After Remodeling

Before   First Floor ·

STABLE
21' x 24'

UTILITY
14' x 5'

CARRIAGE HOUSE
57' x 21'

After   First Floor ·

PORCH
14' x 18'

KITCHEN
15' x 9'

ENT.

DINING ROOM
21' x 11'

UTILITY
14' x 5'

BED RM.
12' x 10'

BATH   LAV.

DOWN   DOWN

LIVING ROOM
24' x 21'

GARDEN

BED RM.
12' x 10'

STUDY
10' x 11'

UP HALL

ENT.

ENTRANCE   TERRACE

DRIVEWAY

Remodeling interior Space   155

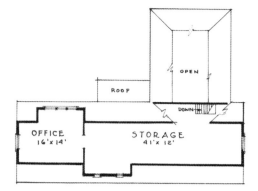

Before   Second Floor

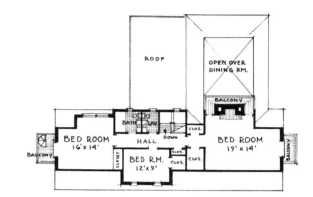

After   Second Floor

On the second floor the bathrooms of the first floor are repeated, built into a new dormer on the back. The master bedroom on the right has an interior balcony that projects over the fireplace in the dining room. An exterior balcony overlooking the fenced garden below is protection for the single French door which allows more sunlight into the room than a window without resorting to additional dormers. Another bedroom has a balcony with a circular stair—a detail as practical as it is decorative.

Before

After

Remodeling Two Ways

There is never just one answer for remodeling your home. Problems of circulation, lack of space for expansion or storage, simply improving the general comfort and appearance—all can be solved in different ways. There are as many moves in remodeling a house as there are on a chessboard, and just as many ways of creating a successful home as there are in winning a game of chess. In remodeling there is no opponent; you play both sides at the same time, balancing a budget, existing conditions, and available materials against basic requirements, desires, and dreams. The size of your budget is not as important as what you do with it. You can play chess with mass-produced plastic chessmen or with hand-carved antique ivory and jade pieces studded with precious stones. There should be as much pleasure and satisfaction in remodeling as in the final result of a remodeled home.

The design of your existing house will determine to a great extent the direction in which the remodeling goes—either to the formal or to the informal. This, in turn, will influence the arrangement of the rooms and how they are furnished. While the façade bears a definite relation to the interior, the number of elements on the exterior of the house and their juxtaposition to each other makes each result individual and gives each remodeled house a character of its own.

In remodeling your house part of the process an architect goes through is to decide the best answers and the correct moves to make. You may know what you want, but he knows the best way to get it for you. An architect knows when to follow the rules and when it is better to improvise. A house can be remodeled economically or lavishly. Within each level of investment there will be variety, but even in the most utilitarian remodeling there should be a bit of extravagance, of daring, of the unexpected. You can play a game of chess by the rules and follow the formal moves laid down by the book, but you may get very bored. You can remodel a house the same way, but it, too, will be dull. There are any number and variety of ways to remodel every house. The results depend only on your capacity to develop them.

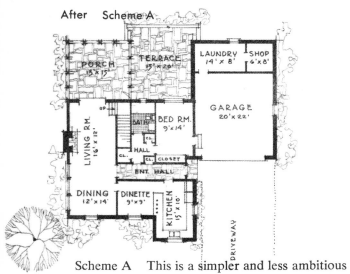

After   Scheme A

PORCH
15' x 15'

TERRACE
15' x 20'

LAUNDRY
14' x 8'

SHOP
6' x 8'

GARAGE
20' x 22'

LIVING RM.
16' x 12'

UP

BATH

BED RM.
9' x 14'

CL.

HALL

CL.

CL.   CLOSET

ENT. HALL

DINING
12' x 14'

DINETTE
9' x 9'

KITCHEN
15' x 10'

DRIVEWAY

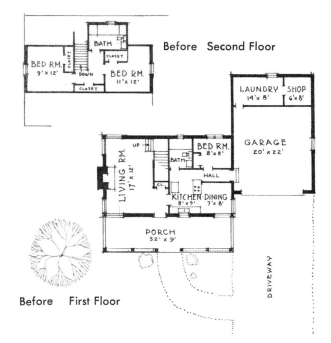

Before   Second Floor

BATH

BED RM.
9' x 12'

CLOSET

CLOSET

DOWN

BED RM.
11' x 12'

CLOSET

LAUNDRY
14' x 8'

SHOP
6' x 8'

GARAGE
20' x 22'

LIVING RM.
17' x 12'

UP

BED RM.
8' x 8'

BATH

CL.

HALL

KITCHEN
8' x 9'

DINING
7' x 8'

PORCH
32' x 9'

DRIVEWAY

Before   First Floor

Scheme A   This is a simpler and less ambitious design that uses only the existing space for remodeling. Here, the porch is enclosed so the downstairs may be expanded. A small projection of about sixty square feet enlarges the kitchen and relieves the exterior of a boxy look. The new entrance gains importance and is protected by a balcony off the bedroom.

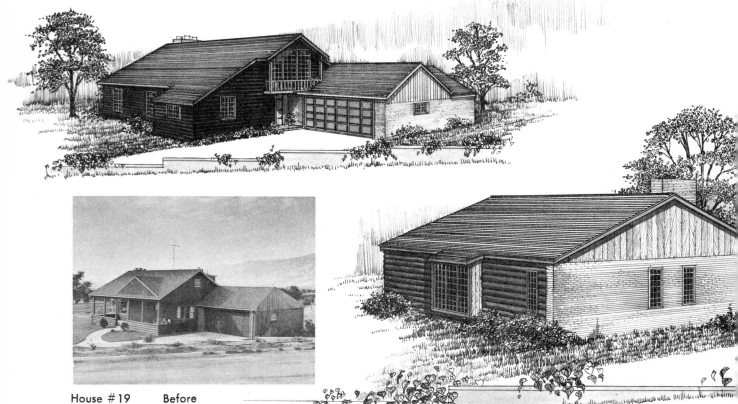

House #19   Before

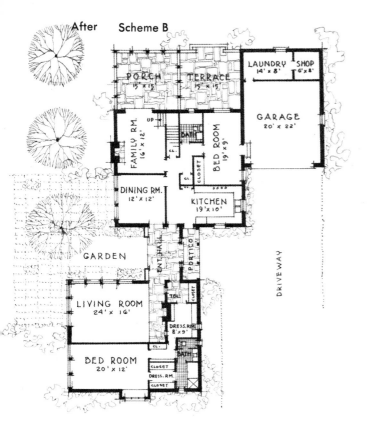

After Scheme B

PORCH 15'x15'
TERRACE 15'x15'
LAUNDRY 14'x8'
SHOP 6'x8'
GARAGE 20'x22'
FAMILY RM. 16'x12'
UP
BATH
BED ROOM 19'x9'
DINING RM. 12'x12'
CLOSET
KITCHEN 19'x10'
ENT. HALL
PORTICO
DRIVEWAY
GARDEN
LIVING ROOM 24'x16'
CLOSET
TOIL
DRESS. RM. 8'x9'
CL.
BATH
BED ROOM 20'x12'
CLOSET
DRESS. RM.
CLOSET

OWNER   I. E. Meacham

LOCATION   Bountiful, Utah

The romance of living in a log house was soon lost as the owners and their growing family faced a serious problem of room for expansion. There was also a challenge in the possibilities of remodeling a contemporary house with as rough and basic a material as logs. The "before" plan has the obvious faults in a house with four lively children—the entrance into the living room, the inadequate kitchen, the cramped dining area, a tiny downstairs bedroom, and the lack of any privacy on the first floor.

The new design leaves the second floor as is. The arboreal façade presents its own exercise. The biggest question was whether to cover the logs with another siding material or to use more logs in an effort to create a sophisticated exterior with an informal and rustic material.

Scheme B   The new living room and bedroom wing is similar in shape to the existing house and is connected to it with a flat-roofed brick portico and entrance. This establishes a separate section for the parents and children with complete privacy from each other. The new master bedroom has two dressing rooms and a compartmented bath. The small antechamber has a guest closet and is also used as a telephone room. Stained glass windows on each side of the fireplace are for decoration and create unusual lighting effects. The same brick of the garage is used in the new section for unity and will be left to weather and fade naturally so the contrast between the brick and the logs is not abrupt.

After   Scheme B

Scheme A

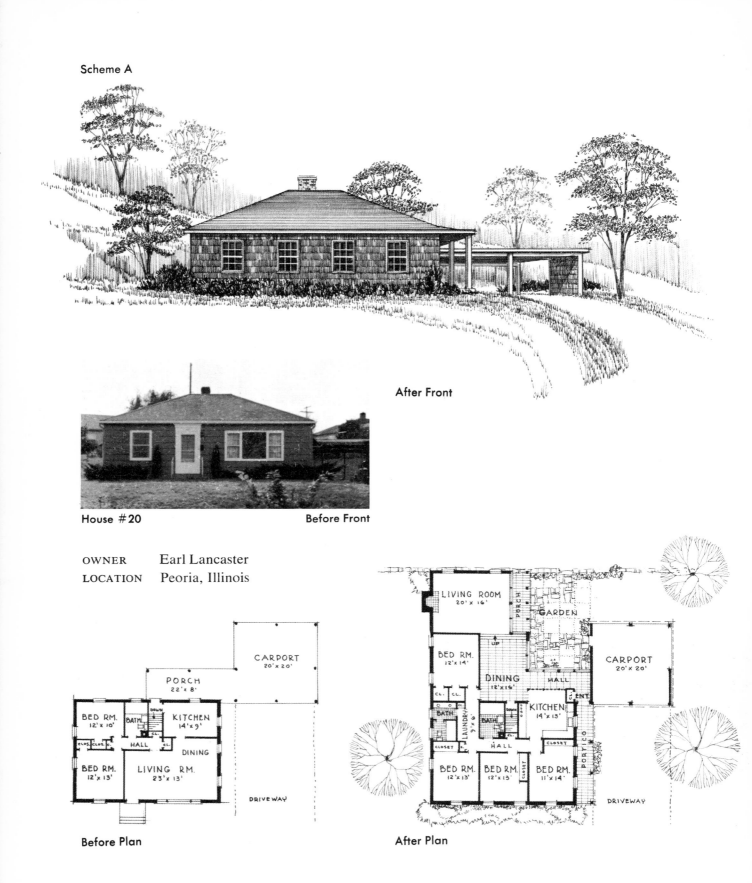

After Front

House #20   Before Front

OWNER   Earl Lancaster
LOCATION   Peoria, Illinois

CARPORT
20' x 20'

PORCH
22' x 8'

BED RM.
12' x 10'

BATH

KITCHEN
14' x 9'

CLOS. CLOS.

HALL

DINING

BED RM.
12' x 13'

LIVING RM.
23' x 13'

DRIVEWAY

Before Plan

LIVING ROOM
20' x 16'

PORCH

GARDEN

CARPORT
20' x 20'

BED RM.
12' x 14'

UP

CL. CL.

DINING
12' x 16'

HALL

BATH

LAUNDRY
9' x 6'

BATH

DOWN

KITCHEN
14' x 13'

ENT.

CLOSET

CL.

HALL

CLOSET

BED RM.
12' x 13'

BED RM.
12' x 13'

BED RM.
11' x 14'

PORTICO

DRIVEWAY

After Plan

Entrance

Although space is limited on a narrow suburban lot, you can still expand; if not out, then up. The first scheme adds two additional bedrooms, a bath, and a dining room with a 720-square foot expansion in the back of the house. The front door is replaced with a window and the "picture" part of the picture window is walled up. Without changing the location of any openings, a balanced façade replaces a jumble of door and windows.

In Scheme A, the front door is placed on a portico off the driveway. The existing rear porch is used to provide an entrance hall and to enlarge the kitchen. Moving none of the existing partitions, two new bedrooms are made out of the living room space. The back bedroom is changed to a large compartmented bath and a laundry. The bedroom and dining room built on the back of the house are flat-roofed, which simplifies the flashing and the connection with the existing flat porch roof. The new living room is roofed with a hip roof that repeats the line of the existing hip roof. The living room is raised several steps, resting on a low retaining wall and enclosing a secluded garden. New roofs, foundations, walls, and long hallways are sometimes the result of major remodeling of this sort, but it does have the advantage of adding just that space you need.

Before Back

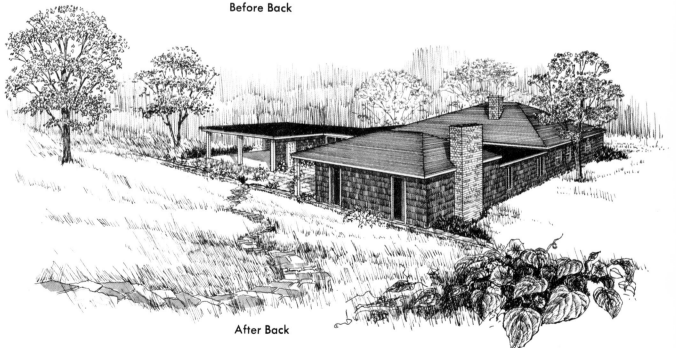

After Back

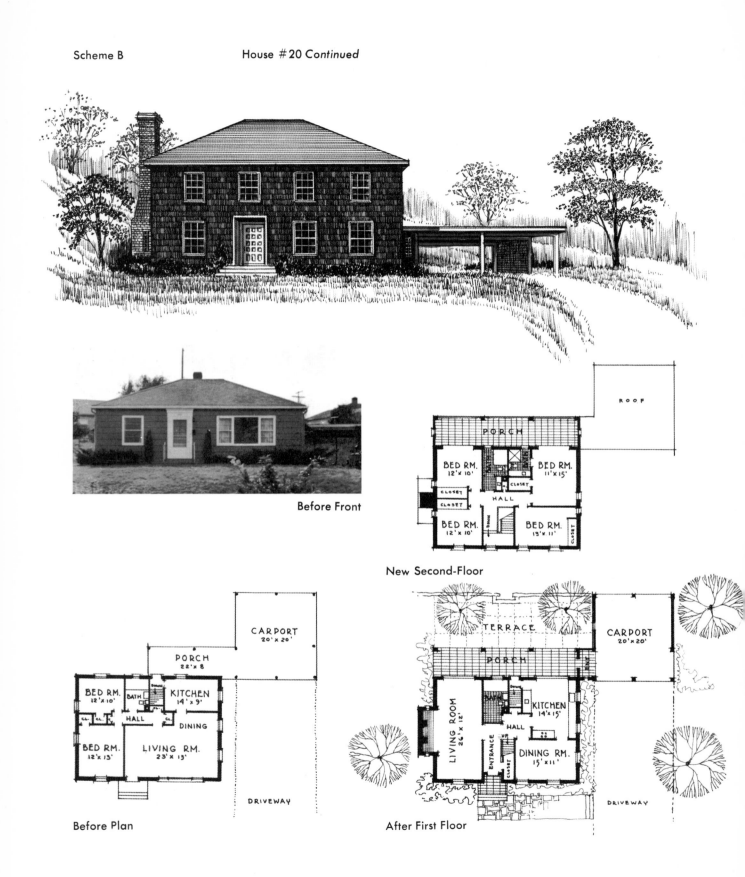

Before Front

New Second-Floor

CARPORT
20' x 20'

PORCH
22' x 8

BED RM.
12' x 10'

BATH

KITCHEN
14' x 9'

CL. CL.   HALL   CL.   DINING

BED RM.
12' x 13'

LIVING RM.
23' x 13'

DRIVEWAY

Before Plan

ROOF

PORCH

BED RM.
12' x 10'

BED RM.
11' x 15'

CLOSET

CLOSET

CLOSET

HALL

BED RM.
12' x 10'

DOWN

BED RM.
13' x 11'

CLOSET

TERRACE

CARPORT
20' x 20'

PORCH

LIVING ROOM
26' x 12'

BATH

KITCHEN
14' x 15'

HALL

ENTRANCE

CLOSET

DINING RM.
15' x 11'

DRIVEWAY

After First Floor

Adding a second floor can double the space inside and cost less proportionally than a ground floor addition because no new footings are required; flashing, plumbing, and heating are simplified; and less floor area is lost to hallways. Sometimes the roof can be lifted and re-used to cover the new floor, or much of the structural material can be incorporated in the new roof.

Two-story houses cost less to heat, and some people feel more secure sleeping on the second floor. But there are disadvantages in having a second story too; there are stairs to climb, the house is noisier than the same size one-story house, chimneys cost more, painting the exterior is more expensive, and in case of fire, escape is more difficult. Usually some of the difficulties are overcome by carpeting the second floor and the stairs to lessen noise, and by using siding materials that do not need paint. Foundations and first floor walls must be strong enough to support the added weight, and an engineer should check the roof to see if it can be lifted economically. The roof structure is reinforced, cut, and raised with a crane. New previously assembled walls are set in place, and the roof is lowered and secured. In a simple structure like this, rough carpentry should take only a day or two.

Again, the picture window is removed, and windows slightly smaller than the existing ones are used in the second floor to keep the façade from having a top-heavy look. The existing back porch is extended into a two-story porch with the ends closed to give additional privacy to the bedrooms. A living room twelve feet wide and twenty-six feet long would result in an unpleasant proportion without the projection and central mass of the raised hearth and fireplace. If the fireplace is omitted, the area should be divided into a living room and a smaller sitting room. Upstairs, two compartmented baths are placed directly over the existing plumbing stack on the first floor. A little over one thousand square feet has been added.

Before Back

After Back

OWNER   LeRoy Rapp
LOCATION   Red Wing, Minnesota

House #21   Before

Before Second Floor   After

Before First Floor   After

Before Basement   After

From Maine to Oregon, Tennessee to Minnesota, this house is typical of farmhouses that are scattered over the countryside. The existing plan is haphazard. It wastes space in the duplication of stairs; it has few closets; there is a bathroom that is almost inaccessible from the bedrooms; and it creates a circulation pattern that leads from one room directly into another.

Beginning with the driveway and using the slope of the hill, a portico is designed leading to an entrance hall in the basement. The basement area was not being used, and an entrance there is a fine and natural place for guests to stamp snow and mud from their boots. Wet coats and umbrellas can be hung in the adjoining laundry to dry. A staircase goes up to the main floor and a small hall that separates the living room from the dining-family room. Off the kitchen there is another entrance to a first floor bath that can be used by the family to shower and change when they come in from their chores. At the top of the stairs on the second floor there is a sewing room that could be used as a nursery. The bedrooms, although small, are well designed for double or twin beds, and there is ample closet space. Two baths are added to the second floor without increasing the exterior perimeter of the foundation.

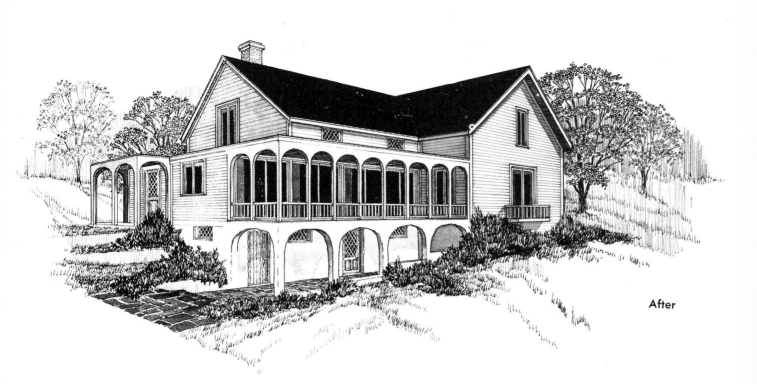

After

Both exteriors use the same remodeling plan, but the first has a cloister with an open porch above. Sliding glass doors along the length of the dining room and kitchen extend the size and visual area. The second exterior has a two-story portico along the front. Small balconies projected in front of the single French doors are decorative and make the windows easier to clean. The laundry door is treated inconspicuously so one is naturally drawn to the more formal front door.

After

House #21 *Continued*   Scheme B

Before Second Floor   **After**

Before

Before First Floor   **After**

Scheme B of the Rapp house is designed to have a new entrance on the main floor off a circular drive. The center hall runs through the house connecting all the rooms to a porch on each floor. The new basement wall lets light and ventilation into the laundry, and the basement will get more and better use than it has in the past. A combination family room and kitchen permit a small study or office on the first floor. The balcony off the master bedroom on the second floor may seem an extravagance at first, but even on the tightest remodeling budget an extra touch such as this is justified by the pleasure and individuality it will contribute over the years.

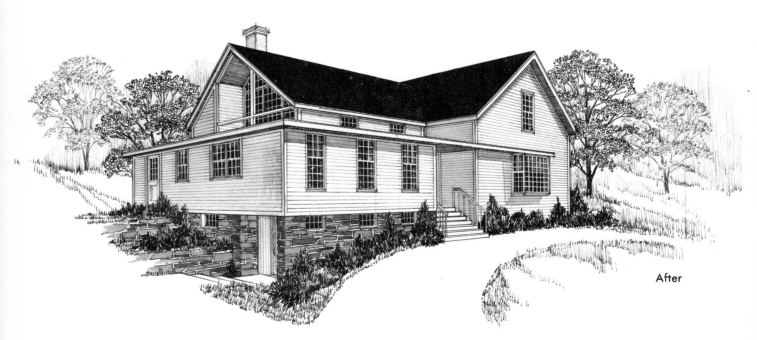

After

What to Add

Deciding just what to add to your home is not as elementary as it might sound. What you add will depend greatly on how successfully you are using your present space. The solution is not simply to go on building additions until the house finally functions in a cohesive pattern. If an additional bedroom is needed, you cannot improve your basic plan by building it so you must pass through another bedroom to get to it. It might be better to change a small living room into another bedroom and build a new living room.

Property lines, setback regulations, zoning ordinances, prevailing breezes, a view, large trees, subsoil conditions, or other site restrictions may predetermine where and how large your addition will be. Your basic house will help determine the style and manner in which the addition is built. Price ranges of similar property in the neighborhood and your own financial situation will govern the amount spent on the new addition.

Whatever you add to your home should do four things: increase the comfort, convenience, value, and appearance of your property. Additions should not create inaccessible rooms, add seemingly endless hallways, overpower the site or neighborhood, or take you to the verge of bankruptcy. Finally, additions should not be built until the present structure is equal to the design and appearance of what you plan to add.

If your remodeling plans do not completely fulfill your desires and needs, or you are not sure of the present condition of your home and any possible restrictions in remodeling, consult a professional architect or qualified builder. You will save time, effort, and needless expense in the end by careful planning in the beginning.

Before Plan

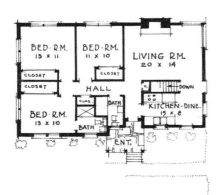

BED·RM. 13 x 11
BED·RM. 11 x 10
LIVING RM. 20 x 14
CLOSET
CLOSET
CLOSET
HALL
BATH
KITCHEN-DINE. 15 x 8
DOWN
BED·RM. 13 x 10
BATH
ENT.

After Plan

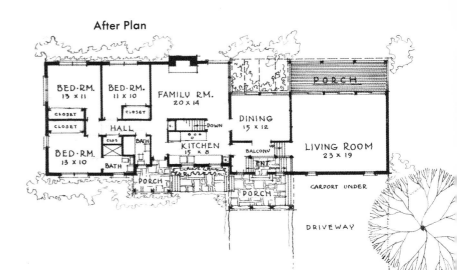

BED·RM. 13 x 11
BED·RM. 11 x 10
FAMILY RM. 20 x 14
PORCH
CLOSET
CLOSET
CLOSET
HALL
DINING 15 x 12
LIVING ROOM 23 x 19
BED·RM. 13 x 10
BATH
KITCHEN 15 x 8
DOWN
BALCONY
ENT.
PORCH
UP
PORCH
CARPORT UNDER
DRIVEWAY

The existing brick house, although basically a sound plan, had become too small for a family with three growing children. They wanted to add a family room, a dining room, and a carport as inexpensively as possible. The house was in good shape and nothing needed to be changed except some cabinet work in the kitchen. The living room is in an excellent location to become a family room. An arbored garden between the family room and the living room grows plants and vines in the summer to keep the sun out of the dining room. The living-room porch shades the high windows that extend into the gable.

The back of the house was originally much less attractive than the front and looked "chopped-off"—as though waiting to be completed. The original roof line is carried over the new dining room, and the living room is roofed with a raised gable which brings the elevation to a more logical conclusion. The high windows of the two rear bedrooms are lowered and protected with a balcony.

Before Back

After Back

Entrance Hall

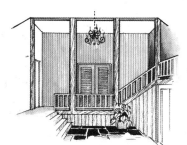

Here the entrance hall is the tie between the carport, driveway, living room, and the dining room. A storage room under the dining room is accessible from the carport so bicycles, garden equipment, and other impedimenta can be kept out of the weather and out of sight. Vertical siding already existed beside the door, making it an easy choice as the material for the new addition, since wood is quicker and less expensive to build with than brick. Brick does not look well suspended over a large opening and should never be cantilevered. If the carport is converted into a garage, the lower portion might be built of brick to match the house. It would be fireproof and lengthen the façade. Low stone walls terrace the lawn down to the level of the driveway and help focus attention on the entrance instead of on the carport.

OWNER   Peter Cassanos
LOCATION   Lynchburg, Virginia

Before Front   House #22

After Front

Although a big house to start, there just did not seem to be enough space for a family interested in hobbies and art. Privacy on the corner lot was not a problem when the house was first built, but soon the neighborhood seemed to surround them. Air-conditioning units set up in front of the windows help screen out the exterior view but they disrupt the basic design of the house and are ugly.

Most of the house stayed as it was—even to the closet in the new entrance hall. An efficient kitchen, two bedrooms, and a bath are the only additions to the interior. This new plan creates a new house built around a courtyard, away from the noise and dust of the street, shaded by trees, and cooled by a fountain. Another enclosed garden off the living room uses shutters to close off the street. Shutters allow the breezes to blow through but keep out sun and rain. Paving is carried off the covered porch into the plants that border the fence to increase the apparent size of the living room garden. A new wall of sliding glass doors makes the garden an integral part of the

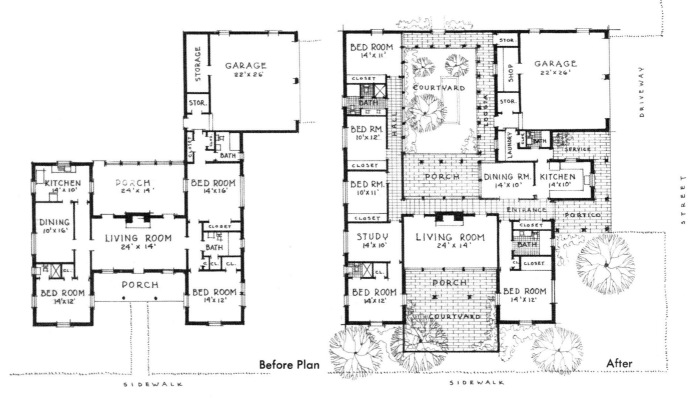

Before Plan

After

Before   House #23

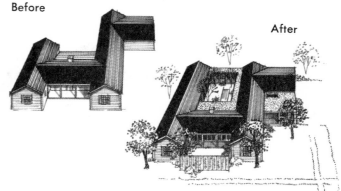

After

OWNER   Alvin Weidner
LOCATION   Gordon, Texas

living room, especially at night when flickering candles and concealed spotlights illuminate the green wall of plants. The new entrance hall is moved to the quieter side street. A dining room is planned, but most of the formal entertaining will take place on the porch overlooking the courtyard. The air conditioning will be built into the attic space, but the house is designed so that the natural flow of air through the rooms from open windows and doors will cool the house in all but the hottest and most humid weather. Room air-conditioning units do not have to be placed in the windows; and if a central system is not needed, it is much more attractive to build the room units in the wall. Porches keep out rain in sudden cloudbursts, and the house never needs to be closed up in hot weather. With access doors locked, the glass walls of the interior can be left open with complete security. It is not enough to simply look out into a garden, you must be able to walk in it also. As refreshing as air conditioning can be, it is not always pleasant to spend your life in an artificial atmosphere.

A bird's-eye view best shows where the two bedrooms and bath were added. The new kitchen is under the flat-roofed section on the right with a skylight over the service door. Flat-roofed porches surround the courtyard which can be enjoyed in all weather. The concept of a residence built around a court is as old as history itself and was used by the Egyptians several thousands of years before Christ. The idea has only recently been adopted in general terms in the United States, but it is a natural outgrowth of more crowded conditions and a search for privacy.

Before Backyard

After Courtyard

After Remodeling

The big tree was mature when the house was new, and now, eighty years later, they are both still in good condition. As the tree grew larger, the house (by today's standards) grew smaller. Some changes in the house had been made in the past; thirty years ago a bathroom was added and running water put in the kitchen. Another member of the family who was handy added a little touch over the front door, and somebody else put on new siding. But now the family is ready to spend some real money on a home in a fine and convenient neighborhood, and the house is ready to begin life over again for at least another eighty years. Of course, the tree stays. Remodeling involved little restoration because the house has no real historical value as Architecture, but a few details such as the addition of corner pieces, the replacement of shutters on the side windows, and the creation of authentic millwork on the entrance, greatly changed the exterior appearance. The planting around the front is replaced or severely cut back, and the house is given a setting to prepare it for the new L-shaped wing to be added to the back.

OWNER   Fred Foppe
LOCATION   Breese, Illinois

House #24   Before

The new entrance on the street is more in character with the house but admittedly will not keep snow and rain off the door, so the front hall is paved with brick. A family entrance to the house is on the auto court, where a small hall with a closet leads to the family room. The brick floor of the hall carries over into the family room and joins the hearth. The double doors between the family room and the living room are opposite the new fireplace so the living room is in view of the fire. The dining room has its own small hearth and is partitioned off from the entrance and the stairs, which also cuts off any drafts from the front door. The existing second floor is about as convenient as could be planned without destroying the Colonial exterior and is left untouched. Two bedrooms and two baths, a breezeway, and a garage are added in the L-shaped wing. There is a bathroom off the hall convenient to the kitchen and family room. The larger bedroom has a dressing room and a walk-in closet. Eventually this section of the house can be converted into a rentable apartment.

When you are remodeling a house with such strong Colonial overtones, it is important not to obliterate them. The second-floor bedrooms, for instance, could have been made larger with a shed dormer on the front, but, as mentioned before, it would have ruined the established character of the house. Additions should be kept simple in line and restrained in decoration, or they will overpower and you will lose the original design. Doors and windows need special attention to avoid a bizarre combination of styles. The entrance detail shown here is only one of many that are available at reasonable prices from almost every lumber yard or millwork company. It is customary now to hang shutters on the exterior solely for color, but they usually look artificial too. It would be much better to have workable shutters such as these, which can be closed in winter on certain windows. In warmer climates, workable shutters can be used to keep the house cool. You will save heat and eliminate the necessity for storm windows which are usually distracting on a Colonial house.

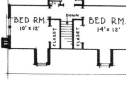

Second Floor

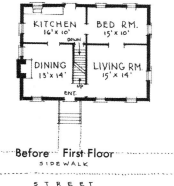

Before First Floor

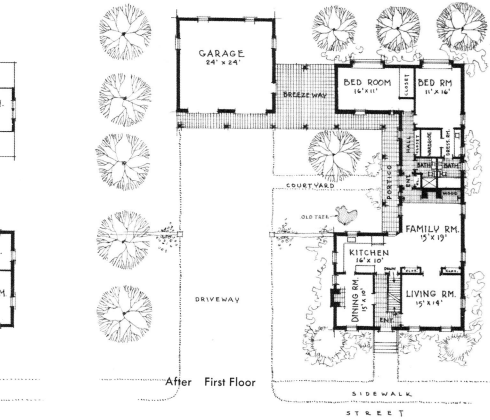

After First Floor

This remodeling presented a special problem because Mrs. Andersen is handicapped by muscular dystrophy. The couple bought "this sad little house" because of its small size and excellent location with the idea of remodeling the first floor. Everything is redesigned so that a handicapped person could be independent and useful even though confined to a wheelchair. The kitchen is planned so a seated person would have full control of food preparation and cleaning up. The counters are low with leg space underneath—just like a desk top. Dishes are easily accessible from low open shelves over the sink. The range top is designed with heating units in a row so there is work space in front of it, eliminating the danger of reaching over a hot unit—a safety feature and design that should be incorporated in many kitchens. Trash cans are in a cabinet with an inside and outside door. Garbage is emptied into cans from the inside and removed from the outside. Above this is another insulated two-way cabinet, where milk and other groceries are delivered from the exterior without disturbing anyone.

House #25   Before

There are a number of special considerations in a design where physical limitations exist. Many of them may well be kept in mind when designing for the elderly. Windows should be lower to minimize the danger of being trapped in a fire, and

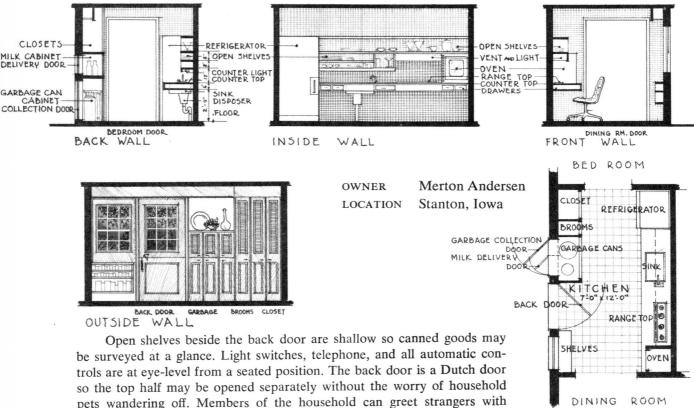

CLOSETS
MILK CABINET DELIVERY DOOR
GARBAGE CAN CABINET COLLECTION DOOR
BEDROOM DOOR
BACK WALL

REFRIGERATOR
OPEN SHELVES
COUNTER LIGHT
COUNTER TOP
SINK
DISPOSER
FLOOR
INSIDE WALL

OPEN SHELVES
VENT AND LIGHT
OVEN
RANGE TOP
COUNTER TOP
DRAWERS
DINING RM. DOOR
FRONT WALL

BACK DOOR   GARBAGE   BROOMS   CLOSET
OUTSIDE WALL

OWNER   Merton Andersen
LOCATION   Stanton, Iowa

BED ROOM
CLOSET
BROOMS
GARBAGE COLLECTION DOOR
MILK DELIVERY DOOR
BACK DOOR
SHELVES
REFRIGERATOR
GARBAGE CANS
SINK
KITCHEN 7'-0" x 12'-0"
RANGE TOP
OVEN
DINING ROOM

Open shelves beside the back door are shallow so canned goods may be surveyed at a glance. Light switches, telephone, and all automatic controls are at eye-level from a seated position. The back door is a Dutch door so the top half may be opened separately without the worry of household pets wandering off. Members of the household can greet strangers with more safety as the Dutch doors discourage them from coming into the house unasked.

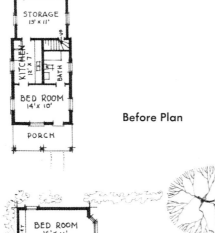

Before Plan

STORAGE
13' x 11'

KITCHEN
12' x 7'

BATH

BED ROOM
14' x 10'

PORCH

BED ROOM
16' x 11'

CLOSET

KITCHEN
12' x 7'

BATH

HEAT

DINING RM.
14' x 10'

ENT.

CL.

LIVING RM.
14' x 19'

PORCH

PORCH

After   First Floor

SIDEWALK

also to allow anyone sitting down or lying in bed to see out. Windows should face the street in several rooms so that anyone confined to the house can share in the activities and life of the neighborhood. It is a great comfort to wave to friends from a window and exchange the latest news. Windows should be easy to open and clean and comparatively narrow for privacy within the room. Doors and hallways should be at least three feet wide without thresholds for easy maneuvering of wheelchairs, and entrances should be designed so you can see who is calling before the door is opened. Raised planters can make gardening fun without much effort, or simply set some big clay pots up on a sturdy bench. A fireplace with a raised hearth also eliminates a lot of stooping and is easier to light and clean. Bathrooms should have plenty of firmly anchored grab-bars around the walls, and the room should be large enough for an invalid to have help when needed. Of course the bathroom and all other floors except the kitchen should be carpeted to cushion possible falls. Slippery floors and loose rugs are a hazard in any home. Even the porch can be covered with exterior grade weatherproof carpet. A built-in vacuum cleaning system throughout the house is a light and easy appliance to manipulate.

SHOP
12'x16'

GARAGE
24'x18'

DRIVEWAY

House #26   Before

Before Plan

PORCH
14'x7'

KITCHEN
14'x14'   BATH   BED RM.
                   10'x14'

CL   UP

LIVING RM.   BED RM.
18'x13'   13'x13'

PORCH

Before Attic

ATTIC
31'x12'   DOWN

After   First Floor

SHOP
12'x16'

GARAGE
24'x18'

LOGGIA

DRIVEWAY

LIVING ROOM
23'x13'

LAUNDRY
10'x6'

CL.

KITCHEN
14'x14'

BATH

BED ROOM
18'x14'

HALL

ENT.

FAMILY RM.
15'x10'

CLOSET

BED ROOM
13'x13'

CLOSET

GARDEN

After   Second Floor

BED RM.
11'x14'

CLOSET

HALL

BED RM.
10'x17'

ROOF

CLOS.

DOWN

CLOSET

ROOF

CLOSET

ROOF

ROOF

OWNER   Robert Corbin
LOCATION   Catlin, Illinois

The dash between the kitchen and the garage was pretty cold on wintry mornings, but the little farmhouse had more serious problems than that. There was no real design, circulation or privacy at all within the house. The entrance to the basement was through a bedroom. From the front bedroom the bath was either through the back bedroom or through the living room and the kitchen. More and better bedrooms and a family room that could be used as a dining room are needed. There was almost enough existing space for everything if you include the unfinished attic. With the addition of a well-designed living room, the present areas are put to better use. The old basement stairs were in very poor location, and they are changed so the same stairwell can be used for stairs to the second floor. The bathroom on the first floor is large enough, but the fixtures are relocated to allow a better bath. The first thing to move is the tub from under the window. This opens things up so several arrangements are pos-

sible. The arrangement used here is duplicated directly above for a second-floor bathroom. A rear entrance off the kitchen is worked out so it also contains the laundry—an advantage on a busy farm when you want to keep soiled work clothes out of the bedrooms. A porch connects with the garage, uniting garage and house into one unit giving the impression that the house is much larger than it really is. The second-floor bedrooms are built into a large shed dormer. A downstairs bedroom is pushed out eight feet so it will hold twin beds. To get light and fresh air into the upstairs hall, a single dormer is built on the front. Another could have been placed in the bedroom to even things up, but it would have shortened the closet space and would not be needed either for light or appearance. The single dormer has much more weight and charm than two ever would. A low stone wall around the entrance is attractive and has practical value by keeping wandering farm animals out of the roses.

House #27   Front   Before

The Bartletts' remodeling problem is shared by thousands of other families who bought houses in Levittowns or similar housing developments all over the country. After years of apartment-dwelling, the low-cost houses were a dream come true. Ten years (and several children) later however, the house that seemed so spacious after a city apartment is too small. The conformity of look-alike neighborhoods is too depressing, but the value of the homes has increased, and what was once almost an experiment in suburban living has become valuable property. In addition, and what is probably more important, the family's friends,

OWNER   Ralph Bartlett
LOCATION   Levittown, Pennsylvania

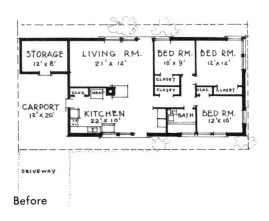

Before

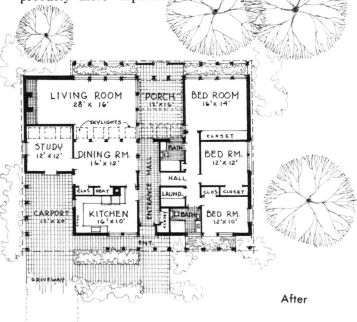

After

schools, church, shopping center, and clubs are in this neighborhood, making it easier and better for the family to remodel than to move.

If nothing else were done, a simple re-arrangement of partitions would produce a better house. An entrance hall with a closet separates the bedrooms from the rest of the house and is so definite an improvement that it is hard to say why it was not done when the house was built. The addition of a living room and a master bedroom with flat roofs in the back of the house circumvents expensive changes in the existing trussed roof. By eliminating some of the openings in the kitchen, the area can be reorganized into cabinets and countertop. The floor-to-ceiling kitchen windows on the front are retained because the room needs the light but they are replaced with mullioned sash. The front door is at the same place as the old one, but at least now the entrance into the house is not through the kitchen even though you may be able to see into it. A skylight and the leaded glass of the door allows sunlight into an otherwise dark entrance hall. A sliding glass door replaces one of the high windows in the front bedroom, but there is still enough space for twin beds. Columns, placed under the existing overhang, hold the façade together instead of letting it split into separate elements. A screened area in front of the bathroom and bedroom windows and between the columns blocks the view from the street into the bedroom and provides a sense of security for the room. The large windows in the back of the house are screened in the same way, and the porch could become the entrance if, as so often happens in developments, the house were turned around and the living room faced the street. The porch is only partially covered, and a row of ten skylights at the intersection of the trussed and flat roofs lights any dark corners of the interior. Columns between the living room at the line of the old wall support the existing roof.

Back   Before

Back   After Remodeling

(House #27 Continued)

An unusual and rather fascinating detail of the Bartlett remodeling is the screened overhang used on the front bedroom and along the back of the house. Instead of screening the windows and doors, the screen is placed at the edge of the roof and supported by columns about four feet on center. The fixed screen is much less expensive to buy and replace than operating screen doors, and rain splashing off the screen cannot get the glass dirty. There is an increased sense of freedom and privacy within the rooms because they can be open to the outdoors without insects, birds, stray animals, or people walking through the house. The narrow corridors along the outside can be heavily planted or used as a passage between one part of the house and another. Lighted at night they can be almost as effective as a wall in creating privacy.

Remodeling Step by Step

Remodeling step by step does not mean that remodeling will be absolutely painless or that you need to plan one stage at a time. Each current step will be less of a shock to your budget, but over a period of years you will have paid more for the entire remodeling than if it had been done all at once. That is, of course, if you pay to have it done. If you can do some of it yourself, or if you hire a helper and can accomplish another step during each season, you may be able to cut the cost of the remodeling by as much as half. Doing it a stage at a time will also mean that the house is going to be disorganized frequently and it requires a very understanding spouse to live through the various stages of construction.

In either case, you will need a meticulous and detailed plan and schedule so that each finished step becomes an integral part of the completed project. Each step must complement the next one but actually be complete in itself. Inevitably there will be elements that are temporary, set up one year only to be removed or relocated as the next stage is approached. Second thoughts and any changes in the plan may have a telling effect on the next step, with unfortunate consequences to the end result.

You must begin the planning by determining the final stage and working backwards. Establish what you hope to accomplish and how far you would like to go with each step. Then, and probably the most difficult part of all, you should work toward the goal that has been set without changing the plans.

House #28   Before

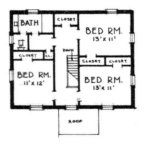

Before   Second Floor

Before   First Floor

OWNER   Ronald Shinabarker
LOCATION   Mansfield, Ohio

Resting in the middle of five-and-a-half acres of valuable rolling countryside laced with four rambling streams, any improvement in the old farmhouse should be a worthwhile investment. Despite its initial appearance this straightforward square house is one of the easiest to develop. There is a lot to work with—the house has a sound structure, good roof, and simple lines. Removing the crude porch and applying a good coat of paint would be one way to begin, but with no neighborhood to restrict the long-range plan, the remodeling is designed to take place in six stages. It was never very clear why the door was built on the second floor, since the porch roof hardly qualifies as a terrace, but with four small children playing about that is the first thing to be changed. The second-floor bedrooms and the large bath are surprisingly well planned and may be left as they are until the fourth stage is reached; even then only the bath receives major attention.

Second Stage of Remodeling

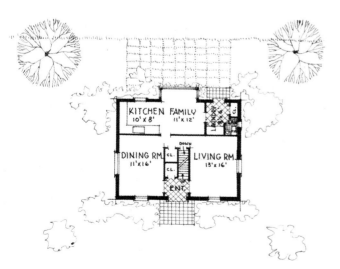

First Floor   Second Stage

After the mechanical side of the house is in top shape (the first step in every remodeling), the second stage begins to show the rewards of careful planning. New weather-stripped windows replace the leaky and disintegrating ones. From a design standpoint it would have been better if the second-floor windows were slightly smaller than the lower ones, but it is less expensive to replace them with windows of the same size as a different size would have required patching. Double Colonial front doors and entrance detail definitely establish the style that will prevail throughout the remaining remodeling steps. With another entrance and windows the style could have been changed to French, Italian or Spanish. A hall closet for coats is backed up with another to hold a baby carriage, card tables, and the children's games. The pass-through from the kitchen to the family room is blocked off and a formal dining room begins to take shape. A square bay window enlarges the kitchen area so it can be used as a combination kitchen-family room. Simple landscaping, to be transplanted later, completes the second step.

Third Stage of Remodeling

Second Floor   Third Stage

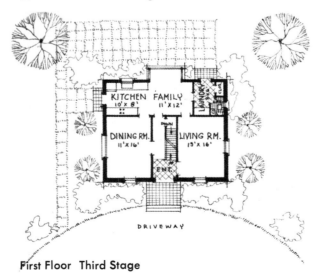

First Floor   Third Stage

Before

The third phase of the remodeling might be used as an alternate plan for the second or combined with the fourth stage. If the remodeling were to stop here, then brick veneer would be the third step. Brick veneer, more expensive than paint, may be cheaper than new siding and paint; and brick also eliminates future painting expense. The condition of the existing siding and the cost of masonry will determine which is the least expensive. However, if the way is clear for a fourth step, brick veneer should be postponed until then. At this point the kitchen is re-designed for additional counter space and in preparation for the new family room addition.

Fourth Stage of Remodeling

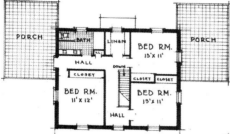

Second Floor   Fourth Stage

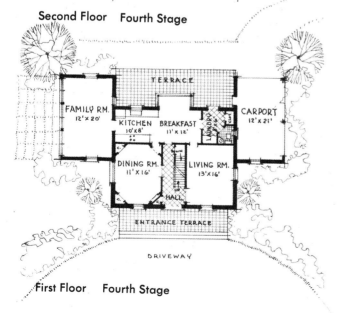

First Floor   Fourth Stage

The development of the wings, one for the garage and one for the family room, begins in the fourth stage. Only a carport is added now because a two-car garage will be needed eventually. The entrance platform is expanded into a wide terrace across the front, and a rear terrace is built between the two new wings. In anticipation of future remodeling, no brick veneer is placed on the exterior of the family room and carport. However, exterior grade plywood sheathing may be added and exposed indefinitely if it is kept painted. The new family room will remove some of the daily wear and tear, so the dining room can be completed with the addition of fine wood paneling and china cabinets to create a formal octagonal or oval room. A small guest closet in the hall is concealed behind one of the cabinets. Upstairs, new doors on the bedroom closets make them more useful and attractive. The bathroom is remodeled, and the existing window is changed into a door for access to the second floor's porch. A large storage closet may be used for linen and off-season clothing.

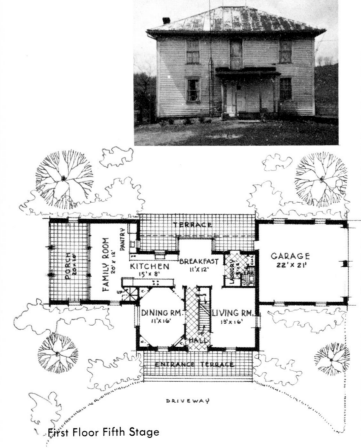

Before

First Floor Fifth Stage

Fifth Stage of Remodeling

The fifth step of the remodeling is the completion of the garage and the addition of a porch off the family room. The kitchen is expanded, and a separate bar for the children's snacks and soft drinks is planned for the family room. The circular stair to the second floor will wait for the final stage of the remodeling. Windows in the closed ends of the porch permit extended use of the area by controlling the air circulation. The completed first floor of the wings may be veneered now or left in painted plywood. On the second floor (*not shown*) no change is planned at this stage except for a balcony across the back connecting the two upstairs porches and sheltering the back doors and the kitchen window. The heating, plumbing, and electrical work has already been done in the walls and ceiling of the garage and family room in preparation for the sixth and final step of the remodeling. The ceiling rafters are sized to support the anticipated weight of the new rooms that will be built above them. The insulation on the ceiling of the family room will not be wasted since it will help deaden the sound transmitted to the new bedrooms. Full insulation should be placed in the garage walls and ceiling in the event that rooms are added here at a later time.

Sixth Stage of Remodeling

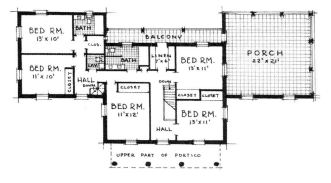

Second Floor Sixth Stage

The sixth and final stage of the remodeling adds bedrooms and baths over the family room and a large sleeping porch over the garage. The two-story portico on the front may be added now or as a later development. The distressed little house we began with has come a long way. It might be called Georgian or Southern Colonial, but it is doubtful if it will ever be called "hopeless" again. With careful planning any house can experience, if not exactly this, a similar transformation.

If more space is needed in the future for more bedrooms, an office, a studio, or even an apartment for grandparents, the sleeping porch can be readily enclosed.

Sixth Stage, from the Back

Front   First Stage of Remodeling

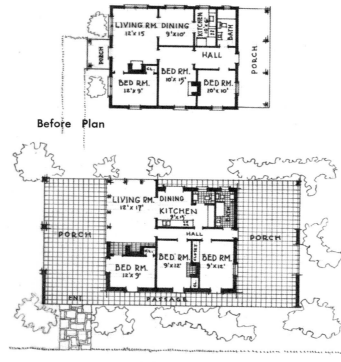

Before Plan

Plan First Stage

OWNER   Mrs. Lois B. Ingram
LOCATION   Moorehead, Mississippi

House #29   Before Front

As different as night and day from the Shina-barkers' traditional remodeling, this country house requires a modern concept. The changes can be broken down into three major stages or many more modest steps. Located in a warm climate, the house looked cramped, stuffy, and hot.

The first step of the remodeling is to open up the house. The living room walls are replaced with sliding glass doors. French doors replace most of the conventional old windows to reduce the feeling of enclosure and permit maximum air circulation. Two of the existing bedrooms are redesigned for more privacy and convenience. The kitchen is taken out of its present small space and given elbow room in the old dining room. Two broad porches shade the windows and siphon the breeze through the house. The economical flat roofs simplify flashing, connections to the existing hip roof, and future additions. The porch on the left will be used as an extension of the living room and the porch on the right as a sleeping porch.

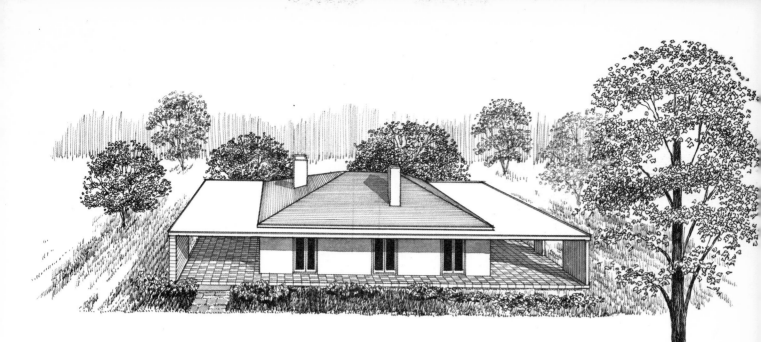

Front   First Stage of Remodeling

The front elevation is unpretentious and completely devoid of ornamentation. Down lights in the ceiling of the porches and overhangs cast a soft glow on the yellow walls and on the tile floors at night. Central heating and air conditioning can be placed in the attic, but in this climate, as in any other, they should implement the natural heating and cooling effects that can be built into a house. Although this is considered as the first step in the remodeling, it could have been broken into five or six smaller stages. The bedrooms might have been the first area to be finished, then the kitchen and bathrooms, followed by the living room and the addition of one or both porches.

The back of the house reflects the same austere façade as the front; however, this is relieved by the verdant foliage of the area. As it was before, this side of the house was ignored but with the sliding glass doors of the living room and the French doors of the kitchen opening onto it, this will eventually become the center of the house.

Before Back

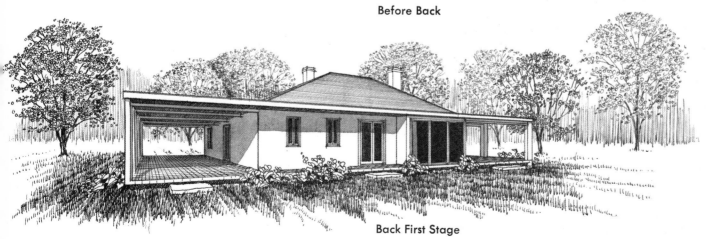

Back First Stage

Front   Second Stage

Front   Before

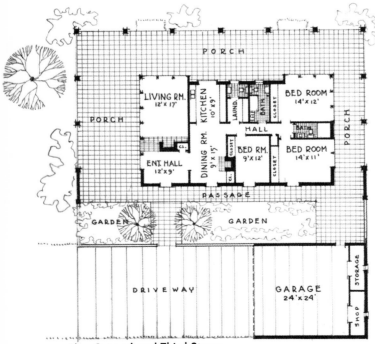

Plan Second and Third Stage

The second step of the remodeling adds two bedrooms and another bath along the porch created in the first stage. The porch is extended along the back of the house and screened so the interior and exterior merge effecting a pavilion atmosphere with the porches furnished and used as outdoor rooms. As the family grows and five bedrooms will not be needed, an entrance hall and a dining room will replace one or both of the original bedrooms. The severity of the façade can be softened with an antique door and sidelights which will also emphasize the entrance.

Front   Third Stage

The final stage of the remodeling includes the addition of a carport and a garden wall at the edge of the driveway. Hollow tile or concrete chimney block can be used to construct the wall which will require no maintenance and will permit the breeze to flow in and around the house with no hot pockets of still air. For this and the other steps of the remodeling, concrete and concrete block have been used to discourage termites and other insects. The flat roof is finished in white marble chips to reflect the heat of the sun and the hip roof is covered in white asbestos shingles. By using fireproof materials the possibility of a destructive fire is avoided. Fire prevention is always a consideration in remodeling a home in a rural district.

Before Back

Back   Third Stage

Aluminum, used properly, can be an excellent remodeling material. It is lightweight, fireproof, and requires little maintenance. Too often, however, aluminum has been badly handled and its positive values are overlooked because of the unattractive results inherent in the misuse of any material. All three steps of this remodeling use aluminum, not the bright shiny kind, or the unimaginative counterfeits of wood, but in designs and colors that have intrinsic value and are handsome in themselves. Walls, roof, windows, sliding doors, garage doors, soffits, and fascia are all aluminum with color baked on to resist weather for years before needing paint. Siding panels are applied directly over the existing siding. If the house is uninsulated, a combination of siding and insulation may be used to sheathe the house walls. Suggested colors are two shades of tan for the walls and pearl gray for the trim and windows.

The bedrooms added to the front in the first stage are down several steps from the existing floor level to get sufficient head room under the present eaves. A sitting room is designed with a low railing overlooking the master bedroom. Narrow windows on the front reduce noise and vision from the street. The existing kitchen and dining room have been redesigned to provide a wide open kitchen, a rear entrance hall, a laundry, and a lavatory. The family room with a charcoal grill can be added without disrupting the rest of the house. When it is finished, the large windows in the present dining room can be removed and the new section becomes part of the house. Another part of the second step of the remodeling is the new entrance hall. The small screened garden is an important projection of the living room.

The new front entrance can be seen from the gate and helps eliminate guess work in finding the front door. Brick paving spreads like a welcome carpet from the driveway through the gate to the entrance. An electric latch and an intercom permit you to interview strangers before the gate is opened.

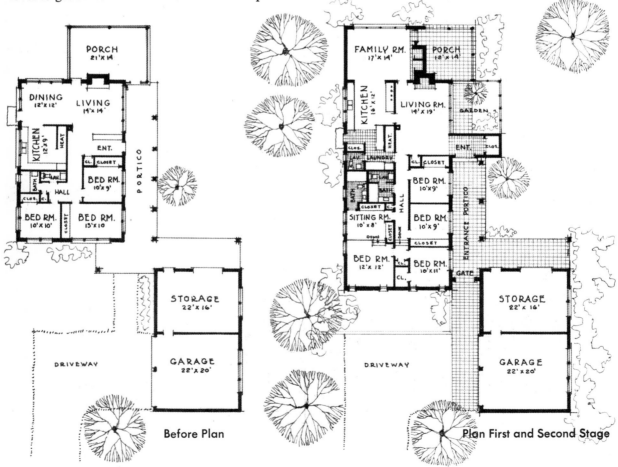

Before Plan

Plan First and Second Stage

Front   First Stage of Remodeling

OWNER   Gene Lightfoot
LOCATION   Westport, Connecticut

Before Front   House #30

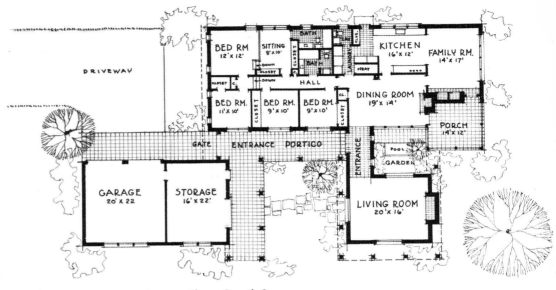

Plan   Fourth Stage

The old garden side of the house looks a bit ragged compared to the crisp simplicity of the remodeled second stage. Most of the existing portico structure remains, but the careful placement of larger columns in relation to the windows helps to organize the space. The third and final phase of the remodeling is the construction of the new living room. Rather than build it against the house which would have deprived the dining room of light, it is built almost as a separate structure connected to the main body of the house by the entrance. The flat line of the portico is carried around at the same height for continuity and to shelter the sliding glass doors of the living room. To gain height on the interior, the ceiling is raised to ten feet. Clerestory windows continue around all four sides of the room. A hip roof is used on the living room to echo the present house roof. The fireplace is designed with a raised hearth so that an ash dump may be accommodated under the fire pit and cleaned from the outside. If a conventional hearth were used, ashes would have to be hauled out through the house. After doing this several times usually one hesitates to use the fireplace because of the bother involved in dumping the ashes and the fireplace falls into disuse. Charming enclosed gardens are formed by the placement of the living room and although this family has a beautiful view from all directions, the same approach would be equally suitable in a crowded suburban neighborhood.

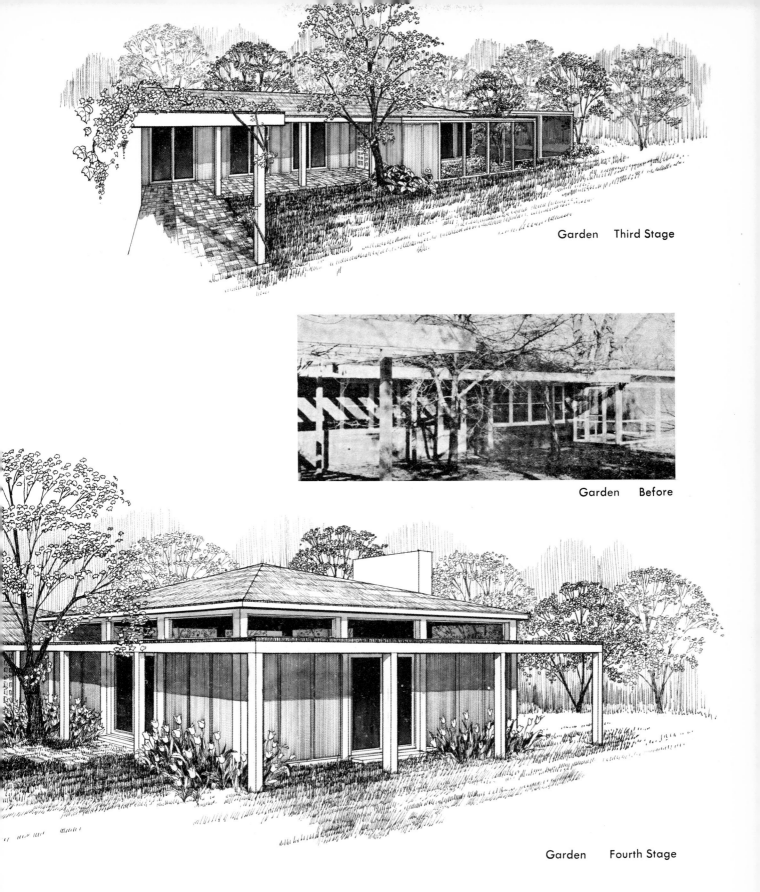

Garden   Third Stage

Garden   Before

Garden   Fourth Stage

The garden enclosed by the living room, the entrance, and the dining room is fashioned after Japanese gardens of similar or smaller size. In winter the entrance is the connecting link between the living room and the rest of the house. However, during the other seven or eight months of the year, the windproof garden would serve as a pleasant transition between the dining room and the living room. Sliding doors can be left open in the dining room and you can enjoy the sound of rain falling in the little pool. Flowers and bulbs will bloom about three weeks earlier and will last about three weeks longer in the protected garden.

Before

After

Complete Remodeling

Complete remodeling is no different than any other except that it is accomplished all at once. What is true of facelifting, remodeling with paint or remodeling interior space, is equally true when applied to the points as they were emphasized in those chapters. A well-designed remodeling can make any old home better than a poorly designed new house. It is one thing to make a lifetime investment in a new house and quite another to create an exciting modern home out of an inadequate old dwelling and do it without spending more than you should. Planning, not money, is the most important part of a remodeling. No one enjoys having a house that is exactly like everybody else's and even in remodeling a tract house you can bring out the non-conformist character inherent in every home by realizing the difference in site, orientation, background, the way the sun strikes it, and, most of all, the family who lives in it. There is no one solution for all houses. Each house has a potential character of its own. Roof line, window placement, circulation, form, together with the structural, mechanical, and electrical features create the total design. Small components are just as worthy of consideration as larger elements. The most economical is not necessarily the least expensive. You must choose what to keep, what to add, and what to remove, both in considering the interior and the exterior so the old and the new enhance rather than detract from each other. It is important to realize that you do not have to demolish everything and start from scratch. Knowing what not to do is just as vital as knowing what to do. There are no cheap solutions. The fine point in remodeling is deciding what you want, knowing what you would rather have if you cannot have everything, and discovering the choices available to you. Whether you remodel bit by bit or all at once you must begin with a comprehensive plan.

Front   After Remodeling

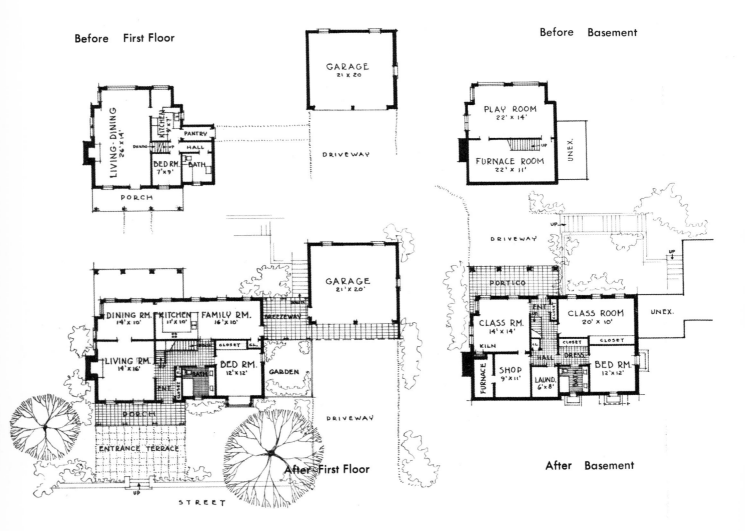

Before   First Floor

GARAGE
21 x 20

Before   Basement

LIVING-DINING
26'x14'

KITCHEN
9'x7'

PANTRY

DOWN   UP   HALL

BED RM.
7'x9'   BATH

PORCH

DRIVEWAY

PLAY ROOM
22'x14'

FURNACE ROOM
22'x11'

UNEX.

UP

DINING RM.
14'x10'   KITCHEN
11'x10'   FAMILY RM.
16'x10'

BREEZEWAY

CLOSET   CL.

LIVING RM.
14'x16'

BED RM.
12'x12'

BATH

ENT.   CLOSET

PORCH

GARDEN

GARAGE
21'x20'

DRIVEWAY

ENTRANCE TERRACE

UP

STREET   After First Floor

DRIVEWAY

UP

PORTICO

CLASS RM.
14'x14'

ENT.

CLASS ROOM
20'x10'

UNEX.

KILN

CL.

CLOSET   CLOSET

FURNACE

SHOP
9'x11'

HALL   DRESS.

LAUND.
6'x8'   BATH

BED RM.
12'x12'

After   Basement

Before Front   House #31

Before Back

OWNER   Charles Donnelson
LOCATION   Arlington, Washington

This house has been turned around, so to speak, and what was once the main entrance is now the private, garden side. The side street and the wrought iron trimmed porch is now used as the family's entrance since Mrs. Donnelson teaches occupational therapy in the basement rooms. The need is for these classrooms, a master bedroom, and family living space on the first floor. Two bedrooms on the second floor were adequate and are not shown in the plans. The natural slope at the back of the house is excavated, opening the basement to light and air, and creating a driveway, parking space, and an entrance to the classrooms. The existing roof is extended into a two-story portico suggesting the hospitality of the owners. The opposite façade, on the family's entrance, has a low sheltered porch and an atmosphere compatible with more intimate family life. An addition to the house is made in the direction of the garage and connected with a porch on the upper level commanding a view of the lovely valley. An exterior stair connects the porch with the classroom driveway area.

Back   After Remodeling

OWNER John Rose
LOCATION Muskegon, Michigan

After Front

How can you convert a lakeside cottage into a year-around home? It is not always easy, especially if it has been changed around, chopped up, added to, repaired, and painted by a succession of owners. To complicate matters, it is on a narrow site and built near the road.

A bachelor, Mr. Rose might not have had to consider the family-type traffic patterns in the

house, but for the possible re-sale value of the house in the future, some of the rules of good sense need apply so the circulation in the house had some drastic revision. In addition, the house needed to be completely insulated, to have a new heating system installed, and to have the exterior changed bringing order to it. Insulation is not as difficult as it could be in an existing struc-

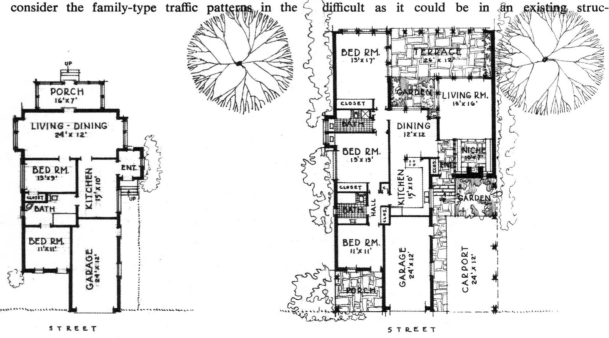

Before Plan

After Plan

Before Front   **House #32**

ture because a living room and a bedroom are added, helping to cut down the exposed exterior walls. The garage and the other few remaining walls are easy to insulate. Heating is designed to be forced warm air and the furnace occupies a corner of the garage since there is no basement. A new flat roof over the front half of the house and on the new additions unifies the façade facing the road. A new overhead garage door, finished in wood shingles, almost disappears and looks like part of the wall; otherwise, the garage door would have been too prominent and made the house look like a gasoline filling station. A carport for guests' cars allows them to park off the road and forms a covered entrance. The garden beside the front door is not roofed so sunlight falls on the plants and the front door, removing the long dark tunnel effect that would have resulted otherwise. Just inside the entrance, but separated from the front door and the hall by an antique wood screen, there is a fireplace niche with built-in couches on both sides. The stone hearth extends to the edge of the living room. Across the back of the house overlooking the lake is a new bedroom and a terrace. Both the bedroom and the living room have direct access to the terrace which could be screened, sides and roof, when the insects become intolerable in summer. The approach to the terrace from the dining room is across an enclosed garden built in the old foundations of the previous porch. The terrace is enclosed on all but one side so it will remain private from the nearby houses on the water's edge.

Before Back

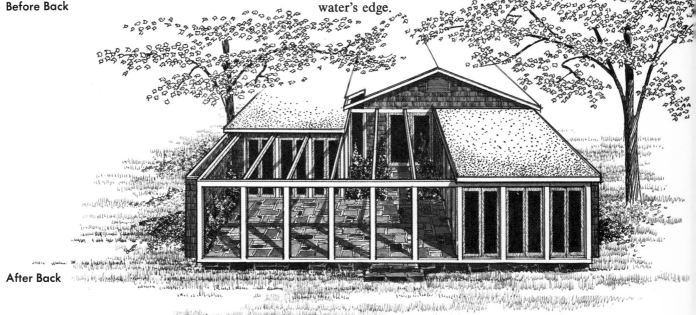

After Back

OWNER   Leo R. Ruscha
LOCATION Verona, Missouri

House #33   Before

Another farmhouse type seen at almost regular intervals from the highway was probably built about fifty years ago and has been added to over the years. It has the bucolic attraction similar to so many other houses built here and in Europe without design or guile by a local carpenter. Appealing as it may be, there are no closets and only one bath off the dining room. The carpenter wasted a lot of space. The entrance terrace, which was to be a porch until he discovered it was impossible to get a roof on it without covering the second-floor windows, never was completed. The front living-room and library windows are changed to French doors so the terrace can be used from the interior and also as an excellent entrance. Old space heaters in the living room and library are replaced with Franklin stoves and the chimneys are widened to accommodate the new and more fireproof flues. Because Franklin stoves throw off

Before Second Floor

After Second Floor

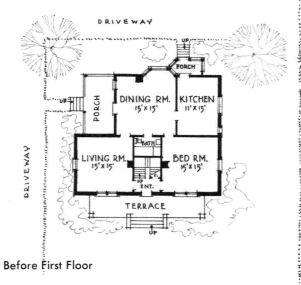

Before First Floor

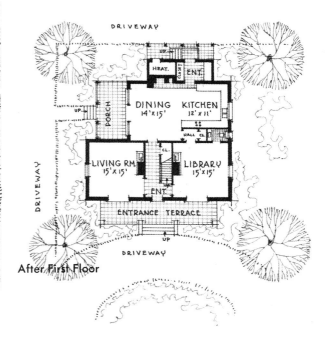

After First Floor

a lot of heat, they have been raised off the floor on marble hearths. The walls behind them should be covered in fireproof marble slabs, brick or thick plaster. The library will also be used as the guest room. The heater is also removed from the back room and a fireplace with an old-fashioned baking oven and a long hearth is built across the end of the room. Central heating is added to the house with the furnace room backed up to the dining room chimney since there is no basement under the house. Large wood beams running from front to back reinforce the dining room and kitchen ceiling. The refrigerator and freezer are in the rear entrance where many people still prefer them. The old bathroom and the twisting stairs are removed and a center entrance hall is built

between the twin chimneys. The large upstairs hall and the staircase is lighted by clerestory windows stretching between the chimneys.

When insulation and new board and batten siding are applied to the exterior a striking change occurs. New doors and windows are set into the existing well-placed openings. The corner posts are cut down and a simple railing is set between them. To retain the simplicity of the house, entrance lights are mounted on the posts. A plain slab door lies behind the screened and louvered storm door. The shutters may remain closed on the large bathroom window over the front door. A whole new personality has emerged from the façade of this house without changing the existing lines except to remove the distracting elements.

OWNER Ronald Evans

LOCATION Crestwood, New York

House #34   Before

There is no problem of over-building the neighborhood with the Evans' home. When the couple bought the house, they had the foresight to acquire an extra lot to their right; now property in this fine Westchester community is more valuable than ever. There are no children in the family but they are cramped for space and a parent often visits, occupying the second floor. The entrance to the house is a full flight of exterior stairs up from the driveway, hazardous in winter and inconvenient at night or when it is raining. The façade, unfortunately, is dominated by the garage door at street level and is particularly unattractive when the door is left open. By using the natural entrance of the old garage, it becomes a formal entrance hall with an interior stair to the first floor. A new garage, with a living room and a dining room above, is added to the right continuing the existing roof line of the house. The old living room is

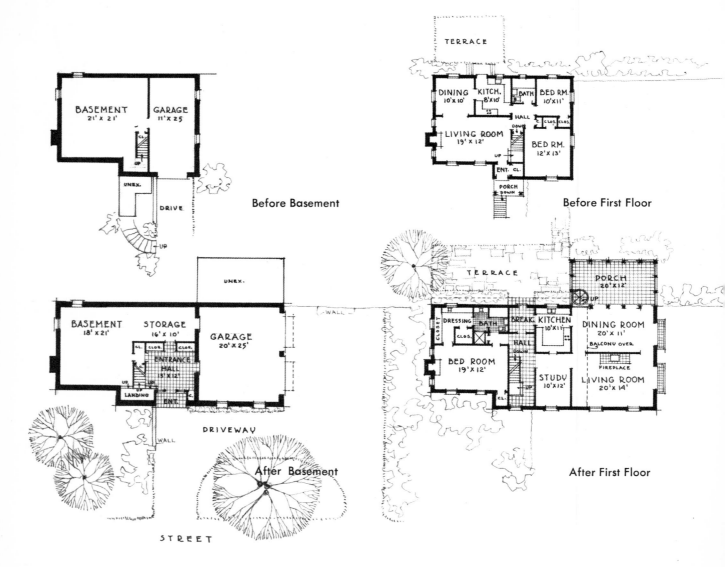

made into the master bedroom with a dressing room and closets in the space previously used as the small dining room. The existing kitchen is changed into a compartmented bath using the same pipes and plumbing stack that are in the wet wall of the old bathroom. A modern kitchen is installed where the back bedroom was. It is interesting to note how few openings and partitions have been changed in the remodeling which is an advantage in keeping the cost low. The open-beamed ceiling spans the living room and dining room which are separated only to a height of seven feet by a wall and a free-standing fireplace set on a raised tile hearth. A balcony off the second floor overlooks the living room and the high transomed French doors and window set in the gable.

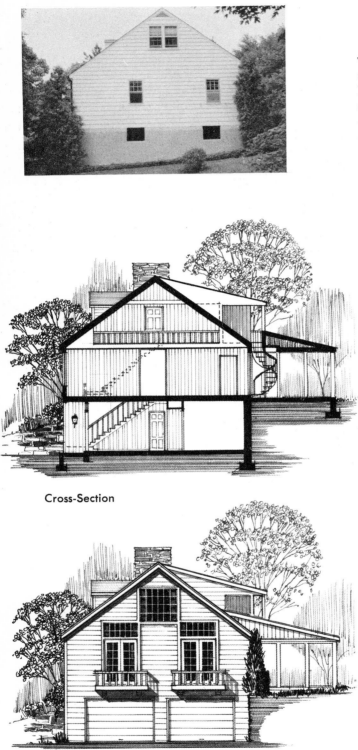

The photograph is of the existing end wall where the addition will be placed maintaining the same height, width, and roof line as the present house. The double window in the gable becomes a door from the sitting room onto the balcony overlooking the living room. The first-floor window on the left is widened to become the entrance into the living room. The window on the right becomes the door from the kitchen into the new dining room. The basement window on the left becomes the door from the entrance hall into the garage and the other window is also lengthened to be the door from the garage into the basement.

In the section—or cut—through the house, just in front of the living-room entrance, the dotted lines indicate the stairs to the second floor behind the living-room partition. The design of the basement entrance clearly shows the advantage of the interior flight of stairs. The new entrance is set within the old garage door frame and recessed to give it some cover. The small balcony of the second floor has no real use except decoratively to increase the apparent height of the open beamed ceiling and define the interesting levels. The stair from the upstairs porch circles down to the porch on the first floor.

Cross-Section

The elevation of the new addition develops the upper floors and leaves the garage doors as inconspicuous as possible. The French doors, with transoms above are bridged by a fixed window that unites the living room and dining room but allows them to function and to be decorated as separate rooms. The two exterior balconies protect the doors, make the glass easier to clean, and shield the interior from the lights of cars parking or turning around in the drive below. The screened porch at the right is projected, with a roof at the same angle of pitch as the shed dormer. More than two angles of pitch on the roof of a house are usually detrimental to the appearance.

Elevation

Garden Before

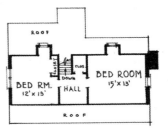

Before Second Floor

The garden side of the house, only partially used before, can be expanded into a green lawn and a terrace adjacent to the screen porch and the breakfast room. A shed dormer across the back opens up the bedrooms and allows them to be enlarged while also providing space for a much needed new bathroom. Next to the bath there is a kitchenette for the preparation of breakfast or a midnight snack. The porch off the sitting room enjoys a view of the garden. The balcony shelters the breakfast-room door, shields the bedroom, and permits easy window cleaning. The circular stair is a shortcut to the second-floor suite or an emergency exit in a fire.

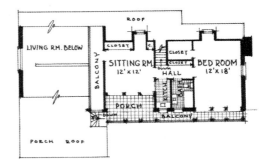

After Second Floor

New Entrance

House #35   Before Front

Before Back

Bare and uninteresting, too small for a family of five, this home is also typical of many prefabricated houses or those built in developments. With no large trees for shade or to break the force of the wind which blows across the open country all year, the remodeling is designed to compensate for these natural elements, by creating an oasis against the heat, the sun, the cold, and the wind. Using the simplest and least expensive materials—unpainted concrete block and handsome rough sawed timber—two new flat-roofed wings are added and surrounded by porches and terraces.

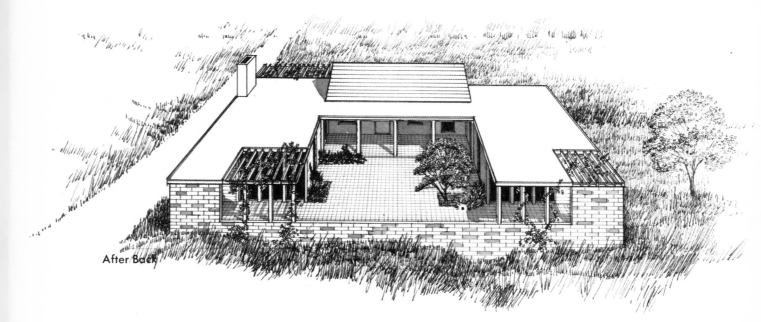

After Back

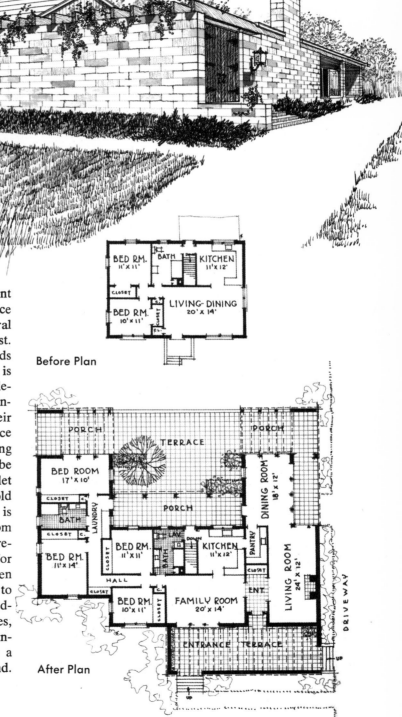

The entrance into the living room and the front door are of particular concern because they face the direction of the strongest winds and several conventional storm doors had already been lost. It should be noted that in areas of strong winds such as the plains (here), or along the shore, it is better to use sliding doors and windows or double-hung windows since projected and casement windows can easily be broken or pulled off their hinges. The new front door is set into the entrance hall between the family room and the new living room. Plank storm doors are used and can be closed in rough weather. Double doors will let a smaller area be opened to the weather and cold drafts. The window in the end of the house is lowered to become the entrance to the family room from the hall and most of the present house remains intact. The bath is compartmented for greater use and privacy, and the closet between the two bedrooms is removed to make a hall to the new wing. The laundry is placed in the bedroom section where soiled towels, work clothes, and sheets pile up. On the other side of the entrance hall, the living room is designed to be a dark and restful refuge from the sun and wind.

Before Plan

After Plan

OWNER   Louis Avondet

LOCATION   Monett, Missouri

House #36   Before

The owners wanted their home to reflect the rural charm of country living and the hospitality of their highly successful Hereford farm. Quietly settled among tall trees the existing house is one that we have seen many times. There was only one bath behind the kitchen for both floors and the bedrooms seemed to be scattered here and there. The living room was too small and no one ever used the front door hidden under the front porch but headed for the obvious and more accessible side door. Organizing the existing space downstairs is not much of a problem because of the established pattern of living. The front porch is torn off and a massive stone wall and fireplace in the living room give an ageless atmosphere. The stairs are reversed to lead to the second floor from the entrance hall. The front door is placed on the side of the house where its spontaneous use will be automatic. The office is made quieter by closing off the door from the kitchen. With another door to the exterior closed, a much better and more efficient arrangement is possible. The plumbing and existing countertop in the kitchen is unchanged, but more cabinets are added to each side to form a wide U. The range top is set in an island counter finished with hard maple wood, like a big chopping block, instead of the conventional sterile synthetic. Steam and cooking odors are removed by a suspended copper hood. A bay window extends the kitchen and is a pleasant place to have breakfast. The old bathroom just off the kitchen is converted into a rear entrance and laundry so muddy work clothes never need get

Before First Floor

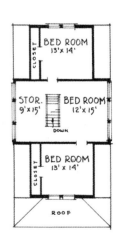

Before Second Floor

further into the house than that. There is a laundry chute in the hall closet on the second floor that drops to the laundry downstairs. The addition of a new master bedroom and bath replaces the bedroom taken over by the expansion of the living room. An attached garage is a better place for the family's personal car than the barn. On the second floor, a new compartmented bath and closets are built and three bedrooms are provided in the existing area. A low wood fence built around the entrance garden limits the flower gardening, and other landscaping is kept to a minimum because of the care and maintenance it requires when more important things need to be done on the busy farm.

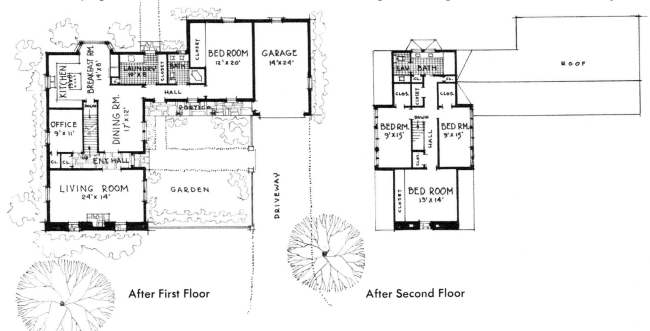

After First Floor

After Second Floor

LOCATION   Greenwich, Connecticut

Before the present owners bought this kennel in a corner of a quiet estate to remodel, it had been home to a famous line of Bedlington terriers. The dogs had their own small hospital, laundry, and kitchen. The groom and his family occupied an apartment on the second floor. A separate garage on the property permitted a second, attached garage to be made into a family room and the street façade to be redesigned with a more residential quality. The door in the gable end of the third floor, where heavy items could be hoisted and stored, is simply protected by a balcony.

House #37   Before Front

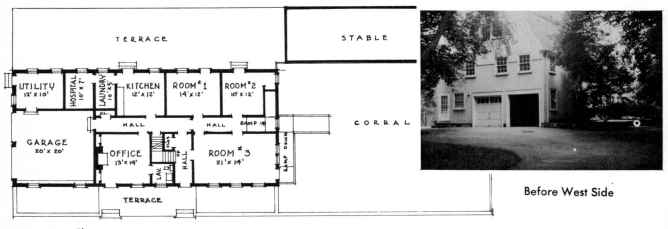

Before First Floor

Before West Side

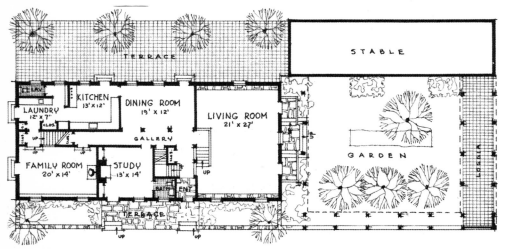

After First Floor

The main entrance façade needed to be changed very little during the remodeling, but heavy foliage prevents a good photograph. Excellent construction on basically French proportions easily influenced the direction of the design—exterior and interior. The side doors, leading to the family room and laundry, are painted the same as the walls so they do not detract from the entrance doors.

Paintings Courtesy of Newhouse Galleries

After Living Room

Decorator Mrs. Karen Barsoe Landers

Photos by Frank Russell

After Master-Bath

The master bathroom replaces the apartment kitchen on the second floor. The door on the far left is to the large tile shower; the second door is to the toilet room. The dressing room beyond had been the apartment dining room and is now lined with closets.

On the right, looking in the opposite direction, twin wash basins are set in a countertop in the same area as the old kitchen sink. Mirrors, edged with lights, are set between the windows over the basins. The tub at the end of the room has a low shelf under the counter for soaps and perfumes. Out of sight on the right there is a closet and a door to the upstairs hall so the room can be cleaned without going through the master bedroom and dressing room.

What had once been the pine-paneled living room of the apartment is now the master bedroom, elegantly arranged with fine detail and colors particularly becoming to the owner's wife. The same carpet, drapery, furniture, and colors are used throughout the master suite.

After Master-Bedroom

Paintings Courtesy of Newhouse Galleries

Decorator Mrs. Karen Barsoe Landers

After Master-Bath

Before Second-Floor Kitchen

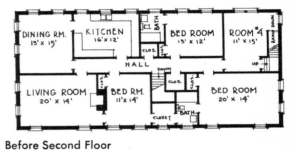

Before Second Floor

Before the house was remodeled the second floor was well designed and insulated from the barks of the dogs downstairs. The biggest change is where the kitchen and dining room replace the master bath and dressing room. Room #4, which was the dogs' maternity ward, becomes part of a two-room suite for the owner's teen-age daughter. The two rooms across the hall are the boys' bedrooms. At present there is only one stair to the third floor, but when it becomes a library and retreat for the owner, a second stair from the dressing room will be added for convenience and safety.

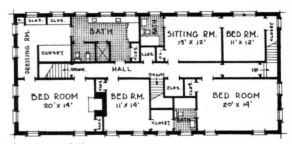

After Second Floor

East Side during Construction

Photos by Frank Russell

Before

A ramp on the east side of the house had led down from Room #3 to a corral adjacent to the stable where the dogs could romp with the saddle horses. Now, with the living room lowered, this area is turned into a cloistered court and formal garden. The second floor of the stable becomes the guest rooms and the first floor is made into outside rooms for informal entertainment. The old stable doors remain so the interior can be completely opened to the garden and court.

The most difficult problem is the low, seven-foot-four-inch height of the ceiling in the living room. With the removal of the structural partitions, the situation is complicated by the even

House #37 Continued

Dining Room

After   Living Room

lower beams that are used to support the second floor. The solution is to lower the floor of the living room which, in this case, adds about one thousand dollars to the remodeling. The entrance to the house is through a small paved entry into this gallery overlooking the living room. The heavy provincial balustrade invites one to descend the richly carpeted stairs. The gallery continues along one side of the dining room defined by massive square columns that replace the structural partition and eliminate the long dark hallway to the family room. The dining room is not isolated but shares a continuity with the living room.

The rough stone walls on both sides of the living room had been the upper part of the basement foundation walls and indicate the depth the floor had been lowered to attain a ceiling height of about twelve feet.

Living Room during Remodeling

In contrast to the sophisticated living room, the family room converted from the old garage has almost a cabin quality. Whitewashed walls, a red tile floor, and a stair wall of bleached cypress with a television concealed under the steps, encourages noise, singing, and dancing. The old Franklin stove is connected to an extra flue of the chimney and raised off the floor on a square brick hearth.

Up two steps from the family room, the laundry also contains, beside the conventional washer and dryer, a bar sink and a counter-high refrigerator for soft drinks and snacks. The back stairs, leading to the center hall on the second floor, are built primarily for convenience, although the need for a secondary exit in case of fire is an important consideration in a three-story frame house almost seventy-feet long.

Kitchen during Remodeling

Photos by Frank Russell

This is a cook's kitchen, straightforward and convenient, with a place for everything and everything in place. The floor and walls are white with pale yellow cabinets and appliances, so it does not look like a laboratory, but there is no lounging around the kitchen table. Cokes and sandwiches can be prepared from the pantry in the laundry while the big refrigerator and the kitchen proper are devoted solely to the preparation of the main meals. The metal cabinets in the old apartment kitchen were refinished at a local auto-body shop and re-assembled in the new kitchen.

The original forty-year-old house was an early prefabricated structure in the shape of an "H" built on a slope above a pond in a grove of tall pines and maple trees. Before the present owners bought it to remodel, a garage had been added and then sometime later a two-story addition had been built with a living room on the first floor and an unfinished second floor. The biggest problem is to relate the living room to the rest of the house and to tie the small separate rooms together creating a feeling of space for informal and relaxed living.

A carport is added on the left for additional sheltered parking. A window, a Dutch door, and an open section at the side of the carport prevent it from being too dark inside. The old kitchen wall is extended to the existing garage wall to provide space for a new kitchen and a breakfast room. The dining-family room is enlarged with a flat roofed section extending over the present terrace to enclose a screen porch overlooking the new living-room terrace and the pond. Because of the close large trees, skylights are set into the flat roofed sections of the family room and kitchen. This is especially effective in the kitchen where round dots of sunlight filtering through the trees move across the white floor.

OWNER   Robert Kelsey
LOCATION   New Canaan, Connecticut

House #38   Before

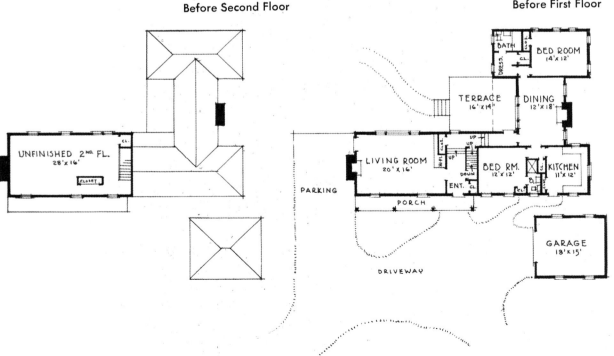

Before Second Floor   Before First Floor

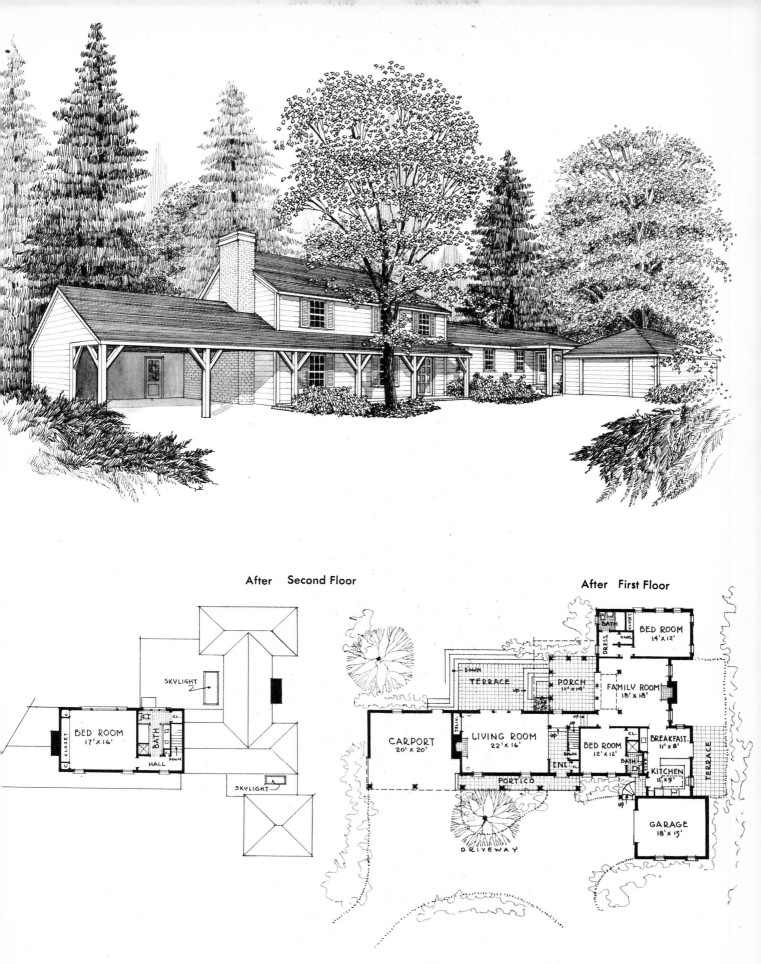

After   Second Floor

SKYLIGHT

BED ROOM
17'x16'

CLOSET

BATH

CL.

HALL

DOWN

SKYLIGHT

After   First Floor

BATH

CLOS.

CL.

DRESS.

BED ROOM
14'x12'

DOWN

TERRACE

UP

PORCH
11'x14'

FAMILY ROOM
18'x18'

CARPORT
20'x20'

TELV.

LIVING ROOM
22'x16'

UP

DOWN

BED ROOM
12'x12'

CL.

BREAKFAST.
11'x8'

BATH

KITCHEN
11'x9'

TERRACE

ENT.

PORTICO

UP

GARAGE
18'x15'

DRIVEWAY

UP

Complete Remodeling   221

Before Entrance

The exterior was painted green-gold with the shutters a slightly darker shade to avoid a jarring contrast. The skinny posts of the portico are made to look stronger and more structural. At night the color of the walls appears slightly warmer, being lighted with low wattage recessed lights behind each post. The soft red brick floor of the portico is lighted and the posts are silhouetted against the lighted walls of the house. The heavy oak door was found in the junk yard and purchased for twenty-five dollars. The pewter hardware cost five times as much, but the combination is elegant. Just inside the front door, the floor changes to black slate.

Photos by Frank Russell

A curved brick stair from the driveway leads to a Dutch door and the skylighted kitchen. The casement window over the sink repeats the geometric shape of the skylight. The overhanging trees, spotlighted at night, and the sky are a part of the interior decoration. White floor, cherry cabinets, and black countertops make a still life from the most casual placement of the groceries. Counter lights under the wall cabinets, pin spot lights, ceiling lights, and a black iron chandelier over the breakfast table can be combined to make very unusual lighting effects.

After Kitchen

After

After from Terrace

Photos by Frank Russell

After Family Room

The back of the house from the pond shows the relation of the porch to the new living-room terrace and the carport addition. The second-floor window is re-used from the old living room.

Before

The family room is as comfortable as an English inn. The orange tree thrives underneath the skylight and bears blossoms and fruit all year. The doors to the porch can open the room completely to the sounds and smells of a summer evening and the flood-lighted pond. Screening is not needed on the doors since the porch is screened which creates an unusual sense of freedom in passing from one area into the other.

The wall with the picture window is removed to expand the new family room. The roof is supported with two square posts which frame the sliding glass doors to the porch and the skylight placed in the old flat roof. The skylight is two clear bubble shaped sheets of plastic with a dead air space that prevents heat loss. Without it, the family room would be dark and gloomy. The four-foot overhang of the porch roof keeps rain off the porch furniture. An opening in the roof over the planter permits light to enter the window of the hall, and wisteria growing through the opening will vine around the bathroom windows on the second floor. The steps and terrace are made from secondhand brick; each brick costs a penny more than new brick because it has to be cleaned, but the aged patina is worth the cost, especially in remodeling where a striking "newness" is usually undesirable.

Before

The old dining room was used as a combination dining and family room but was disconnected from the kitchen. This may be fine in some cases but this family, with sons in high school and college, encourages informal entertaining and buffet dinners after a swim in the pond in summer or ice-skating in winter and at these times no one wants to be isolated in a kitchen. A wide new door was opened behind the sofa into the breakfast room. An easy flow is established between family room and kitchen and, at the same time, in the front bedroom the door is relocated and better closet space is added. When it is desirable, bi-folding doors can close off the kitchen from the family room.

Before Remodeling

During Remodeling

Before the remodeling the kitchen was too small to hold a breakfast table comfortably. The wall on the right is removed and the kitchen is pushed out to the wall of the garage which saves the cost of a new wall. The new space is roofed with a flat section and a skylight. The old kitchen window is replaced by French doors salvaged from the living room. A small bar sink and counter height refrigerator keeps soft drinks and less serious food preparation out of the kitchen area. Multiple lighting arrangements can darken the kitchen and light only the buffet counter; or all the lights except the chandelier over the table can be turned off to create an atmosphere for a formal supper.

After Kitchen

Before the remodeling, the view from the family room toward the living room was down this narrow corridor. The living room itself and its handsome Italian mantel was blocked off from the rest of the house by a closet wall.

After the remodeling, the living room becomes more a part of the house. The stairs lead up to the master bedroom and bath on the second floor and down to the.slate paved entrance hall. The French doors to the right of the fireplace are removed. Television and hi-fi are built into the space, but are covered by louvered shutters painted to match the wall so they do not compete with the mantel.

Before

After   Remodeling

Before   Living Room

During Construction

Looking at the living room from the other direction the result of the removed closet wall is equally effective. The door to the basement under the stairs is covered with the same walnut paneling as the

stair and is now barely visible. The big window is re-used in the master bedroom on the second floor and is replaced with sliding glass doors that overlook the brick terrace and the pond.

Photos by Frank Russell

After

The master bathroom on the second floor is divided with plastic panels and a sliding door. The light weight of plastic makes it very useful in remodeling. It is easier to keep clean than glass and will not break even if struck with a hammer. The same design is used on the shower stall door out of the photograph at left. Twin basins are set in the countertop and lighted with a dropped ceiling panel of white plastic. The apparent size of the room is doubled by the mirror over the entire wall above the countertop. Walls, ceiling, and fixtures are all white; the plastic is light blue and lavender, and the carpet is the same shade of light blue.

Short Cuts in Remodeling

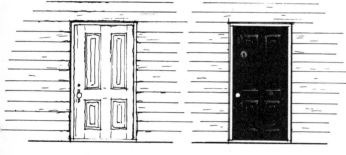

Before   After

Before

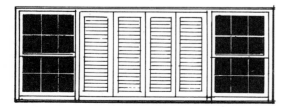

After

The best way to save time and money on your remodeling is to begin with a comprehensive plan and carry it through without changing your mind, whether the work takes six months or six years. There is no substitute for good design and competent workmanship, but there are always several ways of achieving them.

If the exterior paint on your white house is streaked and soiled but really does not need a new paint job for another few years, you can brighten up the appearance by painting the shutters or some of the trim black and making the front door a deep rich color. The door leads the eye away from the walls, and they seem much cleaner and brighter in contrast with the black trim.

Windows can be very inconvenient to relocate and change. If you have blocked up windows on the interior because of new bookcases, partition changes, or new paneling; or if the windows are simply unwanted, they can be simply, inexpensively, and quickly covered on the outside with unlouvered shutters. If an old-fashioned picture window makes your home too public or if you want to keep out hot summer sunshine but still let light into the room, fit the exterior of the window with louvered shutters to control the light and leave the shutters in a closed position.

Studying the modular properties of the materials you are going to use in remodeling can reduce waste and save you money; at the same time, you

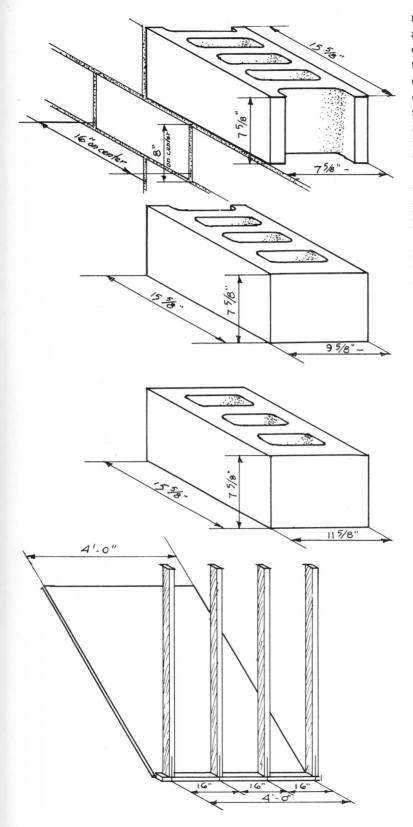

may gain additional space at no extra cost. If you are using concrete block for a foundation, work out the walls in modular units to avoid cutting the block. The blocks themselves are not so expensive, but the saving in time and labor required to cut them to size more than pays for the space gained. For instance, it costs more to build a concrete block wall six feet seven and a half inches long than one an even eight feet long. Keep the courses even, too, so you can avoid filling.

When you are making additions to your house, try to use increments of four feet. If this is not possible, then use increments of two feet so that plywood sheathing, wallboard, or other material can be cut exactly in half and used without waste. A four-foot module is the one most used by architects because most building codes require stud spacing of sixteen inches, although occasionally twenty-four inches are permitted. Three studs on sixteen-inch centers can be sheathed with a four-foot piece of plywood. Plywood, drywall, and other structural and finishing materials are usually 4'x8', and if they can be placed in full uncut sections, the work progresses faster and costs less than if the carpenter must stop and measure and cut each piece individually. For instance, a room addition 12'x16' can cost less to build than a smaller room 10'6"x14'11", and you have the advantage of additional interior space.

In running hot- and cold-water lines to new plumbing fixtures and equipment, it is wise to use copper pipe. The copper may cost more initially, but it can also curve slightly without damage, which means it takes fewer joints and fittings and is easier and quicker to install in an existing structure.

Adjustable steel lally columns can save you time in shoring up a sagging floor or holding up the roof of a new porch. They are used extensively in basements where they are left exposed, but they can also be used in other parts of the house where additional structural support is needed and where they can be concealed in a standard partition. If a wood column of a required size is too large for the particular space, a smaller-size steel lally column, which is unaffected by rot or termites, can be used and furred with wood or other material.

Steel beams are almost the only answer to support roofs and upper floors when a first-floor bearing wall is removed and a ceiling clearance must be maintained. But working with steel is more complicated and expensive than wood, and the joints where the steel meets the wood must be carefully worked out. If clearance or other design factors are not a problem, you can often simplify the carpenter's work by using wood beams.

Windows are a very expensive part of the house, but fixed glass is relatively cheap and does not require weather-stripping, that necessary but costly commodity to keep out wind and rain. Large glass areas facing the garden and the sun can improve almost any house, and the cost can be greatly reduced by using only a minimum of operable openings. You can combine one sliding glass door with a series of fixed glass panels at about one-third the cost of all-operable glass doors or windows. And, in many cases, the fixed glass costs less than a sliding glass door or window surrounded by solid walls. The glass panels not only do not require weather-stripping or screens, but they also eliminate interior and exterior wall finishing and painting. If you use a patterned or obscure glass, you can often eliminate washing the glass and curtains or drapes. Insulating glass does away with cold down-drafts and condensation in winter.

Overhead garage doors can be made to look less commercial and more attractive by covering the panels with plywood, siding or shingles to match your house. The hardware must be re-balanced to compensate for the weight of the added material so the doors operate smoothly. If a new garage door is required, you can re-use the existing hardware if it is in good condition or simply buy new hardware and make a door suitable for the style of your house.

Uneven and cracked walls may be straightened with plywood paneling or drywall, which often costs less than removing the existing wall surface and refinishing it. Simply furr out with batten strips, and apply the new finish on top of the old wall. On exterior walls the dead-air space also acts as insulation and keeps the house warmer in winter and cooler in summer.

Cloth or plastic can also be stretched across an old wall to hide a structurally sound but badly scarred and patched wall surface. Patterned paper or cloth glued directly to the wall hides small cracks, lumps, and imperfections. Plastic is excellent for bathrooms and much softer and less expensive than tile.

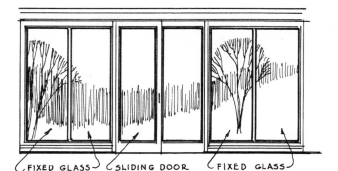

FIXED GLASS — SLIDING DOOR — FIXED GLASS

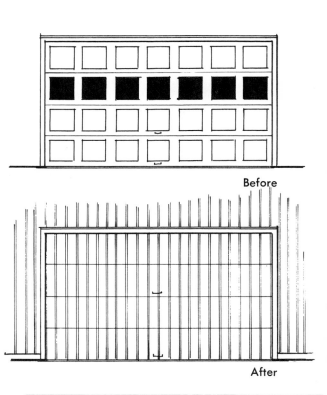

Before

After

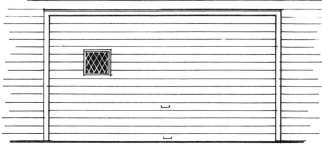

After

Ceilings are difficult, and old cracked and bulging surfaces should be removed. Once the source of the damage has been located and repaired, a new drywall or plywood finish is less expensive to install than extensive replastering and repair.

If you are adding a room and want to have carpet, plan to leave off the hardwood finish floor, and place the underpadding and carpet directly on the plywood subfloor. The saving on the hardwood floor can pay for the carpet. In rooms where the walls have been removed and the floor is patched and in poor condition, you can save time and effort by installing carpet. Since all floors have to have some finish over which you usually have carpet or a rug, it makes sense to eliminate the cost of either the hardwood or the carpet and simplify the care of the surface.

Scratched, scarred, and discolored old wood floors can be improved by staining a dark color. Dark floors show dust and footprints much quicker than light floors, but if kept waxed and polished, dark wood floors are elegant. Many times the application of black paste wax darkens a wood floor just enough to hide imperfections. Repeated applications over a period of years give a fine dark patina.

When you are installing kitchen wall cabinets in an older house, hang them a foot or more below the ceiling. Chances are the ceiling is not level, and you can avoid the work and labor necessary to cut, trim, and patch between the top of the cabinet and the ceiling. Kitchen cabinets are less expensive if built on the job with no prefixed backs. Hung directly on the wall, less material and labor are involved, and many people in an old house prefer not to have two inaccessible surfaces which could attract insects.

If you want to give your kitchen a touch of bright color, paint the inside of the cabinet doors. The surface is easy to paint, it does not get soiled, and you do not see the color often enough to become bored with it.

In the bathroom, prefabricated plastic bathtubs and shower stalls can save several steps in installation. Tub, walls, and ceiling are all in one piece. Shower and tub installations are lightweight and excellent for use on a second floor where the weight of a steel tub, tile walls, and floor may be prohibitive.

Additional closets in the bedroom can be cantilevered over the foundation, eliminating masonry footings and supporting walls, since the weight is carried by the walls and not the floor. Be sure, however, to insulate the walls, ceiling, and floor of the closet.

Another thing not to overlook when you are remodeling is the local junkyard and salvage yards. Very often, doors, windows, shutters, mantels, and railings can be bought at a fraction of the original cost.

SECTION FIVE

Money and Legal Matters

FINANCE—THE COST OF REMODELING

With enough money you can do anything to an old house and make it as grand and as luxurious as you like. Anybody can be elected to be the best dressed person in the world with only a fair figure and a million dollars to spend on clothes. But that is not the point of this book. Good design costs no more than bad design and elegance is less expensive than vulgarity. Your remodeling must be well designed to suit your home, your budget, and your tastes no matter how much or how little you have to spend. It is not enough to say that it depends on where you live and what you want to remodel. You will want to have a clear idea of what your remodeling project will cost and whether your dreams are within the realm of possibility.

The price of materials and the cost of labor in your area are the two biggest determining factors. If you live in a region where local stone is readily available, masonry can cost you less than in an area where stone must be trucked to the site from miles away. In areas where timber is cut and milled, lumber can be inexpensive. Where there is a shortage of skilled labor, the cost of carpenters, plumbers, electricians, and masons may be higher than the cost of the materials.

Local building codes and climatic conditions may also increase the cost of remodeling because they can control the methods and the materials used in remodeling.

The time of the year and the attitude of the contractor can temper the actual cost of the work. If it is wintertime and you want to remodel your kitchen, the contractor may charge you less for inside work. But if it is good weather and you want the work done right away, he may have to hire additional men to do your job and then charge you more. If it is an off-season for him and his help is idle, he may do the work for less to keep his crew intact. These are only some of the reasons it is advisable to get bids on the work from several local contractors.

The larger the scope of the remodeling and the more work you have done at one time, the less it costs for each item. Work done piecemeal usually costs ten per cent more than if the contractor and his crew complete the job when all the equipment and materials are on the job site.

Remodeling work can cost proportionately more than new construction because there is demolition and removal of construction and materials. Remodeling also requires more careful planning, cutting, patching, and filling.

On the following pages there are unit prices for doors, windows, floors, roofs, and cabinet work so you can see some of the relative costs. In every case the prices are for completed work, including labor and materials, on the house so that you will be able to intelligently guess at the amount of money involved in your own remodeling. At least you will be able to know whether you are thinking in terms of hundreds of dollars or thousands of dollars. It is only reasonable that you should know how much it costs to accomplish the remodeling presented in the section of "Case Histories." This will give you an idea of about how much you may anticipate similar changes in your own home may cost.

Because regional price differences for labor and materials vary considerably, and the homes mentioned are located throughout the U.S., all the estimates are based on prices pertinent to Southampton, New York, as of 1966. A similar remodeling in your particular area might cost more or considerably less. The author is indebted to Robert Wilde of Harry H. Wilde Inc. for the prices and estimates quoted.

The only accurate estimate of the exact cost to you is through a local contractor's bid on the remodeling designed for your home. Because of the fluctuation in prices, even contractors' bids or estimates state that the figures quoted are good only for a period of thirty days.

ENTRANCES AND TERRACES (installed, including labor and materials)

Gravel terrace ....$ 0.23 per square foot
Blacktop terrace ....$ 0.25 per square foot
Concrete ....$ 0.45 per square foot
Wood deck ....$ 1.50 per square foot
Brick set in sand ....$ 2.00 per square foot
Brick set in cement ....$ 3.00 per square foot
Portico (including roof, paving and column) ....$240.00 per six feet
Loggia (including roof, paving and columns) ....$250.00 per six feet
Indenting entrance into interior hall $200.00

DOORS (includes door, hanging, and stock hardware; add $25.00 for weather-stripping single exterior door, add $40.00 for weather-stripping double exterior doors)
NOTE: it costs about $50.00 to change a window opening into a door opening plus the cost of the door.

A. Solid core slab door ....exterior—$ 90.00
                                                        interior—$ 45.00
B. Six-panel Colonial door ....exterior—$105.00
                                                        interior—$ 45.00
C. Screened and louvered exterior door ....$ 60.00
        louvered interior door ....$ 40.00
D. French leaded glass, single panel below, exterior $200.00
E. Dutch exterior door (add $35.00 for weather-stripping) $220.00
F. Double five panel exterior doors $400.00
                interior doors $350.00
G. Single French exterior door $120.00
H. Double French exterior doors $240.00
Sliding glass doors for six-foot opening, including weather-stripping $250.00
Sliding closet doors for six-foot opening ....$ 53.00
Mirrored sliding closet doors for six-foot opening $230.00
Bi-folding closet doors (four doors) for six-foot opening ....$ 65.00

WINDOWS (includes window, screens, installation, and weather-stripping)

   NOTE: **it costs about $45.00 to change a door opening into a window opening, plus the cost of the window. Insulating glass will increase the cost of the window prices listed below by 30 per cent. The prices are for windows three feet wide and five feet high.**

Fixed plate glass ....$ 1.25 per square foot
Fixed insulating glass ....$ 1.60 per square foot
Double hung window ....$ 60.00
Casement window ....$ 75.00
Sliding window ....$ 70.00
Awning window $145.00
Hopper window ....$ 45.00
Jalousie window $200.00
Bay window for a six foot opening $485.00
Bow window for a six foot opening $500.00
Doghouse dormer $125.00
Shed dormer ....$ 16.00 per lineal foot

INTERIOR STAIRS

Cutting new stair well in second floor ....$ 200.00
Straight run, nine feet high, oak treads and balustrade, white pine stringers
   and risers; closet underneath ....$ 225.00
Curved staircase; same specifications but without a closet underneath $1,500.00
Four foot circular metal stair ....$ 800.00

INTERIOR NON-BEARING WALLS AND PARTITIONS

Gypsum board (drywall ⅝" thick; spackled three coats; un-
   painted) ....$0.45 per square foot
Plaster (unpainted) ....$0.65 per square foot
Ceramic tile ....$1.75 per square foot
Pre-finished plywood ....$1.25 per square foot
Interior partitions of four inch studs finished on both sides with drywall eight feet high are about $8.00 per lineal foot.

EXTERIOR WALLS (for new finish installed on existing frame house)

Clapboard (including new plywood backing) ....$1.00 per square foot
Stucco ....$0.55 per square foot
Brick veneer ....$2.80 per square foot
Plywood (texture 1-11) ....$0.50 per square foot
Wood shingles ....$0.55 per square foot
Asbestos shingles ....$0.35 per square foot
Board and batten ....$0.50 per square foot

EXTERIOR ROOFS (includes labor and materials for new roof installed on existing roof structure)

210-pound Asphalt shingles ....$0.35 per square foot
300-pound Asphalt shingles ....$0.40 per square foot
Asbestos shingles ....$0.50 per square foot
Wood shingles (includes removing existing roof) ....$1.00 per square foot
Wood shakes (includes removing existing roof) ....$1.10 per square foot
Terne metal ....$1.15 per square foot
4-ply built-up roof ....$0.30 per square foot
5-ply built-up roof ....$0.35 per square foot

FLOORS

Hardwood . . . . $0.65 per square foot
Asphalt tile . . . . $0.75 per square foot
Linoleum . . . . $0.40 per square foot
Inlaid linoleum . . . . $1.25 per square foot
Vinyl asbestos . . . . $1.25 per square foot
Cork tile . . . . $0.80 per square foot
Cork tile with vinyl coating . . . . $1.80 per square foot
Vinyl sheet . . . . $0.35 to $1.15 per square foot
Vinyl tile . . . . $0.60 to $3.50 per square foot
Ceramic tile . . . . $2.00 per square foot
Carpet . . . . $1.00 per square foot

WIRING AND LIGHTING
Electrical Work

New outlets in existing partition—#12 wire . . . . $ 10.00 each
New outlets in new partitions—#12 wire . . . . $ 6.00 each
Single pole switch . . . . $ 6.00 each
Three-way switch . . . . $ 6.50 each
    For silent switches add $1.00 each

Fixtures (includes outlet)

Fluorescent—2-tubes—recessed . . . . $ 35.00
            surface mounted . . . . $ 20.00
Incandescent—recessed, 6″x6″ . . . . $ 21.00
             9″x9″ . . . . $ 25.00
            12″x12″ . . . . $ 28.00
Porcelain pull chain . . . . $ 4.50
Increase service to 100 amperes with circuit breakers $200.00

PLUMBING

New sink installed in same location . . . . $ 90.00
New sink installed in new location $170.00
New disposer installed . . . . $ 90.00
New toilet installed in same location . . . . $ 70.00
New toilet installed in new location $225.00
New bathtub installed in same location $235.00
New bathtub installed in new location $255.00

KITCHEN CABINETS (cost of cabinets includes installation)

New manufactured base cabinets . . . . wood—$ 40.00 per lineal foot
                                 metal—$ 45.00 per lineal foot
New manufactured wall cabinets . . . . wood—$ 28.00 per lineal foot
                                 metal—$ 32.00 per lineal foot
Formica countertops with 6″ back splash . . . . $ 11.00 per lineal foot
Lazy susan corner cabinets . . . . $ 63.00
Vegetable bin . . . . $ 10.00
Tray dividers . . . . $ 4.00
Counter sunk chopping block 24″x24″ . . . . $ 30.00
Wall cabinet for oven . . . . $ 65.00
Broom cabinet . . . . $ 50.00
Range hood with fan and light $140.00

COSTS OF CASE HISTORIES

HOUSE #1—page 126—$2,665 including extension of front wall plus $1,900 for fireplace
   and $100 for fancy brick work on chimney
HOUSE #2—page 127—$2,000 including $300 for demolition
HOUSE #3—page 128—$3,000
HOUSE #4—page 129—$2,000
HOUSE #5—page 130—$1,500
HOUSE #6—page 131—$4,000 including extension of front wall
HOUSE #7—page 132—$5,000

HOUSE #8—page 134—$1,800
HOUSE #9—page 134—Scheme A—$ 200
                   Scheme B—$ 400
                   Scheme C—$ 500
                   Scheme D—$1,000

HOUSE #10—page 137—Scheme A—$2,000
                    Scheme B—$4,000

Due to variables in painting these prices do not include the cost of paint and labor.

HOUSE #11—page 138—Scheme A—$ 600
                    Scheme B—$ 600

HOUSE #12—page 138—Scheme A—$ 300
                    Scheme B—$ 300
                    Scheme C—$ 325
                    Scheme D—$ 350

HOUSE #13—page 141—Scheme A—$ 150
                    Scheme B—$ 200
                    Scheme C—$ 125

HOUSE #14—page 144—$18,000
HOUSE #15—page 148—$ 9,500
HOUSE #16—page 150—$ 8,000
HOUSE #17—page 152—$ 4,500
HOUSE #18—page 154—$34,000 including $2,500 for all new plumbing
                            $2,200 for heating and complete insulation

HOUSE #19—page 158—Scheme A—$ 4,000
                    Scheme B—$12,000

HOUSE #20—page 160—Scheme A—$ 6,000
                    Scheme B—$12,600

HOUSE #21—page 164—Scheme A—$18,000 ⎫
                    Scheme B—$15,000 ⎬ including all new heating and insulation
                    Scheme C—$10,000 ⎭   for $1,900

HOUSE #22—page 168—$ 9,800
HOUSE #23—page 170—$11,000 including central air conditioning for $2,000
HOUSE #24—page 172—$14,500
HOUSE #25—page 174—$ 5,000
HOUSE #26—page 176—$ 8,500
HOUSE #27—page 178—$ 6,000

HOUSE #28—page 182—First stage—new plumbing . . . .$ 600
                                     new heating . . . .$ 1,400
                                     new wiring . . . .$ 400
                        new insulation, patching and repairing . . . .$ 1,000
                                     total . . . .$ 3,400
                        Second stage. . . . .$ 2,500
                        Third stage . . . .$ 2,200
                        Fourth stage . . . .$ 3,000
                        Fifth stage . . . .$ 6,500
                        Sixth stage . . . .$ 4,500
                        portico   . . . .$ 2,000
                                     complete remodeling $24,100

HOUSE #29—page 188—First stage—new plumbing . . . .$ 400
                        central heating and air conditioning . . . .$ 2,600
                        construction and additions . . . .$ 3,500
                                     total . . . .$ 6,500
                        Second stage . . . .$ 6,000
                        Third stage . . . .$ 2,000
                                     complete remodeling $14,500

HOUSE #30—page 192—First stage—Bedrooms and entrance . . . . .$ 2,500
                        Second stage—Kitchen and laundry . . . . . .$ 3,500
                        Third stage—Family room . . . .$ 1,500
                        Fourth stage—Living room and garden . . .$ 3,000
                                     complete remodeling $10,500

HOUSE #31—page 198—$18,000
HOUSE #32—page 200—$ 6,500
HOUSE #33—page 202—$ 8,500 plus new heating ($1,850) and plumbing ($1,700)
HOUSE #34—page 204—$24,000
HOUSE #35—page 208—$11,000
HOUSE #36—page 210—$15,000
HOUSE #37—page 212—$17,000
HOUSE #38—page 220—$19,000

BUILDING PERMITS

Obtaining a building permit is usually handled by your contractor. It is much easier if you have had an architect design your remodeling because he is familiar with the zoning ordinances and building codes and will have seen that everything conforms to the regulations.

Not everything you do under the term "remodeling" requires a building permit. Any changes in the use or basic structure of your house require a permit. But a new roof or finishing off the attic or basement, if no structural work is involved, does not usually require a permit. Building permits are issued under the terms described in your local building code.

If you are in doubt as to whether you need a building permit, consult the building official in your local town hall. He may waive the permit requirement if the remodeling is of a minor nature. If not, you or your contractor must file for a building permit, supplying in your application information on the scope and intent of the remodeling. You are also asked to submit the working drawings of the proposed job.

Many times, even if you plan to do the work yourself, you are required to get a building permit. And here, the building inspector or his office can be especially helpful with advice on safety and sound construction. Before you go off on your own and start tearing out walls or digging foundations, listen to his advice, and follow his suggestions concerning the structural requirements of any work you plan to do.

Getting a building permit usually takes about a week, and you may be asked to pay a fee based on the cost of the remodeling. A typical fee schedule may require three dollars for remodeling costing from fifty to five hundred dollars and a four dollar fee on work running from five hundred to a thousand dollars. Remodeling over a thousand dollars may mean a fee of four dollars for every thousand dollars invested, with the amount of fee increasing in proportion with the higher cost of remodeling.

The building department must be called in to inspect each stage of the remodeling, and the inspecting official signs the construction record, which is tacked up in an obvious location in the house. At the completion of the remodeling, the building official issues a certificate of occupancy.

BUILDING CODES

Just as each district is governed by a zoning ordinance, so every structure built within a neighborhood is governed by a building code. The municipal building-code regulations are in effect to protect the health, safety, and welfare of the public. The building code would, for instance, prevent someone from using inferior materials and workmanship in remodeling a house. Without the regulations you might buy the house later and discover too late that your family is endangered by poor and unsafe construction, a bad plumbing system that could lead to unsanitary conditions, or a heating system that might set fire to the house.

Before extensive remodeling begins, the owner or the contractor who is to do the work must apply for a building permit. The design of the remodeling and the construction drawings are submitted to a city engineer or architect, who goes over them and checks to see that the structure is safe and sound. During the remodeling a building inspector investigates periodically to make sure that the work is progressing in accordance with the approved drawings on file in his office. If it is not, he can require the contractor to remove and redo any work that he considers unsafe. Here again, the building code is for your protection and not a set of rules to be circumvented.

In private residences the code stipulates the size of beams needed to support a floor or roof, the minimum size of structural columns, walls, and footings. It determines the design of a safe roof so that it does not collapse under the snow or blow off in a high wind. The code determines the size of masonry walls and the strength of the mortar used in them so that the wall will not wash away or collapse in the rain.

The code regulates the construction of chimneys, not only so that they do not fall over, but so that fires cannot be started in them and so that fumes are carried out of the house safely. The installation of the furnace and the storage of fuel are supervised so that you do not unknowingly live in a firetrap.

Plumbing fixtures and plumbing systems are regulated so that high sanitary conditions are maintained. This protects not only your own family at home, but it also protects your family from faulty plumbing systems due to your neighbors' negligence.

The building code establishes the minimum safety standards for electrical work to protect you from shock or injury and to prevent your house from catching fire from defective wiring. Both the electrician and the plumber are licensed, and must take out separate permits for their work, which act as a double-check for your protection.

In certain areas of the West Coast where there is a history of earthquakes and in other sections of the country where special problems are known to exist, there are distinct rules governing building and remodeling.

In addition to the structural and mechanical aspect of your remodeling, the building code may also control the light and ventilation required within the rooms of your house, the minimum height of ceilings, and the minimum size of rooms. The size and location of exits, while not usually a problem in private homes, may be regulated by the codes, along with the safe construction and placement of stairs to second floors and basements.

You should not regard the building code, the city engineer or architect, and the inspectors as something or someone to be worked around or avoided. They are there not to harass you, but to help you live in a safer and better house.

ZONING ORDINANCES

Zoning ordinances are drawn up by the town board to restrict and define the use of land and buildings for residences, businesses, and industrial uses. Zoning ordinances, unlike deed restrictions, are almost always written for the protection of the individual property owner. If you feel that your rights as a private citizen are being infringed upon by a particular ruling of the ordinance, you may make application to have the zoning changed or waived in your case.

The zoning ordinance sets aside certain areas of the city or township for residential use, which means that the property next door to you cannot be sold and turned into a gasoline station, rooming house, trailer camp, parking lot, or anything else that would detract from the value of your home as a private residence. Of course, doctors, lawyers, and other professional people may be allowed to use part of their houses to maintain their private practice, but a doctor, for instance,

would not be permitted to turn part of his house into a nursing home or private hospital.

Before you begin the planning of your remodeling in detail, you should be acquainted with the zoning ordinances that are in effect for your property. A copy of the zoning rules and regulations is usually available at your town hall.

In general, zoning ordinances define and regulate the number of families permitted to live in one house. Some areas may allow two families to live in a double house; others may allow you to rent an apartment in your home if you are in residence as the owner; other neighborhoods may be strictly zoned so that only one family with a single kitchen can reside in the house.

The height of your house can be limited as to the number of floors and maximum number of feet the roof may extend over the average grade level. Front, side, and rear yards are designated, and you may not be permitted to extend your house beyond these building lines. The percentage of the lot covered by a structure may be regulated so that light and air can move freely without danger of fire spreading through the neighborhood.

The height of fences and garden walls is usually limited so that pedestrians and traffic are not endangered by blind corners and intersections. The material of the fence or wall may also be specified so that adequate police and fire protection is unimpeded.

The zoning ordinance prevents the construction of shacks, outhouses, chicken coops, kennels, stables, billboards, advertising displays, and so on, that could be a neighborhood nuisance. It may also regulate parking so that the street is not blocked with cars that could prevent a fire truck or an ambulance from getting to your home in an emergency.

The garage may be limited to the storage of two or three cars. Although this may seem too restrictive, gasoline is highly explosive, and a fire in the garage might blow flaming timber and other debris over the entire street or ignite a neighbor's house.

There are other logical reasons for all the rules set down in the zoning ordinance, and they are basically designed and written to protect you, your family, and your property. But there are exceptions to every rule, and if you feel that you cannot remodel your house properly or to your advantage within the existing restrictions, you may apply for a variance. For instance, your neighborhood may require a back yard of seventy feet, but you wish to add a room to your house which will, when completed, be sixty-five feet from the rear property line. The Zoning Board of Appeals meets periodically to review just such cases. Your application is reviewed by the board, and after a few questions at a public meeting, your intention is announced. If any of your neighbors has an objection to your proposal, they are given a chance to be heard, and usually a solution is worked out to everyone's satisfaction.

Zoning ordinances can be enforced, and if anyone builds on or uses property in a way that is counter to the ordinance, he can be fined and made to remove the offending structure.

DEED RESTRICTIONS

Deed restrictions and building conditions are usually written into the deed to your property and may supersede less strict zoning ordinances. The restrictions are placed in the deed to protect you and your neighbors from shoddy building practices and to maintain a level of excellence throughout the neighborhood. You should be familiar with these restrictions before you begin to plan your remodeling. If you have an architect, be prepared to tell him of the restrictions because they can limit the use of certain materials, type of construction, area in which you can extend your house, height of additions, and even the style of architecture.

Building conditions in the deed may state that all new construction and any additions to your home must be of brick or that you must use hand-split wood shakes on the roof. It may limit the size of the windows or restrict you to the use of white paint on the exterior of the house.

You may be prohibited from building an addition using a flat roof or a shed roof. There may

be a construction clause preventing you from building with exposed concrete block, structural glass, corrugated metal, or any number of experimental structural systems. Some restrictions prevent you from using a prefabricated structure on your property or from incorporating the principles of prefabrication in the addition of a garage or extra rooms.

The area in which you are permitted to expand your house may be restricted to the rear of your lot. You may not be able to build a garage on the front of your house, or, if you are, the garage doors may have to face away from the street. You may be prohibited from having your garage doors or back door opposite your neighbor's front door or terrace. You may also be limited to construction over a small percentage of the site so that a certain portion of the property remains free of any construction.

The deed may prevent you from building an addition or raising the roof of your house above a maximum height or number of floors. You may not be permitted to block your neighbor's view or build a structure that robs his windows of sunlight.

The style of architecture of most of the houses in the neighborhood may limit you to remodeling your home in an English half-timber or American Colonial style. Far-out contemporary styles of architecture may be banned so that you or your neighbor cannot build or remodel your home into a flat-roofed, three-story, glass-walled modern structure if all the other houses in the area are one-and-a-half-story Cape Cod cottages.

Deed restrictions are designed to maintain the character and atmosphere of the neighborhood. They are, at the same time, restrictive and prohibitive. With dogmatic reinforcement they can restrict a neighborhood to dull conformity, but with intelligent interpretation, they can also act to stabilize property values and bring about a neighborhood of harmonious consistency.

Glossary

alligatoring. An advanced form of cracking and checking in the surface of paint. The paint pulls away from the wood in vertical, horizontal, and diagonal lines producing a surface deterioration similar to the hide of an alligator.

aspirating registers. Forced warm air registers that suck cool air from the room back through the register to mix it with warm air from the furnace.

asphalt. A mineral pitch used on built-up roofs and basements for exterior water-proofing.

asphalt shingles. Shingles that combine asphalt or tar pitch surfaced with mineral granules.

asbestos shingles. Fireproof shingles composed of asbestos.

atrium. The entrance and "living room" of ancient Roman homes. Today, it refers to a large enclosed space, hallway, lobby, or garden with the principal rooms of the house arranged around it.

awning window. A pane or a series of panes set in frames and opening outward from the bottom.

back splash. Vertical wall covering behind the countertops of kitchen and bathroom cabinets.

baluster. One of the short columns or posts that make up a balustrade.

balustrade. A series of short columns or posts that are used to support a balcony or stair railing.

battens. Thin, narrow strips of wood used to cover the cracks or joints in vertical board siding.

bituminous water-proofing. Mineral pitch or asphalt used to water-proof roofs and basements.

blistering. A failure in the surface of paint whereby the paint film pulls away from the surface.

bow window. Window panes set in a frame on a continuous curve.

brick veneer. A layer of brick, one brick thick, attached but not bonded to the surface of a wall, which carries no load and supports only its own weight.

bridging. Small pieces of wood or metal straps criss-crossed between floor joists to stiffen them and hold them in place.

BTU. (British Thermal Unit) The quantity of heat required to raise the temperature of one pound of water one degree (Fahrenheit).

BTUH. (British Thermal Units per Hour) The unit of measure used to rate the capacity of air-conditioning equipment.

built-up roof. Roofing applied on a flat or slightly pitched roof in layers of felt mopped with hot asphalt.

butterfly roof. Basically, two shed roofs meeting at their low ends.

BX cable. Electric cable encased in flexible metal.

cantilever. The structural overhang projecting beyond the supporting wall or column. A balcony, window or floor that extends over the structure that holds it up and is supported only at one end is said to be cantilevered.

cement. A mixture of Portland cement, sand, and water to be used as mortar for brick and stone or for finishing the surface of masonry floors.

chalking. The powdering of the top surface of the paint film.

check. Hairline crack in wood or paint.

chimney hood. An ornamental covering to prevent rain and snow from entering the flue.

chimney pot. Usually an ornamental clay tile pipe to extend the height of the chimney and improve the draft.

cinder concrete or cinder blocks. Building materials that use clean, well-burned coal cinders instead of gravel as the coarse aggregate.

clapboards. Long boards, thin on top and thicker at the bottom, used vertically and overlapping for exterior siding.

clerestory. A wall containing windows raised over the surrounding roofs.

cloister. A roofed passage around a courtyard.

concrete. A mixture of cement, sand, water, and gravel.

conduction. Transmission of heat from particles of higher temperature to particles of lower temperature in the same body or mass.

convection. Transmission of heat by the natural motion of air or water after it has come in contact with the heat source.

corner boards. Vertical boards used to trim the corner of an exterior frame wall.

cornice. The decorative construction at the intersection of the side wall and roof at the eaves.

crawling. A defect in the paint film in which it breaks, separates, and raises.

crawl-space. The shallow space, usually unexcavated and unpaved, enclosed by the foundation walls under the floor of the house.

dormer. A dormer window built with a small gable projecting from a sloping roof; also called a doghouse dormer.

double-hung window. A window with an upper and lower vertical sliding sash.

down spot. An incandescent light fixture, recessed into the ceiling so that no light is thrown on the ceiling.

dress. To smooth and finish wood or masonry.

dressed-size lumber. The dimension of lumber after it has been cut and smoothed with a carpenter's plane which leaves it smaller than the rough size. Example: a stud 2″x4″ will actually measure 1⅝″x3⅝″.

dry stone wall. A masonry wall laid without mortar.

drywall. This term refers to interior finishing without using plaster. However, it usually means ⅜″ or ½″ gypsum wallboard with the joints taped and finished.

ducts. Usually large, round or rectangular tubes used to distribute air from the furnace or air-conditioning to registers in the rooms. They may be constructed of plastic, metal, asbestos, and composition materials.

easement. An acquired privilege or right to use part of the land belonging to someone else. Usually it refers to the grant to a utility company of the right to lay pipes across your property.

eaves. Part of the roof which projects over side walls.

efflorescence. White powder which forms on the surface of masonry.

elevation. A geometrical drawing of the side of a house or a house wall.

escutcheon. A metal shield or plate placed around the door knob and keyhole to protect the wood of the door.

eyebrow window. A low window between the roof and the floor, almost at the same level as the floor.

façade. The face, the entire appearance of a side, and especially the front of a building or house.

fascia. The flat horizontal board, used by itself or with moldings, at the outer face of the cornice.

fenestration. The design and arrangement of doors and windows in the walls.

fixed-glass window. A stationary window.

flashing. Pieces of sheet metal or other material used at all intersections of walls and roofs, at changes of materials, and over doors and windows, to prevent leakage of snow or water into the structure.

flat roof. A horizontal roof with just enough slope to drain water; the slope does not usually exceed one foot of rise in twenty feet.

footing. The enlargement of the bottom of a column, foundation wall, or chimney to distribute the weight of the structure over a greater area to prevent settling. Footings are usually made of concrete.

French window. A double sash casement window extending to the floor and used as a door; a French door.

frostline. The depth of frost penetration in the soil. Footings should be placed below this depth (which varies), to prevent structural damage.

furring. The act of applying furring strips to provide an air space between structure walls and interior finish or to level an uneven surface.

furring strips. Narrow strips of wood or metal.

gable. The triangular portion of a wall contained between the sloping eaves of a ridge roof.

gable window. A window in the gable.

gambrel roof. A ridge roof with a double slope, the lower slope being the steeper of the two.

garret. The part of the house contained by the sloping roof or the attic.

garret window. A skylight with the glass incorporated into the slope of the roof.

glaze. The installation of glass panes in windows.

glazed doors. Doors with the major portion filled in with glass in contrast to doors which can be entirely glass or glass held in an almost invisible frame.

hardware. Door knobs, door knockers, cabinet latches, hinges, or locks, for doors and windows.

hip roof. A ridge roof with the gables replaced with sloping triangular sections of roof.

hopper window. A window sash hinged at the bottom, and opening into the interior.

hydrostatic head. The pressure of water, usually from a high water table, pressing against the underside of the basement floor and walls in much the same way as the ocean presses against the sides of a ship, forcing water and moisture into the basement.

I-beam. A steel beam in the shape of a capital I. The top and bottom horizontal pieces are the flanges which are often made very wide for extra strength with less height. These wide-flange beams are used many times in remodeling to support floors and ceilings when the structural partitions have been removed.

jalousie window. A series of unframed strips of glass opening out from the bottom to prevent rain from entering.

jerkin head roof. The end of a gable roof with the top portion sloping back to form a small hip.

joist. One of a series of timbers, set edgewise, to support floor and ceiling, and are in turn supported by bearing walls, structural partitions or larger beams.

Keene's cement. An extremely durable, hard finish, white plaster used in finishing bathrooms or kitchens where wear and moisture could be a problem.

knee wall. Low walls that run parallel to the structure in an attic and are used for additional support or to close off unusable triangular sections.

lally column. A steel pipe, usually four inches in diameter, filled with concrete, and used to support beams.

lath. Small strips of wood, or metal, about ⅜″ thick and 1½″ wide, used as the support and foundation for plaster. Wood lath has now been almost completely rejected in favor of metal lath.

lavatory. In this book the term applies to a small room equipped with a toilet and a wash basin. However, builders' and manufacturers' catalogs use the term to apply to wash basins for bathrooms. Contractors often refer to both the room and the fixture as a lavatory, or the room itself as a half-bath.

lien. A legal claim against the owner of a home by a contractor who has worked on, or who has supplied materials for a home, and has not been paid.

light. A window pane.

loggia. A roofed arcade with one side open.

lumber. Wood boards, planks, and beams cut from timber into standard sizes.

mansard roof. A roof with two slopes on all four sides; the upper slope is almost flat and the lower slope is almost vertical to provide a full extra story within the roof. The mansard roof is named for the French architect who first designed and developed it to conform to the height restrictions in the city of Paris during the Renaissance.

millwork. Woodwork finished, machined, and partly assembled at the mill.

module. A variable unit of measure used by architects in designing based on esthetic and economic standards. In the U.S., for residential work, the most common module is four feet; however, other countries vary. For example, Japan, where the people are not as tall as Americans, the module is closer to three feet.

modular construction or design. A logical extension of knowing and working with a module. Studs and other framing materials have been placed on 16-inch centers with a ceiling height of eight feet. Plywood and interior finishes are manufactured in four-foot widths, to cover three studs or framing members, and in eight-foot heights that eliminate waste and time in cutting.

mullion. The division, usually vertical, between a series of windows. In general use for the term, muntin.

muntin. The division, both vertical and horizontal, between window panes.

natural finish. A transparent sealer or varnish applied to wood for protection against damage from dirt and weather, allowing the grain of the wood to show.

nonbearing partitions and walls. Those partitions and walls that do not carry overhead partitions or joists; they support only their own weight and serve to divide space into rooms.

obscure glass. Any glass used in doors, windows or partitions, either patterned, opaque, stained or etched, that does not permit a clear view through the glass.

oriel window. A window, usually in the shape of a bay, projected from the wall and supported by a decorative brace of masonry or wood.

outlet. An electrical contractors term meaning the place where a fixture, plug, switch or other electrical device is to be connected.

overhang. The projection of a floor or roof over an outside wall.

parquet floor. Small pieces of wood set in various inlaid patterns.

penny. The designation of nail sizes which originated in England and indicated the price of one hundred nails which is, in turn, indicated by a "d" because the English penny was a direct descendant of a Roman coin called "denarius." The "d" and the penny now, serve to designate the length of the nail in inverse ratio to the price per one hundred. For instance, a 2d (two-penny) nail is very light and an inch long; a 10d (10-penny) nail is heavy and three inches long.

perspective drawing. A sketch of a building taken from a particular vantage point to indicate its height, width, and depth. There is enough detail so that a photograph of the building from the same position would be similar.

pilaster. A rectangular column or a section of column attached to a wall.

pivoted window. A casement window that pivots either vertically or horizontally.

pin spots. Incandescent lights recessed in the ceiling with only a small aperture, usually about an inch. These lights are used to light sculpture, flower arrangements, or for special effects.

plasterboard. Gypsum that is covered on both sides with paper; it is sometimes called gypsum board or more often, drywall.

plate. A two by four, or larger board, placed on top of a stud wall; attic joists and rafters are fastened to this plate. A plate is also used on top of masonry walls to which floor joists are fastened.

plate glass. Polished, high-grade glass, thicker than usual window glass.

ply. One thickness of the material used to build up several layers.

porch. A covered section of house projecting from the main wall with a separate roof.

radiant heating. A system of heating which uses the floor, walls, or ceiling as heating panels with pipes or wires imbedded in them.

rafter. The sloping member of the roof structure.

rendering. A finished perspective drawing of a building, usually in black and white, sometimes in color.

rheostat. An electrical device for regulating the current to light fixtures in a room, so the amount of brightness can be controlled from a single switch.

rough floor. The subfloor which will serve as the base for the finished flooring.

rough opening. The crude and unfinished opening in which the frame of a door or window will be placed.

rug. Floor covering placed on top of the finished floor in contrast to carpet which covers the entire floor from wall to wall and is the finished floor.

sash. The frame for one or more window panes.

scale. An architect's scale is a sort of expensive ruler used to measure ¼″ to the foot, ½″ to the foot, and various other dimensions for detailed drawings. Architects also speak of scale in relation to proportion: the appropriateness of elements within the design of the building. If something is out of scale it is either too large or too small for the rest of the house making it unsuitable.

section. An architect's drawing of the house seen as if it were sliced at a given point in much the same way as a loaf of bread can be seen by cutting through the middle of it.

shake. A heavy, handmade wood shingle.

shed roof. A roof sloping in one direction with a uniform pitch.

side lights. Small vertical panes of glass on each side of a doorway.

single-hung window. A window with an upper and lower sash, with usually only the lower one operable.

sliding window. A window in which one or more of the sash slide on tracks vertically.

soffit. The underside of a part of the house, such as a staircase, but not the ceiling.

soil pipe. A vertical drain pipe carrying waste matter from the toilet.

stud. A vertical piece of lumber, usually 2″x4″. It is used in a series to form the interior walls and the interior partitions of a house.

subfloor. The rough boards or plywood applied directly to the floor joists. When all rough work is finished on the house, the finished floor is applied on top of the subfloor.

sump. A pit in the basement or ground floor of a house that is used to collect excess water. A pump is then used to remove the water to prevent flooding.

terrazzo floor. A mixture of marble chips and cement, ground and polished smooth and then given a high polish.

terne plate. A coating of an alloy of tin and lead.

timber. Heavy lumber with a minimum dimension of five inches in width or thickness.

three-way switch. An electric switch that controls a light that can be turned on or off from two places.

transite. A combination of asbestos and cement manufactured into fireproof sheets and panels.

transom. A small window over a door or another window.

truss. A combination of members usually arranged to form a triangle for supporting roofs or other loads over a long span.

valley. The intersection of two roofs.

vitreous. A term used to describe a material that is hard, shiny, and resembles glass.

variance. Written permission from the local zoning board to build or remodel in a manner that is not permitted within the strict limitations of the existing zoning ordinance.

wet wall. A term sometimes used to refer to walls that have plumbing pipes and drains running through them.

winders. Treads of steps cut considerably wider at one end than the other, and are used where stairs are carried around corners.

Index